LORDS OF THE RINK
The Emergence of the Natio...

No sport is as important to Canadians as hockey. Though a great many things may divide Canada, the love of hockey has long been a unifying force. Before the latest labour unrest in the National Hockey League, however, it was easy to forget that hockey is also a multi-million-dollar business run, not by the athletes or coaches, but by corporate boards and businessmen. *Lords of the Rinks* documents the early years of hockey's professionalization and commercialization, and the emergence of a fledgling NHL.

As the popularity of hockey grew in Canada in the late nineteenth century, so too did its commercial side, and players, club directors, rink owners, fans, and media alike developed deep emotional, economic, and ideological interests in the sport. Disagreement arose about how organized hockey, especially at the elite level, should be managed and it became apparent that governing bodies were required to maintain a semblance of order. These early administrative bodies tried to create a structure that would help to coordinate the various interests, set standards of behaviour, and impose mechanisms to detect and punish violators of governance. In 1917 the NHL held its first games and by 1936 it had become the dominant governing body in professional hockey.

Having done extensive research in the NHL archives – reviewing league meeting minutes, letters, memos, telegrams, gate receipt reports, and other documents – John Chi-Kit Wong traces the commercial roots of hockey and argues that, in its organized form, the sport was rarely if ever without a commercial side despite labels such as amateur and professional. *Lords of the Rinks* is the only truly comprehensive and scholarly history of the league and the business of hockey.

JOHN CHI-KIT WONG is an assistant professor in the Sport Management Program at Washington State University.

Lords of the Rinks

The Emergence of the
National Hockey League, 1875–1936

JOHN CHI-KIT WONG

UNIVERSITY OF TORONTO PRESS
Toronto Buffalo London

© University of Toronto Press Incorporated 2005
Toronto Buffalo London
Printed in Canada

ISBN 0-8020-3725-9 (cloth)
ISBN 0-8020-8520-2 (paper)

Printed on acid-free paper

Library and Archives Canada Cataloguing in Publication

Wong, John, 1955–
    Lords of the rinks : the emergence of the National Hockey League,
    1875–1936 / John Wong.

    Includes bibliographical references and index.
    ISBN 0-8020-3725-9 (bound)   ISBN 0-8020-8520-2 (pbk.)

    1. National Hockey League – History.   2. Hockey – Canada – History.
    3. Hockey – United States – History.   I. Title.

    GV847.8.N3W65 2005   796.962'64'09   C2005-900742-7

Front cover: Newspaper photograph of a hockey game, ca. 1933–5. The teams are likely
the New York Americans and the Detroit Red Wings. (Hockey Hall of Fame Archives)
Back cover: Photograph of the Board of Governors of the National Hockey League
during their meeting of September 1933 at the Windsor Hotel, Montreal: (left to
right) Bill Dwyer (New York Americans); Leo Dandurand (Montreal Canadiens);
Charles Hughes (Detroit Red Wings); Redmond Quain (Ottawa Senators); Bob
Parsons; Frank Calder, President; Charles Adams (Boston Bruins); Major Fred
McLaughlin (Chicago Blackhawks); John S. Hammond (New York Rangers); Conn
Smythe (Toronto Maple Leafs); and James Strachan (Montreal Maroons) (not shown –
James Callaghan of the Philadelphia Quakers). (Hockey Hall of Fame Archives)

University of Toronto Press acknowledges the financial assistance to its publishing
program of the Canada Council for the Arts and the Ontario Arts Council.

University of Toronto Press acknowledges the financial support for its publishing
activities of the Government of Canada through the Book Publishing Industry
Development Program (BPIDP).

Contents

Illustrations follow page 112

Acknowledgments

In writing and publishing a book, there are inevitably contributions from many people besides the author. This book could not even have been attempted without the generosity of the National Hockey League in granting me access to its previously unexamined archives. For this stroke of fortune, I wish to thank the NHL commissioner, Gary Bettman. Mr Brian O'Neill and Mr Darrin Burke in the Montreal office generously gave me their time and assistance, for which I am grateful. There are also other generous individuals who shared their research holdings with me. Mr Len Kotylo of the Society for International Hockey Reseach located and sent me the court cases involving E.J. Livingstone. Mr Birger Nordmark contributed the meeting minutes of the Ligue Internationale de Hockey sur Glace and articles dealing with the 1936 Winter Olympics hockey tournament. I am also indebted to the Hockey Hall of Fame for providing me with a copy of early NHL meeting minutes and to the staff of the National Archives of Canada, the Ontario Archives, and the Library of Congress for their assistance. Dr Michel Vigneault, arguably the foremost authority on early hockey history in Montreal, has consistently been generous with information and encouragement.

This work began as my doctoral dissertation at the University of Maryland. A special thanks must go to the members of my dissertation committee, Drs Keith Olson, Donald Steel, and Joan Hult, who provided valuable comments that improved the original work. I owe my intellectual development to two other members on the committee, Dr Nancy Struna, who was my advisor, and Dr Stephen Hardy. Steve, now at University of New Hampshire, had been my advisor in my masters studies at Robert Morris University and had inspired me to pursue my doctoral degree. Nancy has been a beacon in the vast ocean of learning. More often than I would like to admit, she has managed to refocus my attention to the forest when I have been staring at the trees. Any errors in this book, of course, are my responsibility.

viii   /   *Acknowledgments*

I also want to thank the University of Toronto Press for taking on this project. I especially want to thank my editor, Len Husband, for his humour and patience with this neophyte in the publishing world. The editorial staff at the Press, in particular John St James, have made this book considerably more readable.

Lastly, I have to thank all my friends who have supported me over the years with their undying friendship. I cannot end these expressions of gratitude without a word for my love ones. My parents, my siblings, and their families were supportive all through graduate school and the writing of this book, even though such a journey can only be undertaken alone. To the One in my heart, this journey would not have occurred without you coming into my life. I dedicate this book to you.

LORDS OF THE RINKS
The Emergence of the National Hockey League, 1875–1936

Chapter 1

Introduction

On March 23, 1894, the *Toronto Daily Mail* reported on the first Stanley Cup championship match at the Victoria rink in Montreal the previous night. According to the reporter, there 'was never before in the history of the game ... such a crowd present at a match or so much enthusiasm evinced. There were fully 5,000 persons at the match, and tin horns, strong lungs, and a general rabble predominated.' The report went on to describe the match as 'a hard struggle' and 'a great contest' in which Montreal defeated Ottawa by a score of three to one.[1] For many hockey enthusiasts and writers past and present, this was a watershed event for several reasons. First, the trophy and the competition have withstood the test of time as the symbol of supremacy in the sport. In today's parlance, that supremacy is equated with professional hockey. Second, the governing organization of professional hockey, the National Hockey League (NHL), has always proudly claimed that the Stanley Cup is the oldest championship trophy in professional team sports.[2] To generate excitement for the sport, promoters of hockey often referred to stories of past struggles in the quest for this trophy. Thus the trophy stands as a symbol that connects the present to the past. One connection that has persisted through the years is that the players have always competed for the honour of being champions. All else is secondary. This love-of-the-competition story resonates especially well for those who may have become sceptical – perhaps even cynical – about professional athletes and team owners in today's heavily financed and marketed sports world.

Despite the sentimentality later generations have for the first Stanley Cup, there is one unmistakable but often overlooked facet of this first match. It was a commercial undertaking. Five thousand spectators paid admissions and the newspapers promoted the match. Furthermore, rumours of paid athletes in this supposedly amateur sport appeared by the end of the century. Even as the two competing teams contested the first Stanley Cup match under the banner of amateurism, monetary exchanges occurred among clubs, rink owner, fans, and media. In other words, elite-level hockey had been a business early on.

This book has its genesis as a study of the NHL as a business organization before the Second World War. While conducting my research, I found it impossible to discuss and analyse the NHL without understanding its roots in commercialized elite-level amateur hockey. The result is a business history of elite-level hockey that follows the sport's development from its commercialization to professionalization, and the establishment of the NHL from a regional Canadian business to a dominant North American sport cartel. The story begins with the formalizing of hockey under the amateur ideal in the late nineteenth century, then traces the emergence of commercial interests in the sport, the tensions that led to the subsequent split between the amateurs and professionals, and the rocky road that eventually established the NHL as a powerful organization by the late 1930s. In this journey, various individuals and groups crossed paths. They formed alliances that competed against each other to capture the hockey market. Some of these alliances did not survive. Others re-formed into new organizations, with changes in the composition of membership and/or organizational structure. A major underlying force that guided these changes was the power politics within and between groups of hockey entrepreneurs. Throughout the development of elite-level hockey, power relations played an important role.

In titling the book *Lords of the Rinks*, I intend to examine the people and groups of people who shaped the commercialization and professionalization of hockey both before and after the formation of the NHL. These stakeholders formed a network that included those who affected, and were affected by, the development of the hockey industry. Besides the obvious participants, such as players and club directors/owners, other groups within the hockey network included the media, rival organizations, rink owners, fans, and the different levels of governments. Not all of these groups exerted their influences at the same time. Some appeared in the process for only a short time, while others had a much more enduring presence. It is true that the NHL eventually assumed leadership, or as Robert Stern labelled it, 'a linking-pin role,' in this network; but the various groups all left their imprints. Thus, this book departs from the many studies in professional sport in general and professional hockey in particular, which have focused on the relationships between players and club management. By examining commercial and professional hockey through a network of stakeholders, I hope to provide a broader perspective of the hockey industry.[3]

Lords of the Rinks does not merely broaden the field of investigation. The title also suggests the existence of power relationships among stakeholders. Since stakeholders' interests and values varied, competition to control the development of hockey existed among groups. Of course, the influence of each stakeholder group fluctuated over time. Despite their differences, stakeholders held financial, emotional, and ideological investments in the sport, which wore them into a hockey network. In pushing their own agendas to promote their versions of hockey, various stakeholders formed alliances in order to control the flow of information and resources. One manifestation of these struggles for influence can be found in the development of hockey's governing bodies. Reacting to opportunities and threats from others in the hockey network, officials of these governing bodies made decisions to guard and advance their interests. As historian Stephen Hardy argues, the decisions of hockey promoters shaped the development of organizational forms that 'produce and distribute three-part commodities.'[4] Thus, changes in the administrative structure of a governing body and the game-form divulge important information about power dynamics among the stakeholders within the hockey network. Power relationships, in turn, influence and are influenced by the expansion and contraction of the hockey network.[5]

As much as I take an expansive view regarding stakeholders in hockey, this book is not an all-encompassing story about the business of hockey. Instead, the story focuses on, first, the elite amateur hockey in Canada's central provinces, then the dominant professional hockey organizations produced after the hockey network was split between amateurs and professionals into two subunits, and finally the NHL. This choice excludes hockey played by women and by non-whites, and that in lower-level organizations. In the context of the late nineteenth and early twentieth centuries, women and minorities did not constitute a major force in influencing elite-level hockey. I also make no attempt to cover spontaneous hockey as played by many on the frozen ponds and lakes in North America. Nevertheless, these groups made up part of the hockey network. Many were supporters and, as such, they belonged to that important group of stakeholders – fans. Although excluded from this book, the stories of organized and spontaneous hockey as played by women, minorities, and men with lower levels of skill are by no means unimportant. But they are beyond the scope of this book, which focuses on formalized and organized hockey as played by highly skilled, white males.

I also make a distinction between commercialized and professionalized hockey. Often, when referring to professional sports, the general public labels as professionals athletes who are paid for their performance. While financial compensation to the athletes constitutes a legitimate definition of professional sports, Bruce Kidd has refined the term professional by proposing two distinctions – the '"not-for-profit" or "community" teams and leagues, on the one hand, and "full market" or "capitalist," on the other hand.'[6] These labels address the ownership of the organizations, clubs, and leagues. Whereas a sense of community pride motivates the operations of the former, the latter follows market forces and may desert one community for another in search of a better bottom line. Although this distinction certainly has held true in the development of professional sport ownership, a further clarification must be made in order to acknowledge situations that do not fall within the two classifications and can be applied to both ownership and the status of the athletes.[7]

In the examination of professional sport and its development, one must not forget that these were commercial ventures. Monetary transactions and economic considerations were important. Yet, not all commercialized sporting activities could be called professional sports. Early tavern owners provided sports as part of their business. Certainly, these commercial sports providers had their roots deep within the community, as taverns were central to community life in the early days. Still, they did not fit the 'not-for-profit' category. In the nineteenth century, a different sort of commercial sport operator emerged. They were independent contractors who sold their skills to an audience, for a chance to wager, or to the highest bidder. Prize fighters, circus acrobats, jockeys, and even early baseball and hockey players fell into this category. While their motive was undoubtedly profit-oriented, one could hardly call them professionals, for some of them had other careers. And often their other careers or their preference of one community over another took precedence over pay-for-play sports.[8]

In the early days of commercialized sports, there existed a loose relationship between owners of capital and the producers of labour. At times, an individual could be both. If separate, owners of capital often had multiple roles in the business. They acted as marketer, talent scout, accountant, and manager. The role of producers could also be multifaceted. More importantly, they retained a great deal of control over their labour.

Out from the undifferentiated world of commercialized sports, however, both elite amateur and professional sport organizations emerged and became more centralized, specialized, and bureaucratized. In the process, the distinction between owners of capital and producers of labour became increasingly clear, especially for professional sports. To promote and improve their products, owners established a chain of command that often reduced the producers of labour (athletes) to the role of employee. Thus, the road towards professionalization encompassed increasingly a more complex organizational form that invariably defined precise individual roles and responsibilities, outlined a clear organizational hierarchy, and prescribed clear lines of authority. This organizational restructuring helped to organize people and resources to perform in an orderly manner in their daily operations.

A similar process occurred in the professionalization of amateur sports at the elite level as well, but there were differences. First, the distinction between club management and members resembled less that of an owner-employee relationship and more the workings of a fraternal organization. While the line and staff functions of a professional team seldom mixed, it was possible for amateur club management to involve itself in the product, such as acting as officials during games, and for the players to assume policy-making power via their membership in the club. A second difference had to do with sharing the profits. In the professional game, both parties received remuneration; and for the successful leagues that also controlled the labour market, the owners generally took the larger share. For the amateurs, the players supposedly received no financial compensation. All profits went to the club to pay for current and anticipated operating expenses and, occasionally, honoraria for club officials. Still, elite amateur sports required the same kind of formal organization in terms of their functionality.

Perhaps the demands of maintaining the elite status, vis-à-vis being a competitive if not leading organization, necessitated some degree of orderly efficiency. The road towards this end, however, was treacherous, filled with unexpected barriers and resistance in both professional and elite amateur sports, because the division of labour meant the division of power and control. Moreover, an organizational structure that promoted order and efficiency did not necessarily ensure that the people within it would follow the formal organizational procedure. A strong corporate culture based on shared values, however, will assure adherence to organizational protocol.

Creating a corporate culture, however, often makes for a contested terrain. Members of the organization, such as owners, coaches, and players, seek to alter or defend organizational regulations and performance standards in attempts to consolidate, maintain, and redefine their spheres of influence. Moreover, outside agencies such as the courts, the press, and fans also influence this process. These power struggles are especially difficult for a young organization searching for its identity and creating its unique corporate culture. In the early days of amateurism, factions struggled to define just what the appropriate behaviour and performance standards were. This occurred at both the club and association level. Until there was some general agreement and strong enforcement mechanism on how to reward the faithful and punish violators of the amateur code, professionalization could not even begin to occur. This was true for sports as for any other disciplines and professions. In other words, professionalization of hockey began when organized amateur hockey developed a formal organizational structure, a code of behaviour, and mechanisms to monitor members. Hence, professionalization is a work in progress, with its own internal tensions and continuous negotiations and adaptations.[9]

In North America, commercialized sports had long been a fact of popular culture. Professionalization of sport, however, first appeared in the late nineteenth

century. In the case of hockey, the rise of amateurism, a relatively new phenomenon, expedited its emergence. More importantly, amateur hockey provided a
model for the development of professional hockey. As an exclusionary practice
based on one's social standing, amateurism drove a sharp wedge between those
who advocated sport as an avocation and those who openly took money in
exchange for their performances. Amateur sports, however, were by no means
non-commercialized. Clubs could not exist without adequate support, in terms
of both talent and funding. But by the early twentieth century, the excluded
professionals had taken a separate road to establish their own organization. Instead of employing an exclusionary policy based on social class, professional
sports emphasized profit margins and player skills. Given professional hockey's
lineage from commercialized elite amateur hockey, an examination of commercialized sports in North America before the emergence of organized amateur
sports should be a useful starting point.

Commercialized entertainment involving contests and displays of physical
skills appeared early in eighteenth-century North America. In the United Sates, a
vibrant and varied sporting life often flourished in the social centre of a locale,
the town tavern. Willing owners provided both equipment and space for animal
baits, horse racing, prize fights, and other activities. At times, they even arranged
matches to entertain locals and travellers alike. One could argue that tavern
owners were the first sport entrepreneurs. By the late eighteenth and early
nineteenth centuries, some entrepreneurs began to stage circus acrobat shows and
invest in pleasure gardens catering to the growing middle class in the cities.[10]

In the United States, commercialized sports grew rapidly during the nineteenth century. Especially during the second half of the century, they blossomed
with the emergence of modern sports. Much of this development occurred in
the growing cities in the industrial northeast. The population of the United States
received a major boost through successive waves of immigration in this period.
Immigrants provided a ready source of cheap labour to fuel the emerging
American industrial economy. This growing economy sharpened the distinction
between work time and non-work time. Unlike the case of the traditional rural
agricultural economy, where work and leisure were not separate entities, leisure
activities, including commercialized sports, now belonged to the domain of non-
work time. Important infrastructure improvements that were vital to an industrial economy accelerated this transition from a rural agricultural economy. By
1840, there were 3326 miles of canals in the United States transporting goods and
people. Steamboats shortened distances within the country and for international
travel by mid-century. Expansion of railroads began in earnest during the antebellum years. By 1869, the Union Pacific Railroad connected America from
coast to coast. The invention of the telegraph in 1844 greatly sped up the

dissemination of information. Telegraph lines linked San Francisco to the Atlantic coast by 1861. In 1866 the trans-Atlantic cable bridged the communication gap between the United States and Europe. Advances in the printing process made newspapers affordable to the public, and therefore events of significance could reach a larger readership. Coincidentally, these technological advances in transportation and communication also helped to popularize sports.[11]

By the mid-nineteenth century, urbanization had fuelled the growth of commercial sports in the United States. Population increases put pressure on land use. Traditional recreation spaces such as open fields and empty lots were fast disappearing. Sanitation and pollution problems compounded the deteriorating living conditions. A growing urban middle class began to search for solutions to improve their conditions. In their quest for health, they distanced themselves from tavern sports, which they criticized as immoral, violent, and disorderly. Some urban leaders advocated the building of city parks as replacements for recreational spaces lost to urban development. More importantly, many turned to organized modern sports as a means to improve their health.[12] The development of baseball is instructive, as some of its developments would later influence the growth of hockey.

First mention of baseball in the press appeared during the antebellum period. Initially, social class served as the basis for membership in organized clubs, as can be seen in the New York Knickerbocker Base Ball Club. It connected a group of middle-class New Yorkers who shared similar interests. The club's emphasis was on intra-club rather than inter-club activities. As more urbanites in New York and other cities took to the game of baseball, clubs based on occupations and neighbourhoods proliferated. A movement to formalize and standardize the game occurred as clubs banded together to form associations. These voluntary associations were a result of increased competition among clubs. They acted to standardize rules and, as the competition became fierce, to monitor and arbitrate player eligibility.[13]

Several developments also appeared as competition grew intense. Games began to arouse interest from people other than members of the rival clubs. As winning took on increased significance, some clubs began actively recruiting players by offering financial inducements. While players did not change clubs for that reason alone, pay-for-play had certainly become a feature in baseball before the Civil War. Benefit games were an early form of financial compensation for a club's star players. Eventually, the better players received direct payments from the clubs themselves. As independent contractors in demand, good players possessed quite a bit of bargaining power. Yet they were not the only people who benefited from commercialized baseball. Facility owners also saw an opportunity in the baseball craze. Initially, open fields, empty lots, cricket grounds, and race tracks served as playing facilities. Club member subscriptions probably helped to cover the rental of the facility. As the popularity of baseball spread and payments to players became more prevalent, clubs realized the necessity of charging admission fees to recoup expenditures and perhaps maintain their competitive stance when it came to bidding for players. At the same time, facility owners also recognized the potential revenues generated by the spectators, and so the relationship between the club and the facility owner became increasingly intertwined. Despite growing commercialization, baseball clubs remained largely a loosely organized group in the first decade after the Civil War. Each club set up its own schedule of games and players could change clubs with relative ease. Professionalization of the sport did not arrive until 1876 with the establishment of the National League.[14]

Studies on pre-Confederation Canadian sporting practices are scant. The early development of sports in Canada was probably similar to that in the United States. Whereas similar trends in immigration, industrialization, and technological improvements occurred north of the border in the nineteenth century, they were on a much smaller scale and often their development lagged behind that in the United States. As late as Confederation, in 1867, industrial capitalism was not a major economic force in Canada. By the beginning of the American Civil War, the United States had 392 urban areas, with 9 cities having over 100,000 inhabitants. By contrast, Montreal, the largest city in Canada, had just over 90,000, while about 56,000 resided in the second largest city, Toronto. After Confederation, the new Dominion government began aggressively fostering the development of the young nation via a set of economic and immigration policies. Yet, significant population increases did not occur until the end of the century. Just four years after Confederation, the 1871 census counted only 3.6 million people in Canada. While business interests and the fear of American annexation of western Canada prompted the government to encourage immigration, many immigrants considered Canada as a stop before heading to the United States, where economic opportunities looked brighter. The government's land-grant incentive to entice immigrants also proved to be too unattractive, as recipients often found themselves in isolated farms at a time when the transportation system was still trying to catch up with the vastness of the country.[15]

The growth of commercialized sports in Canada also developed along lines similar to those in the United States. After Confederation, taverns continued to be social centres that provided leisure and sports to the urban working class. Cockfighting, a sport associated with taverns, persisted to the end of the century. Entrepreneurs built facilities or arranged sport contests in hope of a profit from the gate receipts and gambling. A group of investors, for example, financially backed Ned Hanlan, the great Canadian oarsman, who toured North America and Europe. They, in turn, hoped to recoup their money plus a profit through wagering. Even upper-class sportsmen often competed for purses, cash prizes, and wagers in horse racing and billiards. At times, exclusive facilities also became available to the general public because of dire financial conditions. In 1862, a group of Montreal Anglo-Canadians built the Victoria rink as a socially exclusive gathering place for themselves in the winter time. A variety of factors, especially the costs of maintaining a facility idle for nine months of the year, finally convinced the directors of the rink to open their facility to outside users by the early 1870s. Although the rink still hosted events catering to the upper and middle classes, some of them were unmistakably non-amateur in nature.[16]

By the 1870s, a growing sporting culture began to appear in the two largest Canadian cities, Montreal and Toronto, as well as some parts of Ontario that were benefiting from industrialization and technological advances. As federal protective tariffs jump-started Toronto's and English-speaking Montreal's industries and banks, more people were moving into these and other cities in the two provinces. Between 1871 and 1891, the Montreal and Toronto city populations grew by over 105 and 223 per cent respectively. Unlike the case in the United States, however, local elites rather than the urban middle class exerted a strong influence on the development of sports. They formed sport clubs and built facilities. Living in the largest and most prosperous city in Canada, Montreal's elites played an important role in the history of Canadian sports. As early as 1807, local merchants formed the Montreal Curling Club. British soldiers stationed at garrisons brought their sporting tradition from the old world to British North America, and were generally one of the first groups to organize matches among themselves and against the locals. By the last quarter of the nineteenth century, university students, especially those from McGill in Montreal, helped to popularize and modernize football and ice hockey. Participants pre-arranged contests via the challenge method, and matches occurred irregularly. In the 1870s however, these elites began to adopt the emerging British sport ideology, amateurism. Given their British heritage, this was not a surprising development.[17]

Such was the state of the sporting culture in North America by the 1870s. The following chapters continue the examination of this sporting culture in one particular sport, ice hockey. It begins with the emergence of hockey as an organized activity and the shaping of a network of stakeholders in organized hockey in the last quarter of the nineteenth century.

Chapter 2

From Fraternal Hockey Clubs
to Closed Corporation

Richard Gruneau and David Whitson have argued that "the needs of and interests of specific groups" played an important role in driving the institutionalization of sport.[1] Such was the case in the early history of hockey. Organized in upper-class institutions in the last quarter of the nineteenth century, hockey first developed in amateur sport clubs with their culture of fraternal fellowship and gentlemanly sportsmanship. As they did in other club sports, upper-class and, later, upper-middle-class young men formed hockey clubs to compete against and socialize with one another. To facilitate inter-club competition, they organized hockey clubs into associations that sought to institutionalize hockey through formalizing a governing structure, standardizing playing rules, regulating eligibility, and adjudicating disputes. In this process, these voluntary organizations also adopted and adapted the British sporting ethic of amateurism. The institutionalization of hockey under the aegis of amateurism restricted participation to those who subscribed to the same philosophy.

This fraternal culture of gentleman hockey at the elite level did not last very long. The commercialization of hockey, the infusion of participants from other social backgrounds, and the perceived representational status of the hockey clubs gradually redefined the criterion for belonging to the hockey brotherhood from one of social class to that of skill. As these forces fed on each other, they contributed to the popularity of hockey and placed increasing demands for the senior clubs to assemble strong squads. At the same time, the willingness of some elite-level players to depart from the amateur ethos and market their skills as a commodity further fuelled the changing hockey fraternity. Thus, a network of hockey stakeholders based on economic, emotional, and ideological interests slowly emerged.

When players shared in the spoils of commercialized sports, amateur sport governing bodies, including hockey organizations, reacted by labelling such behaviour as professional, despite the fact that early hockey players could never rely on hockey to make a livelihood. Beginning in the 1880s, amateur proponents developed a paternalistic system of governance in order to monitor players and punish offenders of the amateur ideal. From the few on the executive board came the guidelines and judgments as to who was the good boy, the amateur sportsman, and who was the bad boy, the rogue professional mercenary. In the process, these men fostered the development of organizational power through the amateur organizations' bylaws in the name of protecting the integrity of sport and its participants. By doing so, they were also professionalizing the business of amateur hockey in setting operational regulations and standards. The emergence of a paternal culture in the governing bodies, however, did not immediately replace the fraternal bond that existed among members and directors of the early organizations. Still, the dual processes of institutionalization and commercialization in amateur hockey slowly eroded that tie, and thus began the process of separating players from administrators.[2]

Organized hockey grew out of upper-class institutions within a small clique of sportsmen in Montreal. Although there is evidence that a game played with stick and ball on ice existed in North America at the beginning of the nineteenth century, most writers of hockey have pointed to the March 3, 1875 game between two teams played in the Victoria rink in Montreal as the first recorded match of modern ice hockey. Each side had nine players who played two half-hour periods. Since the rink did not have side boards to separate the players and the spectators, the players decided to use a wooden puck instead of a lacrosse ball to avoid it 'going to the spectators to their discomfort.'[3] Writers generally credited James George Aylwin Creighton, a Haligonian studying law at McGill University and captain of one of the nines in that game, as being the 'father' of modern hockey. Not only did he organize that Montreal game, he also published the first set of rules in 1877.[4] Still, hockey did not elicit much enthusiasm in Montreal or elsewhere by the end of the 1870s. Newspaper reports on hockey were rare, and when an announcement was made, it usually appeared in the city news section rather than the sports and pastimes section. At least until the early 1880s, the popular winter sports in Montreal were snowshoeing and skating.[5]

There was no question of the upper-class roots of hockey at that 1875 Montreal match. Built in 1862, the Victoria rink had been the social locus of wealthy citizens of Montreal in the winter time. According to the notice of the match that appeared in the *Montreal Gazette*, the players were 'chosen from among the members.'[6] While the follow-up report next day in the newspaper noted the score, two games to one, its tone emphasized the skills and efforts of the players. It described the match as a 'well-contested affair, the efforts of the players exciting much merriment as they wheeled and dodged each other, and notwithstanding the brilliant play of Captain Torrance's team Captain Creighton's men carried the day.'[7] This by no means suggested that the match was not competitive nor that winning was unimportant. Still, the absence of any complaints or commentary on rough play and hinted at adherence to the amateur ideal of sportsmanship by the participants.

As a further indication about expected behaviour in gentlemanly sporting conduct, early hockey rules, as conceived by Creighton and his peers, supported the notion of fair play. Within the first set of published rules there were no provisions for penalties for any infractions. Instead, rule number 6 allowed for a restart if any player committed a foul. Because a restart did not guarantee any team an advantage, early hockey players, at least as far as Creighton was concerned, assumed infractions were unintentional, and thus there was no need for punishment. Since sport was to be an avocation, no gentleman would intentionally take advantage of his opponent. When an infraction did occur, however, albeit unintended, a restart giving neither side an advantage seemed to be the fairest solution. A further glimpse of the promotion of amateur sportsmanship appeared in one of the few reported matches of the 1870s. In a match between McGill University and the Montreal Club played at the Victoria rink in 1879, the reporter noted approvingly the '[g]ood play, whether on the side of "town" or "gown," receiving hearty applause.'[8]

At least in western Quebec and eastern Ontario, the popularity of hockey as a winter sport increased in the 1880s. A major catalyst was its inclusion in the first Montreal Winter Carnival in 1883, when two Montreal teams, the Victorias (organized by the upper-class Victoria rink) and McGill University, and one Quebec City team competed in a round-robin tournament on a scraped surface on the frozen St Lawrence River. To accommodate the Quebec team, which had only seven players, the two Montreal teams agreed to play seven a side. This became the preferred format in the next year's carnival and seven-men hockey caught on. By 1885 the tournament during carnival time grew to six teams, one from Ottawa and five from Montreal. Besides the two original competitors from Montreal in 1883, the Crystals (organized by the commercial Crystal rink), the Montreal Football Club, and the Montreal Hockey Club (part of the Montreal Amateur Athletic Association, MAAA) also vied for the tournament honour. In the same year, local enthusiasts in Kingston, Ontario, formed a league. Hockey had begun to spread.[9]

By the 1890s the popularity of hockey as a winter sport extended beyond Montreal, migrating with the population westward across the Laurentian Shield to places such as Rat Portage and Winnipeg. McGill students and other Montreal hockey enthusiasts who left the city took the game with them. James Creighton, for example, started a team when he went to work in Ottawa. At least four hockey clubs existed in Toronto by 1889, and in the next year, there was sufficient interest in Ontario to form the Ontario Hockey Association (OHA). Manitoba followed suit in 1892, establishing its provincial organization. At the end of the decade, the OHA had grown to include sixty-three teams in three divisions. The sport also spread southward. Again, students played an important part. Yale students began to play hockey in 1893, and a Johns Hopkins student from Montreal invited a team from Quebec to play a group that he organized in Baltimore.[10]

Concurrently, other groups began to take part in this once exclusively Anglo-Canadian sport. From the mid-1890s on, French- and Irish-Canadian hockey clubs began to appear. Both the French and the Irish players followed their Anglo counterparts' route to hockey – via educational institutions. Students from two bilingual colleges, Ste-Marie and Mont St-Louis, formed the core of an Irish hockey club, the Shamrocks. Although French-speaking students attended both institutions, only the Mont St-Louis team had French players. In 1894, a group of French-Canadian businessmen decided to organize an association to promote sports to the French-Canadian population. L'Association athlétique d'amateurs nationale or Le National had two hockey teams consisting of mainly students from Mont St-Louis. Until 1904, these and other French-speaking teams were never really competitive. A language barrier, the late start, and possibly discrimination might account for their dismal records. However, they did plant the seeds for a vibrant French-Canadian hockey culture.[11]

Early hockey competition came from upper-class sports clubs and university clubs. Members of these early clubs scrimmaged among themselves. Occasionally they accepted challenges from other clubs within the city. Early challenges involving mostly players in the senior category usually implied the players were of a certain age and had attained a fairly high skill level within the club. However, unlike the case in the National League in professional baseball in the United States, which had established a regular schedule since 1876, these infrequent contests followed the challenge format that prevailed in the Canadian sports world. While these early affairs were competitive, they were also jovial social events much like the intra-club games. In a rare detailed account of an early hockey match between the St James and the Metropolitan clubs, the reporter lauded the players' efforts and averred that the dinner given after the game 'will be a good one and about which we presume there will not be two opinions.'[12]

Efforts to regularize competition began in the late 1880s. Four Montreal clubs – the Montreals, the Crystals, the Victorias, McGill University – and one Ottawa club wished to formalize their hockey season from the irregular challenge format and the one-week Carnival tournament to a more structured and regular schedule. In 1887 they formed the Amateur Hockey Association of Canada (AHAC). The emphasis thereby began to shift from intra-club competitions to inter-club contests. Again, unlike baseball south of the border, rather than deciding the champion based on the number of victories accumulated, the AHAC retained the single-game challenge system favoured in individual sports such as boxing and wrestling. Thus, every match was a championship match in the AHAC's inaugural season and the team winning the last match of the season became the champion of the league. In 1891, the Montreal Hockey Club became the AHAC champion when it won the last match – its only victory that season.[13]

Wishing to avoid a repeat of this rather absurd situation, the AHAC adopted a regular schedule in the following season that declared the team winning the most games the champion. It was apparently a satisfactory arrangement in terms of the race for the championship as well as financial considerations. Reporting the results of the 1892–3 season, the secretary-treasurer told members that the new format was a success in both the senior and the intermediate divisions, 'keeping [fans'] interests in the matches until the end of the season ... also giving them [the clubs] the benefit of gate receipts.'[14]

During the inaugural season of the new AHAC championship format, senior hockey in the Montreal region received a boost from Frederick Arthur, Lord Stanley of Preston, Earl of Derby and Governor General of Canada. Lord Stanley, an avid sportsman, hockey fan, and father of two hockey-playing sons and one hockey-playing daughter, wished to promote hockey within the Dominion. Since there were a number of regional organizations in existence, he donated a cup costing ten guineas to 'be held from year to year by the leading hockey club in Canada' because of 'the interest that hockey matches now elicit, and the importance of having the games fairly played.'[15] Although Canada had shed its colonial status at Confederation, its deep ties with Britain made a trophy donated by the Crown's representative a prestigious one. In a sense, hockey thus had Royal approval, and the AHAC was the chief benefactor because Lord Stanley instructed that the Montreal Hockey Club, 1893 champion of the AHAC, be the holder of the trophy. This effectively raised, if only for this one season, the status of the AHAC in the world of hockey.

The connection between the Stanley Cup and the AHAC continued after the initial season, and its competition fit with the emphasis on achievement popular with the growing urban business and professional elite in the late nineteenth century. This emblem of hockey supremacy seldom left the AHAC and its later reincarnations. Lord Stanley wanted the leading teams in various associations to challenge for the cup. Theoretically there could be several Stanley Cup matches within a single hockey season. Since his term as governor general was up, he appointed two trustees, Sheriff John Sweetland and Philip Dansken Ross, both avid sportsmen from Ottawa, with broad power to oversee all matters with respect to the challenges. The two trustees then proceeded to lay down the regulations that governed the Stanley Cup competition. More importantly, they designated the annual champion of the AHAC as the holder of the cup, who was to defend it against outside challengers as approved by them. It could be that the trustees were from Ottawa, which had a team in the AHAC, and thus they were more familiar with the AHAC brand of hockey; or it might be that they were deferring to Lord Stanley's opinion of the AHAC. Nobody knew why the trustees favoured the AHAC over the other hockey organizations, but their decision positioned the AHAC to become the premier association in the country.[16]

When one compares the trustees' regulations to the original hockey rules, there are some noticeable changes in the presumed behaviour of the potential participants.[17] While the trustees' regulations were relatively minimal when compared to the hockey rules of the AHAC, they nevertheless had taken into consideration disputes on gate money, locations, dates, and choice of officials. These were a far cry from the genteel understanding of the early hockey participants. The trustees' anticipation of potential trouble would not be surprising at all on closer examination of the Canadian sporting world in the late nineteenth century.

Commercialization of winter sports in Canada began before hockey became popular. By the early 1860s, the social elite in Montreal built the Victoria rink for their skating socials. Sensing the commercial possibilities, some entrepreneurs also started to take advantage of the demand for skating facilities in growing cities where traditional recreational spaces had begun to disappear. Together with the increase in urban population, the lack of recreation space and facilities within city limits raised a concern for order and the safety of citizens. Authorities frowned upon those who persisted in pursuing their recreational activities outside approved areas. In 1878, for example, a boy was fined for 'sliding and coasting' on the streets in Montreal.[18]

Competition for clientele grew with the number of skating rinks. Many of these rinks modelled their programs after that organized at the elite Victoria rink. They held skating parties complete with bands, annual carnivals, and masquerades.[19] In part, pressures on land use and rising property values in the city increased the expectations for economic return by landowners. Privately owned sport facilities that failed to meet their expenses, such as the Montreal Gymnasium, ceased to exist.[20] Even the wealthy Victoria rink had to give in to economic pressure and opened its doors to some middle-class patrons. In light of the economic realities, rinks that did not have the backing of wealthy members had to cater, by necessity, to a wider variety of customers. Even the poorer east-end residents in Montreal could enjoy commercialized skating in a rink located in an old reservoir on Upper St Elizabeth street.[21]

Searching for additional revenues, rink owners began to incorporate hockey in addition to skating as part of their regular program as the sport became more popular by the late eighties. One way to ensure this new source of revenue was to start a hockey club bearing the rink's name. The Victorias and Crystals were two examples.[22] They also rented space for practice and games to other clubs. The Montreal Wanderers, for example, rented the Crystal rink for the club's practices and matches.[23] The institutionalization of amateur hockey also provided a steadier source of league games, allowing both the rinks and teams to share in the gate receipts.[24] The increasing number of clubs and leagues, however, placed a heavy demand on ice time. The sport that these demands affected most was skating: beginning in the 1890s, it steadily declined as a favourite winter sport in commercial facilities in Montreal.

Four parties shaped the commercialization process in early amateur hockey. Consumers of commercial leisure expected a quality product. Rink owners, by contrast, needed a product that would draw paying customers and sustain interest. Prompted in part by their own economic interest to increase circulation, the media provided advertising outlets for amateur hockey by reporting on upcoming games, commenting on past contests, and editorializing the state of the sport. As providers, club directors found that the shared gate receipts became increasingly an important source of revenues for maintaining the clubs' operations and improving club facilities. A formalized hockey governing body such as the AHAC, of course, enhanced the coordination of the interests of these parties, and consumers identified the brand of AHAC senior hockey as being of top calibre.

Before the 1890s, players had little stake in the economic aspects of commercialized amateur hockey, other than the prestige of the competition. As late as the early twentieth century, hockey seasons lasted about three months, and remuneration, if any, from hockey only supplemented a player's income. Players usually came from an upper-class or later, middle-class background. Whether or not they had already subscribed to the amateur ideal, they had other careers that were financially more rewarding and stable than hockey. Moreover, the line between players and club management was not distinct in early hockey organizations, since players' interests in commercialized amateur hockey were similar to those of the clubs.

In early commercialized senior amateur hockey, one of the contentious issues for the press and spectators alike was that hockey games seldom started on time. On the day of a semi-final game between the Montreal Hockey Club and the Victorias, a newspaper report pleaded, 'It is to be hoped, too, that the record will be broken and that for once a match be started on the advertised time.'[25]

never competed for a money prize, or staked bet, or with or against any professional for any prize, or who has never taught, pursued, or assisted in the practice of athletic exercise as a means of obtaining a livelihood.'[32] Furthermore, the Association also restricted membership to those who were over eighteen years of age. According to the MAAA, then, an amateur sportsman must refrain from disorderly and impetuous conduct that brought immediate self-gratification. Such behaviour might be tolerable in youth, but certainly not in a gentleman athlete. The Association's membership dues of ten dollars and, later, an added initiation fee of ten dollars were well beyond the reach of most of Montreal's working class. Thus, being an amateur also carried a social-class bias.[33]

Frank Cosentino suggests that by the late 1880s Canadian amateurism proponents did not necessarily frown upon the receipt of money by the clubs as long as the athletes were not paid to play.[34] Certainly, the MAAA members set up an organizational structure that ensured the sound financing needed to operate its activities. Within the Association, an elected executive board ran a two-tiered membership system consisting of the first five affiliated clubs and other connected clubs. The difference between the two categories lay in the power to make decisions. Only affiliated clubs could vote in the MAAA, and each of the five elected three men to serve on the executive board. The MAAA constitution guaranteed the autonomy of each club in running its own affairs, but the executive board controlled, among other things, the Association's finances, which consisted of all the member clubs' funds and assets. Member clubs applied for funding and the directors voted on the requests in their weekly meetings. Elected directors were always 'prominent active businessmen' in Montreal, 'and underlying their every decision was a concern for the "bottom line."'[35]

Partly because of its initial debt obligation, the MAAA focused on finances from the beginning. The executive board's vision of its financial strategy also extended beyond the present, predicting in the 1882 annual report that 'if we can continue to increase our capital every year, we shall soon become a *wealthy* [emphasis added] corporation.'[36] This might seem like a boast, but the MAAA had instituted an organizational structure that supported its vision early on. While the MAAA structure centralized the decision-making process in the hands of the executive board members, most, if not all, of the elected board members were also active sport participants. Thus, the distinction between the administrators and the other members was not always clear cut. This held true for other sports organizations, as well as those in hockey, until the end of the century.

As a major sport organization in Montreal and, indeed, Canada, the MAAA was instrumental in creating a network to promote amateur sports by establishing the Amateur Athletic Association of Canada (AAAC) on April 11, 1884. In part, the establishment of the AAAC marked a determined effort to facilitate competition between different clubs. It was also a reaction to the creeping commercialization of sports in the late nineteenth century. As its membership and the concern over money's influence in amateur sports grew, the AAAC changed its name to the Canadian Amateur Athletic Union (CAAU) in 1898. In 1902 it claimed authority over track and field, basketball, bicycling, ten-pin bowling, handball, hockey, lacrosse, skating, snowshoeing, swimming, wrestling, and rowing, even though lacrosse, bicycling, and rowing all had their own powerful national organizations.

At the heart of the CAAU's legitimacy was its rigid stance on amateurism. In 1902 the CAAU redefined an amateur as

> a person who has not competed in any competition for a staked bet, monies, private or public or gate receipts, or competed with or against a professional for a prize; who has never taught or assisted in the pursuit of any athletic exercise or sport as a means of livelihood; who has never, directly or indirectly, received any bonus or a payment in lieu of loss of time while playing as a member of any club, or any money consideration whatsoever for any services as an athlete except his actual travelling and hotel expenses, or who has never entered into any competition under a name other than his own, or who has never been guilty of selling or pledging his prizes.[37]

This redefinition broadened the categories of what an amateur could not do and, besides forbidding the athlete from accepting money, prohibited amateur athletes contact with any professional − a player who accepted remuneration for his athletic ability. This stance effectively drove the lacrosse organizations away, because at the time individual lacrosse players had already openly accepted money for playing. Despite pleas from the lacrosse associations to allow the mixing of both amateur and professional players on the same team, the CAAU remained steadfast in its stance. In an ironic twist, the CAAU lost the support of the high-profiled lacrosse organizations.[38]

Yet the loss of the lacrosse associations' support did not hurt the CAAU. Although the presence of professional players became more or less an accepted fact in the Canadian national game of lacrosse, and hockey had established its first openly professional league in the early 1900s, the CAAU diligently cultivated grass-roots support in encouraging the establishment of provincial associations. Its efforts came to fruition by 1906 as membership jumped from 36 to 465 clubs and associations. By 1909, the CAAU had a membership of 900 clubs and associations, consisting of over 6000 card-carrying members.[39]

These new recruits joined the CAAU in droves in part because they were confused over the many definitions of an amateur provided by the different sport governing bodies. The varying array of definitions of amateurism was especially difficult for athletes in small towns and rural areas, where most athletes played more than one sport owing to the smaller population base. Multi-sport athletes also existed in large cities. Thus, one could be an amateur in one sport and a professional in another. The Canadian sporting public was looking for a central organization that could bring some order to the chaos, and the CAAU readily accepted the responsibility. This numerical increase in membership gave the CAAU tremendous influence, as its members, at least for the time being, sub-scribed more or less to the CAAU's version of amateurism.[40]

As the CAAU grew into prominence in the mid-nineties, the issue of paid players, which would split commercialized sports into two distinctive paths, had finally reached the breaking point. Backed by its increasing influence, the CAAU continued its hard-line approach in its stringent definition of an amateur. While some senior lacrosse associations had given up hope of negotiating a compromise with the CAAU to allow both paid and non-paid players to compete together, many sports, including ice hockey, decided to remain inside the CAAU. This spoke volumes about the success and influence of the CAAU's grassroots move-ment. Although not all of the CAAU membership subscribed to the same rigid definition of an amateur, many sports associations, such as the MAAA, were bound to the national organization because they had members who participated in more than one sport. Until sports like lacrosse could offer their players sufficient compensation to leave the amateur ranks, none would desert the CAAU. Some hockey clubs, however, would soon follow lacrosse's path.

As the dual processes of institutionalization and commercialization contributed to the popularization of amateur hockey, the once closed circle of upper-class, gentleman's hockey began to show signs of cracking by the mid-1890s. One of the last gasps of gentleman's hockey at the elite level occurred on February 2, 1895, when the AHAC voided a Crystal club win against Quebec because the Crystals, the only non-upper-class-rink sponsored club, had merged its team with the Shamrock club. At the time, the Shamrocks, an Irish sports club, was not a member of the AHAC. This merger of the two clubs made the new club stronger and apparently angered the rest of the AHAC clubs, which disapproved of such ungentlemanly conduct in pursuit of victory. Then, the AHAC had to call a special meeting two weeks later to discuss a rough match between Quebec and Ottawa. Not only did several players exchange punches during the game, but the Quebec fans also dragged the officials back to the rink after the game was over and wanted them to declare the contest a draw. The Ottawa contingent further complained about the verbal abuse directed by the home fans towards them despite the presence of lady supporters. Because the integrity of the officials must be maintained, the AHAC passed a motion to suspend the Quebec club for the remainder of the season.[41]

The row over the Quebec club also demonstrated the role of the media as civic boosters. By this time, hockey's growing popularity as Canada's winter pastime had made it a powerful symbolic representation for different locales. Its tie to civic pride offered 'an opportunity to share a common passion as well as to rehearse old rivalries.'[42] After the AHAC suspended the Quebec club in the 1894–5 season, the Quebec media defended the home club, even though the club stood to miss only one game and was in no position to contend for the championship of the Association. Boosterism by the media occurred in other hockey cities as well. When the Winnipeg Victorias challenged for the Stanley Cup for the first time, Winnipeg newspapers arranged live telegraph coverage of the games in Montreal. The *Winnipeg Free Press* proclaimed that the city would become 'the hockey center of the world' with a successful challenge, and urged the 'seven of the prairie capital's most stalwart sons to do battle with the representatives of the 200,000 people who inhabit Canada's greatest city.'[43] After the Victorias won the Cup, the *Free Press* was beside itself. It exalted the home team's victory over 'the champions of the effete east.'[44] Like it or not, the media's emphasis on the importance of victory promoted senior amateur hockey and its players as defenders of civic pride.

The media's self-prescribed role of civic booster did not come by coincidence and the rapid growth of daily newspapers in the late nineteenth century was a contributing force to an increased interest in local happenings. Whereas early weekly and biweekly newspapers catered to a small literate elite, the 'dailies' targeted the urban masses as their customers. To reach their target market and compete for advertising revenues, the dailies' editors sought to appeal to the taste of urban readers by sensationalizing stories of crime and scandal. They also favoured the reporting of local events and included entertainment and leisure news. Reports of dramatic struggles between two rivals in sporting contests fit into the overall marketing strategy of the dailies. By the late 1880s reports of hockey matches appeared more frequently. As the newspapers provided more coverage of sports, editors moved these reports from the city news section to an expanded sports section. Since the dailies targeted local readers, most of their reporters, not surprisingly, tended to favour the local club against visitors from other cities.[45]

While the media equated success in the rink with the reputation of the city, some reporters did not lose sight of the dominant amateur ethos that stressed gentlemanly conduct. As early as 1886, criticisms appeared in the *Montreal Gazette* about rough play in hockey. After a game between McGill University and the Crystals, the reporter lamented that the 'worst feature of (rough play) is that the boys playing are all of the same class' and insisted that there should be 'no room for differences of any kind.'[46] For this reporter, at least, the presence of rough play among upper- and middle-class participants was particularly distressing. Rough play in amateur hockey was not the only concern from the media's point of view. Reporters also noticed a pattern of behaviour that strayed from the spirit of the game. Since the days of the Montreal Carnival tournament, when Quebec did not bring the requisite number of players, it had been the custom for the home club to accommodate the visitors in the spirit of good sportsmanship. During a game between the Crystal and Quebec clubs in 1886, a Quebec player sustained an injury and was unable to continue. Since the Quebec club did not have a substitute player, it asked the Crystals to drop a player and continue the game with six a side. Behind in the score at the time, the Crystal club argued that the rules did not demand such a practice, and it refused the request. Subsequently, the referee declared the game for the Crystals. Disgusted with the Crystals' unaccommodating stand, the *Montreal Gazette* sport editor questioned the value of winning the championship via such means.[47]

As winning became more and more important, even that bastion of amateurism the MAAA succumbed to the practice of adhering to the letter of the rules rather than the spirit of the competition. During a game in the 1892–3 season, the Montreal Hockey Club refused to allow a ruled-off Crystal player to return in the overtime period. The Crystals subsequently filed a protest. Nor was the Montreal incident the only disagreement among AHAC clubs during that season. In fact, the AHAC had to call a special meeting near the end of the season to deal with the various protests lodged by the clubs. In light of these developments, the *Montreal Gazette* chastised the tactics used by the various clubs in search of victory.[48]

After having its internal squabbles published and criticized by the media the AHAC took action. During the annual meeting the following season, the AHAC secretary, J.A. Findlay, acknowledged in his report the protests in the previous season and the fact that the game had changed. He then suggested the group use the occasion to revise the constitution. This they did, but in the process member clubs failed to address the behavioural problems. Most of the revisions dealt with the operational procedures of the Association and the playoff format. Thus, most AHAC executives seemed confident of their product's marketability and did not see a real need for any meaningful changes.[49]

The erosion of gentlemanly conduct in amateur hockey continued. During the 1894 Stanley Cup final, the play of two players, one from each opposing club, as well as the conduct of the referee came under fire.[50] By 1904, a critic lamented that a Stanley Cup playoff series between the Ottawa Hockey Club and the Winnipeg Rowing Club did not live up to the standards of the past because there was 'too much of the win or die spirit.' He associated this development with the professional ranks, 'where the players are hired men ... [who] consider it necessary to catch the man so that he may be hurt; he must be stopped, stop him any way.'[51] The age of the gentleman player was on the wane.

The increasing emphasis on winning was by no means the only contributor to the changes facing the AHAC. Early on, clubs had recognized the revenue potential of senior amateur hockey. This tie between revenue and success slowly pushed hockey into a development similar to that experienced by baseball in the United States almost half a century earlier, when some amateur baseball clubs began actively recruiting players outside their membership base. Further, some clubs had begun to resort to paying skilled players.[52]

To maintain a competitive if not a winning team at the senior level, hockey club directors recognized the need to search for talent. Traditionally, members filled the various hockey squads because a key objective of most sport clubs was to provide sport and recreation for its membership. Intra-club competitions were common practices. These internal affairs fostered fellowship among members. With the increasing emphasis on winning and its corresponding financial considerations, the distinction between the skilled and the less-skilled players became important. Intra-club contests became less and less frequent and only the better skilled players played in the senior squad. For the less-skilled club members, the chance to play with skilled players and, thus, to improve their own skills lessened. In effect, this trend created a wider gap between the senior-calibre players and the rest. This was true at the club level as well as the association level. Rarely did a hockey club in the intermediate division make it to the senior rank after the establishment of the AHAC. Furthermore, the separation of players based on skills also meant that it would take the less-skilled players longer to achieve competency in the senior rank. When the older, skilled players retired, a club might not have anyone of similar calibre to replace them. For some club directors, the easier way to maintain a successful hockey club was to broaden the search for players, even if it meant including players who came from different social backgrounds and locales.

The problem in the search for talent by competing clubs and associations first became noticeable in the OHA. At the level of hockey skill, the OHA clubs could not match those in the AHAC. The best club in Ontario, the Ottawas, played in the AHAC. When a Toronto newspaper suggested that the OHA clubs would soon be good enough to challenge the AHAC, the *Montreal Gazette* editor sneered at the idea.[53] Hence, the OHA was particularly wary about player movements within the organization as some clubs tried to secure the services of skilled players by providing jobs for their recruits. At its 1899 convention, it passed an amendment requiring players to establish residency.[54] In the same year, rumours of paid players began to circulate in hockey circles.[55]

A consequence of the emphasis on winning and the commercialization of hockey was the creation of a hierarchical division of teams. From its inception, the AHAC had been a voluntary organization that, theoretically, clubs could join or leave at any time. In reality, any club wishing to join the Association had to submit an application that would be subjected to the close scrutiny of the AHAC executive committee. Since the champion of the senior clubs within its ranks defended the Stanley Cup and the honour of the AHAC against all outside challengers, the senior clubs increasingly became leery about the process of admission into the Association and especially into the senior series. Admission to the AHAC called for a vote from all members, and the senior clubs were clearly the minority within the Association. Furthermore, rink owners wanted senior hockey as their marquee attraction. In general, AHAC hockey at the senior level drew good crowds. When the Ottawa Capitals, a team of doubtful quality according to the senior clubs, gained admission into the senior rank in 1898, the five senior clubs from the previous season withdrew and formed a new organization, the Canadian Amateur Hockey League (CAHL). This effectively created a closed corporation and excluded all except those in the senior series. From this point on, the affairs of the senior, intermediate, and junior clubs were to be governed by separate bodies. In its first annual meeting, the CAHL secretary, George R. James of the Montreal club, proudly announced that it had been 'a year of prosperity' for the organization 'composed exclusively of senior clubs ... without any reference to the intermediate clubs.'[56] He noted the CAHL's successes in gate receipts and in defending the Stanley Cup. A year later, the CAHL forbade its members from competing with any outside teams without first receiving sanction.[57]

This separation and concentration of top talent would become a double-edged sword as the battle waged by the CAAU against what it saw as the evil of money rose to its peak at the beginning of the new century. As elite-level hockey drew more and more fans, the need to operate the CAHL in a manner that befitted the skill level exhibited on the ice became more and more apparent to the clubs and rink owners. Moreover, fans and the media demanded a more business-like approach in the running of the CAHL's affairs. Tardy starting time, sloppy play, and other unbecoming conduct came under intense scrutiny. The CAHL and its later derivatives increasingly spent a great deal of time attending to the commercial elements of elite amateur hockey by restructuring the organizational framework and revising the constitution and bylaws. The professionalization of hockey had begun.

Chapter 3

The Hockey Front in
the Athletic War

Even before the turn of the twentieth century, economic interests and the emphasis on victory took on increasing significance in Canadian hockey circles and drove the Montreal-based CAHL to reorganize the way it conducted its business. The CAHL had established an organizational foundation that separated itself from those whom it deemed unworthy. Under this hierarchical division, the CAHL and its later derivatives attempted to corner the market of highly skilled hockey players during the first decade in the new century. In maintaining this leadership position in the developing commercialized hockey network, senior amateur hockey in Montreal contributed to a larger struggle in the Canadian sporting world between the ideologues of strict amateurism and proponents of a more liberal interpretation of the amateur athlete.

Alan Metcalfe and others have written about the efforts of the amateur purists' crusade, known as the 'Athletic War,' to fight against the evil of money in Canadian sport at the beginning of the twentieth century. At the heart of this struggle was the definition of an amateur. Amateur purists wanted a strict interpretation and adherence to a definition that expanded the prohibitions of what an amateur could not do. Given the already close connections between commercial interests and several popular sports at the elite level, this restrictive definition created a schism in the Canadian sporting world.[1]

As arguably the most popular winter sport, amateur hockey in Canada in general, and in Montreal in particular, became part of the terrain in this ideological struggle. The commercial success of elite-level amateur hockey drew others to enter into the hockey business and no doubt fuelled amateur purists' war cry against the influence of money in sport. Yet it also created a vibrant market. Competition among the different hockey organizations for players increased demand and helped to develop an emerging labour market for expert players. Indeed, the first decade of the twentieth century was a transition period for elite-level commercialized hockey, and the hegemony of the once exclusive Montreal-based hockey governing body faced an uncertain future as the Athletic War raged on.

Amateur ice hockey continued to define and redefine behaviour and standards during the first decade of the twentieth century, when a war against money's influence began in earnest. As the premier organization in commercialized amateur hockey, the CAHL worked to improve its product packaging and its organizational structure. In its fifth annual convention, the CAHL amended its constitution by instituting a ten-dollar fine for late start of games, a persistent problem that had been plaguing the organization, and a one-hundred-dollar fine for defaults. Whereas default fines had gone to the CAHL in previous years, they now went to the other team, thus signifying the importance of the financial consequence of a default to the aggrieved club. Potential financial consequences became increasingly important in arriving at the League's decisions and policies.[2]

The importance of economic considerations also showed up in the relationship between the CAHL and one of the hockey network's stakeholders, the Montreal Arena Corporation. Unhappy with the pattern of late starts in the past, the rink's management undoubtedly had been urging the CAHL to present a more professional image. As the CAHL attempted to do so, it also tried to renegotiate the gate split with the Arena, where many of the games were played. But the Montreal Arena was one of a kind as far as seating capacity and consumer comfort were concerned. With the CAHL games drawing well, the larger capacity of the Arena certainly gave a better return to the clubs. Furthermore, demand outstripped supply with so many hockey associations, besides the CAHL, in existence and so few suitable rinks to accommodate them. Not surprisingly, the CAHL failed to convince the Arena Corporation to rework the gate split. This issue, however, remained a sore point between elite-level hockey organizations and rink management for years to come; and eventually, before the age of public subsidies, some teams financed their own arenas. Still, the days when the clubs did their own bidding had passed. The CAHL was assuming more and more responsibilities.[3]

Competitive and commercial successes seemed to justify the CAHL's increasingly centralized role in the administration of senior hockey affairs. With the exception of the 1900–1 season, its members captured the Stanley Cup four out of the first five years. More importantly, business had been good for the CAHL. In the second game of the 1901 Stanley Cup final, a crowd of over 4000 showed up, even though the rink had raised the admission, and the gate receipts totalled $2700.[4]

While the CAHL valued the financial windfall and prestige of the Stanley

Cup, its directors also worried that Cup challenges interfered with the League's scheduled games because challenges could occur at any time during the hockey season. When the Stanley Cup trustees ordered the Montreal Hockey Club to defend its title in the middle of the 1902–3 season, the CAHL refused to release the Montreal club from the league schedule to defend the title. It reasoned that the Stanley Cup series would affect League game attendance adversely. After much negotiation between the League and the trustees, as well as some internal wrangling among the members, the League relented. The best-two-out-of-three series held in late January yielded $14,000, and the two competitors received $3000 each.[5]

The economics that underpinned the arguments over when a CAHL club could defend the Stanley Cup demonstrated the prominence of commercialization in elite Canadian amateur sport since the turn of the twentieth century. Elite-level hockey clubs had been successful financially. To maintain quality play, clubs tried hard to retain their skilled players. Despite the residence rule and other controlling mechanisms, skilled players still managed to move from city to city. This was true in hockey as in other popular commercialized amateur sports such as rugby and lacrosse. Hence, clubs offered day jobs to skilled players or secretly paid them so that the players would stay put. A Kingston reporter chastised the OHA executives for turning a blind eye to clubs in large cities that were whittling players away from smaller towns by offering them 'lucrative positions' and '$15 a week during winter.'[6] Reacting to this and other similar complaints, amateurism proponents began a campaign to curb the influence of money in amateur sports; hockey was not exempted in this ideological battle. One measure advocated was the enforcement of a strict definition of an amateur that forbade an amateur athlete, among other things, to associate with any pro-wfessional (paid) player.

Not everyone in amateur sports agreed that this was the solution to counter commercialism in amateur sports, however. Acknowledging the realities of running a top-flight sport organization, the MAAA, the parent organization of the Montreal Hockey Club, favoured a more liberal definition of an amateur by allowing the intermingling of professional and amateur players. In part, the MAAA member clubs, such as its hockey and lacrosse clubs, increasingly found that the pre-eminence they had once enjoyed in the sport world was eroding. As the MAAA and some defenders of amateurism saw it, the problem was the increasing presence of payment under the table by clubs to retain and recruit players. Moreover, many athletes in a sport association such as the MAAA partici-pated in more than one sport, and some sports such as lacrosse allowed payments to players. Thus, the CAAU rule that forbade the intermingling of amateurs and paid players would taint many athletes. Attempting to address the dilemma in

1904, the MAAA delegates to the CAAU convention proposed a constitutional amendment that allowed amateurs to compete with and against paid players without jeopardizing their status as amateurs. This moderate stance, however, met with staunch resistance, especially from amateur purists in Toronto, such as those in the OHA, and the schism grew between proponents of the status quo and the reformers.

In the world of amateur hockey, the OHA began to position itself as the defender of pure amateurism. The OHA had adopted the bridge-burning position of once-a-professional-always-a-professional on amateurism when the first openly professional hockey league, the International Hockey League (IHL), started its first season of play in the Lake Michigan region in 1904. This was not an unexpected move by the OHA, for it had been a strong opponent of pay-for-play hockey. Although the IHL had only one Canadian franchise, in Sault Ste Marie, Ontario, most hockey players in that league came from Canada and many hailed from the OHA. In the face of what he considered as the creeping menace of professional hockey, the OHA president, John Robertson, in a lengthy address, chided the CAAU for ignoring its responsibilities during the OHA's annual convention, and blamed the Montreal faction for the corruption in amateur sport.[7]

While the OHA and its president were staunch defenders of amateurism, their rigid stance against professionalism also had something to do with the dismal record of the Ontario champions in challenging for the Stanley Cup. Until 1904 Ontario teams, with the exception of the Ottawa club from the AHAC, had appeared in and lost six Stanley Cup series. Many of the losses were lopsided, and the gate receipts sometimes did not even cover the clubs' expenses.[8] The IHL's recruiting efforts in Ontario undoubtedly drained top talent from the OHA and would not help to improve the poor performances turned in by the Ontario senior amateur hockey clubs against the CAHL teams. Through a restrictive definition of an amateur, the OHA hoped to discourage, if not stop, its skilled players from leaving the province's top amateur clubs.

While civic pride had been evident in inter-city games, the Stanley Cup competition also presented an opportunity to boost regional superiority. By the turn of the century, Ontario had become increasingly industrialized and politically powerful. Under the Liberal premiership of Oliver Mowat, the provincial administration 'was becoming ever more modern, better able than any other regime in Canada, federal or provincial, to accommodate the tremendous and dynamic developments of the twentieth-century Canadian society.'[9] Still, Montreal remained the centre of the Canadian sports world. To some in Ontario, the losses in Stanley Cup competition did not fit the rising status of Ontario. Worse, the champions from the Manitoba Hockey League drew much more attention in

Montreal than the OHA representatives in Stanley Cup contests in past years. The Montreal media gave the Manitoba challengers more coverage and, in general, the games drew a much larger crowd than those of the Ontario challengers.[10] This had to be a slap in the face to many in Ontario who considered Manitoba to be in that wilderness between industrializing Ontario and the Pacific coast and certainly inferior to Ontario economically and politically.

The reputation of the OHA had further been plagued by constant turnover of its membership. Clubs appeared and disappeared. A 1903 *Montreal Gazette* editorial attributed the poor quality of OHA hockey, in large part, to its liberal policy in admitting clubs to the senior division. Many of these clubs folded within a short time, which certainly did not bode well for the OHA's image as a stable organization. To safeguard its own interests and to improve its prestige as an elite league, the OHA's harsh approach to prevent an exodus of its top players to the IHL was a logical choice.[11]

As the OHA looked to maintaining hard-line amateurism as a strategy to bolster its prestige, the commercial potential of hockey had nudged the CAHL further away from its amateur roots. In order to sustain its status as the premier amateur hockey entertainment and therefore maintain premium prices, the CAHL decided to continue its exclusive membership policy, which was drifting further and further away from a criterion based on social class to one that emphasized the calibre of the competition. As hockey spread to other parts of Canada, the Stanley Cup competition became a symbol of prowess for the victorious cities and the organizations to which the victors belonged. Since the CAHL received an automatic bid for the Stanley Cup, the exclusionary market positioning strategy effectively placed the Montreal-based association in the top rung of the hockey world by setting up the CAHL as the authority on the worthiness of a new applicant's entry; and there was no lack of applicants for the CAHL. In 1899 the CAHL even turned down an application from McGill University, a traditionally aristocratic institution that played a key role in the development of organized hockey in the early days, to join the senior circuit.[12]

To be fair to the CAHL, other considerations also made the exclusionary practice logical, if not unavoidable. Facilities, in particular, presented a major difficulty. Demand outstripped supply as more and more hockey clubs formed in the Montreal region. Practice and game times were at a premium. At the senior level, revenue considerations further reduced the number of rinks capable of hosting the matches. Montreal-based CAHL clubs had played most of their matches at the Arena ever since it opened, and to admit a new member meant straining the already crowded Arena calendar.[13]

Technological limitations further complicated the facility problem. Although artificial ice-making technology existed and there were rinks that employed this technology, none of them were in Canada. Hockey seasons in Canada still depended on cold weather to keep the ice surface in playing condition. In Montreal, and even in farther north Ottawa and Quebec City, that meant approximately a nine-week season from late December to mid-March. Since players held regular jobs, they could not travel frequently during the week. In many League meetings, scheduling usually took up much of the time as teams bickered about the dates on which they were willing to travel. A short season with limited facilities restricted the number of out-of-town games in the CAHL scheduling and made the inclusion of new teams almost impossible.[14]

Despite all the limitations, exclusion elicited resentment from those who were left out. In 1899 rumours of a new organization consisting of several rejected clubs, including the Nationals of Montreal and the Ottawa Capitals, began to circulate. Nothing came of the rumours, but the exclusionary practice continued. In the following year, the CAHL moved to forbid its members from arranging exhibition matches during the season without the consent of the League. At the 1902 annual meeting, the CAHL directors again rejected two more applications for admission and forbade its League champion from defending the Stanley Cup before the season's end.[15]

The zealously guarded exclusive membership of the CAHL collapsed in the 1903–4 season when several rejected applicants to the senior series (league) formed a new organization, the Federal Amateur Hockey League (FAHL), on December 5, 1903. Besides the continual practice of gate-keeping by the CAHL, several contemporary developments prompted the creation of the new organization. Early in November, the CAHL rejected an application from the Cornwall Hockey Club, even though the Cornwall team was relatively successful in the OHA senior series and, geographically speaking, was closer to Montreal than both the Ottawa and the Quebec clubs.[16]

At about the same time, player troubles within the CAHL surfaced. Several players on the Montreal Hockey Club were unhappy with the club's directors and challenged their authority. In this particular case, the directors introduced a new constitution at its annual meeting and quelled the disaffected faction. The manner in which the Montreal club directors handled this challenge, however, left the players bitter.[17]

By the beginning of December 1903, rumours of a new hockey governing body appeared in the press. The new organization supposedly included the Nationals of Montreal, the Capitals of Ottawa, the Cornwall Hockey Club, all failed applicants to the CAHL, and a fourth team called the Montreal Wanderers, which was formed from the disillusioned players from the Montreal and Victoria Hockey Clubs. While the first three teams consisted of mostly untested players in the CAHL series, the Wanderers assembled a top-quality seven with four Montreal Hockey Club defections, including its captain, and two Victoria players. Almost immediately, comments appeared in various hockey cities regarding the new organization, the FAHL, and the CAHL. Most writers agreed that the CAHL had been operating as a closed corporation for too long and criticized it for not recognizing the growth of hockey. At least one reporter, however, doubted the credibility of the new hockey governing body.[18]

In line with its elite status, the CAHL's initial reaction to the FAHL was one of condescension and indifference. Even though the new Wanderers club had decimated the Montreal Hockey Club, CAHL President Harry Trihey, himself a former top-notch player from the Shamrock club, dismissed the new organization as weak and accused it of 'introducing to hockey an element dangerous to the welfare of the best traditions of the game.' He further defended the CAHL policy of exclusion by submitting that 'in one instance only was a worthy club refused admission.'[19]

Trihey might have had good reasons to remain nonchalant about the new rival. The CAHL still had the Ottawa Hockey Club, which had won the Stanley Cup the previous year, and from all indications, the new organization seemed reluctant to confront the CAHL. William Foran, the FAHL president, stated that the new circuit would not compete with the CAHL for players and playing dates. Besides, rumours of new hockey organizations had appeared before, and often they disappeared just as quickly.[20] When it became apparent that the new circuit was for real, the CAHL hinted that it planned to expand its current membership with some of the clubs in the FAHL. By then, it was too late. The CAHL was punished for its own arrogance when the Cornwall club refused to desert the FAHL.[21]

The prestige of the CAHL as the premier hockey organization was clearly evident when the FAHL proceeded to organize its affairs for the first season. Even though it was a competitor in the marketplace, the FAHL chose not to confront the established CAHL. Perhaps realizing that most of its players were unknown to the hockey public, Foran announced that his organization would not schedule any game on the same night as the CAHL. Attempting to present the league as a credible hockey association, the FAHL executives adopted the CAHL's constitution, but with two important deviations. It relaxed the requirement for new membership. Whereas the CAHL needed a unanimous vote to admit a new member, the FAHL constitution required only a majority vote. In order to control player movement, the FAHL included an expulsion clause banishing any player who defected to a different organization. The second point was notable for what it did not say. It did not mention a residency requirement like that of the OHA. In effect, the FAHL acknowledged the existence of a labour market and the possibility of player movement, as long as it was within the same organization.[22]

For the first time in senior amateur hockey in Montreal, two organizations competed in the same marketplace. Yet the appearance of a challenger to the CAHL hardly affected the labour market. While the new FAHL recognized that quality players would give credibility to the League, its adherence to the amateur code forbade it from openly bidding for players. Players were also apprehensive about the viability of the new organization, and many of them still regarded the CAHL as the premier circuit. Furthermore, three of the four FAHL clubs already had their full complement of players before the CAHL rejected their applications to join the senior circuit. These clubs, of course, believed their squads would be competitive in the senior series. As the 1903–4 season opened, early pronouncements seemed to confirm the superior calibre of play in the CAHL. Still, the newcomers were fairly successful in drawing a crowd initially.[23]

By about mid-season, the FAHL received an unexpected hand in legitimizing its status as a governing body on a par with the CAHL. The old problem of starting games late created internal bickering in the CAHL and led to the resignation from the League of the defending Stanley Cup champions, the Ottawa Hockey Club. A crowd of 5000 waited for one-and-a-half hours for the arrival of the Ottawa club at a game in Montreal with the Victoria Hockey Club. By midnight, the match remained unfinished, with the Ottawas leading by a score of four to one. Both teams agreed to discontinue the match. In accordance with the CAHL constitution, the League levied the ten-dollar fine against the Ottawa club and discussed the tardiness of teams at a special meeting. To deter such behaviour in the future, the League voted to increase the fine from ten to fifty dollars, and demanded a replay of the Ottawa-Victoria match. Ottawa objected. At the time of the incident, the Ottawa club was far ahead in the standing and felt that some of the clubs were conspiring to halt its winning streak. The Ottawa representative made an attempt at compromise and offered to replay the match if the league championship depended on the outcome of that one game. Given the strength of the Ottawa club, the others voted the compromise down. When the motion demanding a replay was passed, the Ottawa club resigned.[24]

Economics undoubtedly influenced the decisions made by the Ottawa and other CAHL clubs. For them at the time, the Stanley Cup series yielded extra revenues beyond those received from the scheduled CAHL games. Since the Stanley Cup rules dictated that the defending champions should play on home ice, challengers had to travel to the defender's city. Thus, in contrast to regular-season games, the defending champion incurred no travelling costs, but stood to gain from its split with the rink. After its resignation from the CAHL, the Ottawa club vowed to finish the season by playing the Stanley Cup challenge series only.[25]

The importance of the Stanley Cup in both prestige and financial rewards led to wrangling about the ownership of the trophy between the CAHL and the Ottawa club. The opening shot, however, came from one of the Cup trustees, P.D. Ross, publisher of the *Ottawa Journal*. He declared that Ottawa remained holder of the trophy until dethroned by a challenger. This led to the CAHL questioning his decision, arguing that it inherited the role of defender of the Cup by virtue of its connection to the defunct AHAC. Now that Ottawa had resigned, the CAHL demanded its current champion be declared the Cup holder. Not to miss a golden opportunity to position itself as a legitimate heir to the trophy, the FAHL chimed in to welcome Ottawa to join its group and suggested that the Montreal Irish club, the Shamrocks, would soon follow. Local newspapers were all busy laying blame.[26]

Although Ottawa had vowed to carry on by playing exhibitions and the Stanley Cup series, it had to realize that the strategy did not make any economic sense. A regular-season schedule provided a steady source of revenues that sustained an elite-level hockey club, and the Ottawa club had no wish to go back to the old challenge system. Hence, it joined the FAHL, but its admission would not be effective until the following season. Recognizing that it was in a precarious situation, the CAHL attempted to lure the Wanderers into the fold, but was rebuffed.[27] In the meantime, an improbable scenario existed: by the end of the current season, there would be a champion from each of the respective organizations as well as the Stanley Cup holder, which had only completed part of its season schedule. Amidst the confusion one writer suggested to 'throw the old cup away.'[28] Quickly, though, he conceded that the economic interests of the various stakeholders in senior hockey made this proposition difficult. The whole quagmire finally ended when Ottawa successfully defended the Stanley Cup.[29]

The commercial aspects of amateur hockey seemed to be an open secret. It was only a matter of time before the proverbial straw would break the farcical camel's back. Meanwhile, rumours flew again by the end of the season that the Shamrocks would join the FAHL. Given the close relationship between French and Irish hockey organizations in the past, there emerged the distinct possibility that the CAHL would only have three senior teams by the next season. The Shamrocks denied the rumours, but it seemed that the CAHL's days were numbered by the end of the 1903–4 season.[30]

The early demise of the CAHL was greatly exaggerated; at least, it did not occur during the following season. At the beginning of the 1904–5 season, the CAHL manoeuvred to bring some degree of credibility to itself now that the Stanley Cup resided with its rival. It managed to add two new clubs for the coming season, one of which, the French-Canadian Nationals, came from the rival FAHL. Perhaps the most important move came when the CAHL attempted to snare the two strongest clubs in the FAHL, the Ottawa and the Wanderers hockey clubs. If these two other FAHL clubs switched sides, the FAHL could not possibly survive. Still, harsh feelings from the past resurfaced when the Ottawa representative reportedly presented his plan on amalgamation in a somewhat dictatorial tone. His callous attitude towards dropping other fellow FAHL club members, something a gentleman certainly would not do, also did not sit well with some in the CAHL, despite their desire to end the competition for hockey patrons. Finally, the elected CAHL president, Fred McRobbie of the Victorias, accused the Wanderers of being a professional team. He apparently had not forgotten that the Wanderers had two of the former Victoria players. Thus, the hockey war between the CAHL and the FAHL continued when the season began in December.[31]

The commercial successes of the AHAC and then the CAHL demonstrated that elite-level hockey in the Montreal region could be a viable business. However, the struggles between the CAHL and the FAHL also illustrated that the region could not support two senior hockey associations. Especially in Montreal, the seven clubs from the two circuits saturated the market during the 1903–4 season and affected gate receipts. Only seven hundred spectators showed up for a game between the Victorias and the Shamrocks. Even the Stanley Cup champion, the Ottawas, drew only 'a handful of spectators' against the FAHL Capitals. The post-game report described a 'small crowd present' at the CAHL's final season game between the two oldest clubs, Montreal and Victoria.[32] In order for senior hockey to prosper again, its organizers had to reduce market competition first and foremost. They also needed to make other changes that addressed the efficient running of their operation. Since senior hockey was still under the aegis of amateurism, labour costs had not been an operational concern, or at least the issue had not been addressed openly. Yet, other developments opened discussions and changed policies on the issue of labour.

As the CAHL and FAHL prepared to carry on their competition for hockey patrons in the Montreal region, a professional hockey league, the International Hockey League, appeared in 1904. The IHL granted franchises in the copper-mining region of Lake Michigan as well as one in Pittsburgh.[33] While it had only one Canadian franchise, in Sault Ste Marie, the IHL was actively and successfully recruiting players in Canada. When the manager of the Canadian franchise went to Toronto to recruit players, he openly accused OHA teams paying players, just like the IHL, and said the OHA was hypocritical in allowing these shady deals. Rationalizing and justifying the professional-hockey business model, he maintained that the IHL would 'be run on the strictest business basis' with 'a salary limit,' and would offer other jobs to those players who wanted them. Furthermore, the players were under contract that regulated their conduct in and away from the arena. The home team would receive 60 per cent of the gate; in addition, 'the visitors are given a guarantee of expenses in case the 40 per cent does not reach the expenses.'[34]

The IHL departed from the operational model used by the Canadian hockey associations, for whom contracts and salary limits did not exist. Moreover, the control of players extended beyond the matter of whom they could play for. The professional contracts included provisions governing player conduct during as well as outside the games. Another notable fact about the IHL was that, with the exception of the Pittsburgh club, all franchise locations had relatively small population bases. Unlike the elite-level clubs in the CAHL and FAHL, which drew support from membership in sizable markets, mining profits and enthusiastic promoters backed the IHL enterprise.[35]

No one really knows if the creation of the IHL had any immediate impact on the eastern hockey circle. For some of the players at least, the IHL offered an alternative to under-the-table payment in amateur hockey as the Athletic War raged on. Many established players from Canada jumped to the IHL because the salaries offered were attractive and, perhaps best of all, they did not have to hide the fact that they were salaried. The IHL also offered a number of French-Canadian players an opportunity to play elite-level hockey.[36]

While the IHL turned to open professionalism, the two Montreal-based organizations still clung to amateurism, at least in theory. Even though the IHL lured Canadian players away from their clubs, the CAHL and the FAHL were not overly concerned about losing their players, nor did they consider turning professional to prevent the exodus of players. In the context of the Athletic War, no Canadian hockey governing body was prepared to make the leap into professional hockey because that would effectively bar hockey players from other sports. Since the MAAA's proposal of allowing the intermingling of amateurs and professionals could still be a reality, many hockey executives, especially those in Montreal, were still holding out hope for liberalizing the definition of an amateur. Even if a club lost most of its senior squad, as the Montreal Hockey Club did in 1903, it could always draw from its intermediate club or 'persuade' a player from a different club to join as a replacement. Besides, the IHL drew many more players from the OHA than from the CAHL and the FAHL.[37]

The urgent problem at the beginning of the 1905–6 season for the CAHL and the FAHL was the overcrowded market, especially in Montreal with seven clubs.[38] To solve this dilemma, a number of the established clubs in the CAHL and the FAHL proposed to join forces and form a new organization in that season. Six clubs, the Victoria, Quebec, Montreal, and Shamrock hockey clubs of the CAHL and the Ottawa and Wanderer clubs of the FAHL, formed the new

Eastern Canada Amateur Hockey Association (ECAHA). This effectively reduced the Montreal senior hockey market to four clubs, as the ECAHA dropped the two Montreal-based clubs that finished at the bottom of the CAHL standings the previous year. Since there were few suitable rinks for senior hockey in Montreal, the formation of a separate hockey body by the excluded clubs seemed unlikely. With the powerful clubs lined up in the ECAHA, the major facility provider, the Montreal Arena, could not possibly be interested in granting the weaker, excluded clubs any ice time.

The economic motivation behind the formation of the ECAHA was perhaps clearest in the initial discussions about, and the ultimate decisions on, which Montreal teams would be included in the new organization. Westmount of the CAHL was originally one of the four Montreal clubs included when the idea of the ECAHA first surfaced, but Ottawa suggested the Wanderers, its FAHL colleague and rival, because it was the stronger team, and their matches usually drew large crowds. The Montreal Hockey Club, which was still fuming about its defected players in the Wanderers club from the previous season, vigorously objected. It held out for the inclusion of Westmount. Knowing that Ottawa had tremendous drawing power, as it had won the Stanley Cup in the three previous years, others weighed in to try to persuade the Montreal club to change its mind, but the club held firm.[39]

As the clubs quarrelled over the selection of which Montreal clubs were to be admitted into the new organization, the Arena Company intervened. Even before the question of the composition of the association was settled, the Arena Company announced that it had reserved six Saturday nights for the Wanderers' games. Three weeks before the start of the season, Arena president Eddie Sheppard voiced his displeasure at the clubs' continuous bickering. He delivered a not-so-subtle hint of his support for the Wanderers in the proposed merger, noting that the Arena received more revenue from the Wanderers' games than from those of the entire CAHL.[40]

Economic considerations eventually decided the issue. After Sheppard's comment, both the Montreal and Westmount clubs immediately suggested that they would play elsewhere. As the hockey season was less than a month away, no practical solution without a substantial financial loss was in sight. Besides, the Arena had the largest crowd capacity. It seemed, after all the squabbles among the clubs, that the rink management had the trump card. During an acrimonious CAHL meeting held on Saturday December 9, accusations of treachery flew freely. Knowing that it would be one of the sacrificial lambs, Westmount accused the others of backing out from a signed agreement to stay together. Sensing a deadlock, a Montreal delegate called for an adjournment. But over the weekend, six clubs apparently reached an agreement. On Monday, with William Northey of the Arena acting as chairman, the ECAHA came into being in a secret meeting before the adjourned CAHL meeting resumed later that afternoon. The National and the Westmount clubs were out. A gentlemen's agreement mattered little in the face of potential financial success.[41]

The back-stabbing and rancour in the formation of the ECAHA led to the restructuring of the new organization. In past hockey governing bodies, member clubs' directors took turns in assuming the president's post. With the lesson of the dismantling of the CAHL and the war wounds of the inter-league struggle still fresh, suspicion ruled the day. The only thing that the delegates could agree on in its first meeting was to elect a chairman who 'should be one of prestige in the hockey world, but not actively connected with any of the six clubs.'[42] They selected Howard Wilson of Montreal, and contacted him by phone to ask for his acceptance of the position. A former executive of the Victoria club, Wilson was no longer active in running the Victorias by 1905. The election of an impartial chairman immediately proved to be a wise move, because the six clubs were divided equally into two camps during the nomination process of the first and second vice-presidents. The older, established clubs – Montreal, Victoria, and Quebec – formed one bloc, and the Ottawas, Wanderers, and Shamrocks constituted the other. With a disinterested party as president, neither bloc could count on the president's vote for the disputed positions.[43]

Distrust among ECAHA members persisted, however. In a later meeting, on December 20, 1905, the Association decided to do away with the two vice-presidential positions that were elected in the initial meeting and made the secretary-treasurer a paid position. For this latter position the ECAHA also chose an outsider, William Northey of the Arena Company. With the top administrative positions held by people outside the member clubs, the president of each club formed an executive committee. Whereas executive officers were elected from member clubs in previous league organizational structures, this development represented an experiment towards removing the administration of the Association's daily affairs from the member clubs. While the ECAHA executive committee still had a powerful voice in the Association's affairs, its separation from daily operations moved the executive committee towards becoming a consulting and legislative body. Still, this was not an inevitable step towards centralization and bureaucratization in the development of an organizational structure in hockey. Given the alliances and oppositions within the ECAHA, the lessening of the clubs' involvement in the administrative duties was a compromise solution to deal with the distrust in the new group. With the chief operating officer and the secretary-treasurer having no ties with any member clubs, the new structure would, at the very least, give the appearance of an unbiased administration. In the following year, however, the ECAHA abandoned the experiment and nominated from member clubs to fill these positions.

Fearing that bad feelings might disrupt the new organization's operation, the ECAHA adopted and amended the CAHL constitution with safeguards. To deter any further unnecessary bickering, the EACHA executives added a clause that required a fifty-dollar fee accompanying any official protest; the fee would be forfeited if the protest was unsuccessful. In a curious twist, the Association reduced the fine for delaying the start of a game from fifty to twenty-five dollars, though this was still higher than the ten-dollar penalty preceding the incident that led to the defection of the Ottawa club to the FAHL. Recognizing the alliances within the league, the ECAHA adopted the FAHL requirement for a three-quarter majority of the executive committee to admit new members into the Association.[44]

The blatant commercial interests that led to the creation of the ECAHA and the manner in which the deserted clubs in the old leagues were treated elicited immediate criticisms. In a scathing letter mocking the ECAHA's avowed goal to 'improve, foster and perpetuate the game,' an irate fan faulted rampant commercialism in senior amateur hockey that led to the breakup of the old associations. He cautioned that the back-stabbing would continue given the way the ECAHA was formed.[45]

While some fans were angry about the intrusion of commercial interests in amateur hockey, others were irritated about the hypocrisy of commercialized amateur hockey. One fan charged that the '[o]fficials and players are all trying to gull the public with yarns about elevating the game, splendid form of exercise for young men, club loyalty, etc., when as a matter of fact, none of these things ever enter the minds of the majority – at present.' He argued that '[i]f there is a place and demand for professional hockey, let us have it, but if not, let us do away with the conditions which will allow the club with the cleverest bookkeeper to pay the most out – to players.'[46]

Commercialized senior amateur hockey did not turn professional just yet. While criticisms and pleas to change senior hockey appeared in the press, the ECAHA was content to keep the status quo of a closed corporation composed of a small clique of elite-level teams run under the banner of amateurism. The kind of amateurism that the ECAHA practised allowed the clubs to pay players under the table. Since not all players demanded payment as an inducement to stay with the clubs, the payroll would not be as large as it would if the ECAHA turned professional. This strategy seemed to be financially rewarding to the member clubs. The dramatic two-game Stanley Cup series between the Ottawa and Wanderer clubs in the ECAHA's inaugural season further proved the selection of the Wanderers over the Westmount club was a wise move. Besides the two clubs' own supporters, fans in other parts of the region took special trains to witness the final. The Wanderers won the title in front of a large crowd that included Governor-General Earl Grey and Lady Grey at the Ottawa home rink.

The final series pointed to the continuing trend of bringing in players just before big matches. Newspapers had long been reporting these movements. For whatever reasons, the articles seldom indicated whether these moves were for legitimate change of employment or whether employment was dependent upon the hockey skills of the employee. These movements certainly did not escape the notice of some in the general public. A fan questioned the seemingly uncontrolled movement of players and wondered how certain 'players from Montreal can go to that town and play amateur after receiving an offer of $15 per week.'[47]

Within the larger ideological debate between proponents of pure amateurism and those who wanted a liberal interpretation of the amateur's definition, the ECAHA was moving towards professionalizing hockey. To maintain a stable of skilled players in an increasingly competitive labour market, some clubs decided to shift their strategy in procuring talent. To secure top-quality talent, a club had to entice the players to join its rank. Inducements other than direct payment to the player still existed within the ECAHA. Older clubs such as the Victorias and the Montreals were able to retain some of their players because of their social origins and their allegiance to the amateur ethic. A secure government job had been the lure for the Ottawas. Other clubs found it necessary to pay the players directly, if not openly. While the amateur code forbade such practice, a large portion of the paying public did not seem to mind, if gate attendance was any indication. Thus, following the footsteps of lacrosse, senior amateur hockey in Montreal decided in its 1906 annual meeting the following season to allow clubs to pay their players openly. This shift in policy played its part in fuelling the Athletic War.

Between 1906 and 1909, the Athletic War shifted into high gear. Before the 1906–7 season began, the prominent controversy in Canadian sports concerned the possibility of whether an amateur player could maintain his amateur standing in the CAAU if he played with and against paid players. By this time, the CAAU had adopted the OHA's all-or-nothing principle and labelled such behaviour unworthy of the amateur badge of honour. At its annual meeting, the ECAHA fanned the fire of the Athletic War by voting to allow the coexistence of paid players and amateurs if each club furnished the Association with a list of its players and their status. This list would in turn be made public through the news media. While the Wanderers announced that they would have 'at least one professional,' the Victoria club maintained that it would have 'a strictly amateur team.' This important policy shift, however, received less than five minutes of discussion by the executives. The matter had apparently already been sorted out in a private caucus before the main meeting. Yet from the discussion on the admission of the National club into the ECAHA, it was clear that at least Montreal and Victoria were unsure about this new route.[48]

What complicated matters for clubs such as Montreal and Victoria was their affiliation with a larger parent association that encompassed other sport clubs besides hockey. Some of these sport clubs opposed a liberalized definition of an amateur. During the MAAA semi-annual meeting, a member reminded the organization that its constitution and by-laws explicitly restricted participation in the various clubs within the Association to members only. The president replied that 'the men in question were not members of the association, but *hired employees* [emphasis added], and that the association has received assent of the members in permitting these to play.'[49]

A new direction required adjustments in league operation. Now that the decision to allow paid players had been made, the ECAHA began preparing itself for this new experiment. While the Association still maintained its exclusionary practice in admitting new members, the ECAHA executives attempted to organize the officiating crew, a bone of contention among clubs in senior hockey. Up until this point, players and club officials usually took on the role of the referee. Although this was not a paid position, the referees did have their expenses covered. For the actual appointment of the game officials, the competing clubs usually submitted the names of three persons whom they could get to referee the match. Both teams then had to agree on one of the nominees. Because of rivalries and current league standings, teams were always leery about the nominations from their opponents. For the first time, however, the ECAHA attempted to have a set pool of referees at the beginning of the season. While the teams still retained the custom of nominating referees for the matches, the president could now appoint one from this pool if there was no agreement. Although the suggestion did not pass, the Association did set a standard fee for referee travel.[50]

On the more important matter of controlling player movement, the ECAHA toyed with the idea of a list of reserve players. On this issue, the two three-club coalitions within the Association broke down further into three groups. As noted, Montreal and Victoria were at best hesitant to allow paid players into the game; they did not really care one way or the other whether there was a reserve list. Of the remaining four clubs that were keen on this new adventure, two, the Quebec and Shamrock hockey clubs, had weak teams. Quebec had won only three games the previous season, while the Shamrocks did not record a win. Hence, they saw the reserve list as a hindrance to their bidding for players. By contrast, the Association's two strongest clubs, the Ottawas and the Wanderers, saw the list as necessary to protect their positions. Ottawa had already made a head start by stockpiling players. With the issue deadlocked, the reserve list would not appear until 1911.[51]

Without an agreement to institute a reserve list, players had leverage in negotiating their contracts. By allowing paid players in the Association, the ECAHA offered a reprieve to the exiled IHL hockey players, who could now return to

Canada to ply their trade. A trickling of players began to migrate back north. The return of skilled players did not, however, suppress their economic value. Since clubs were competing for their services, players could test the market. This they did, and in at least one case, one player signed with two clubs.[52]

With the stockpiling of players and the latter incident, the Victoria club tried to reverse the practice of mixing amateurs and paid players. But the Wanderers pointed out that its club had already signed players based on the new approach. Bitter arguments ensued. The Shamrock representative compared the paid players to parasites. In the end, the old guard lost this last-ditch effort, and the ECAHA sided with the Wanderers. When the list of players' status finally reached the press, the Wanderers' roster showed five out of nine as paid players. The Shamrocks had three and the Ottawas had one. Montreal, Victoria, and Quebec all claimed to be amateurs. A newspaper commented sarcastically that 'it was bad enough to have Montreal, Victorias and Quebec deny professionalism, but it was really stretching things when Patrick, Russell, Blachford and Kennedy (all members of the Wanderers) were called amateurs.'[53] Apparently, the press had known for a long time what the Association pretended did not exist.

Now that the leading hockey organization allowed the intermingling of amateurs and professionals, many top clubs in other parts of the country lost all pretension of maintaining the amateur code. In a January Stanley Cup challenge series, Kenora (formerly Rat Portage), fortified by its own hired guns, won the Cup from the Wanderers. Immediately after winning the ECAHA title in early March, the Wanderers set out to recapture the Stanley Cup. As ECAHA champion, the club issued a Cup challenge to Kenora, and a barrage of bickering followed. The two sides quarrelled about the dates and location of the series, and the selection of officials. Most important of all, each accused the other of assembling 'ringers,' paid skilled players, at the last minute for the series. Thus far, the trustees of the Stanley Cup had been silent on the issue of salaried players. But when the two sides brought their grievances to William Foran, the acting trustee on behalf of P.D. Ross who was away in England, he threatened to withdraw the Cup 'if the teams were going to gather professionals from all over to contest it.'[54] Somehow, the two teams found middle ground, and the series went ahead. The Wanderers recaptured the Stanley Cup, and rough hockey was the order of the day. Violent behaviour was not the exclusive domain of professional hockey. Amateur hockey had had its fill of rough play since the early days. But the negative connotations associated with the professional game magnified its importance as part of the brand.

During the next season, the bidding war for players continued. An unintended consequence of the ECAHA allowing the mixing of amateurs and paid players was the demise of the IHL. Without the IHL, more players were available. For the players, 1907 was a bonanza year. Although the IHL had folded, another professional league, the Ontario Professional Hockey League (OPHL), sprang up in Canada. Four cities in western Ontario, Toronto, Berlin (now Kitchener), Brantford, and Guelph, decided to form a hockey league. By this time, the region represented by these four cities was experiencing a boom in population and industry. Furthermore, they were in close proximity to each other, which effectively cut down on travelling expenses.[55] While the OPHL did not have the same prestige as the ECAHA, hockey players had at least two choices of paid hockey careers, not to mention the fact there were other teams in other leagues that would make special financial arrangements for them.[56]

Within the ECAHA, labour problems continued in the second season of the new experiment. Clubs were arguing about the signing rights of players, and some players were leveraging their positions by playing one club against another. Several players signed with one club and then tried to renege on their contracts so that they could sign for higher pay with another. Ottawa experienced a similar player revolt as the one that Montreal had four years earlier. The crux of the trouble, it seemed, was the players' dissatisfaction with their pay at the end of the previous season.[57]

The uncontrolled labour market began to affect the clubs' financial positions. The Wanderers, by far the most aggressive of the clubs when it came to protecting their player assets, lost six hundred dollars in the 1906–7 season. Montreal had also lost money, but the MAAA organizational framework allowed the parent association to absorb the hockey club's debt. With the competition for players and the high cost of using the rink, some of the clubs teetered on the edge of bankruptcy. Rumours appeared in the press that some of the Wanderers' executives wanted out. The distrust among clubs did not ease the situation. Amidst all the turmoil, the Victoria club reaffirmed its stance to be purely amateur. Interestingly enough, it posted a positive balance on its ledger. The move towards professionalizing hockey seemed to have created financial disasters for many of the ECAHA clubs – ironically, especially those that were committed to the cause.[58]

Chapter 4

Leagues of Their Own

Uncertainty and anxiety about the direction of commercialized amateur hockey at the end of first decade of the twentieth century prompted a reorganization of the hockey network. As the Athletic War was coming to an end, commercialized hockey was split into two camps, amateur and professional. Each group sought 'partners ... perceived as most legitimate and ... reliable, either because they are constrained from staging a coup or because they share the orientations and goals of the organizers.'[1] Advocates of open professionalism formed their own leagues. In the Montreal senior circuit, many clubs took their best players down the professional path. With many of the clubs in the elite Montreal circuit turning professional, the city lost its status as the leading elite-level amateur hockey centre in Canada, and this created a power vacuum. At the same time, Montreal became the centre of the professional hockey network, and its leadership would remain until the last quarter of the twentieth century. Since the ideologues of pure amateurism had won the day in the Athletic War, the development of professional and amateur hockey went on their separate paths from this point onward.

By no means did the split of the commercialized hockey network into two sub-networks ensure the survival of each. Especially for the professionals, this division required changes in the network's operations and policies. As much as professional baseball existed as a model, professional hockey marched to its own rhythm in its development as a viable enterprise. Issues such as control of players, franchise memberships, and markets became contested grounds among different groups of stakeholders. Despite these conflicts, the emergence of professional hockey ushered in a development phase that began to separate players and clubs into the roles of employees and employers respectively.

Uncertainties and apprehension in the path towards professionalizing hockey finally led to a split in the ECAHA just before the 1908–9 season began.

Montreal and Victoria, both reluctant on the idea of mixing amateur and paid players from the start, resigned from the Association and formed a new amateur hockey governing body, the Interprovincial Provincial Amateur Hockey Union. Without the objections of any more amateur proponents among them, the remaining ECAHA clubs committed themselves to professional hockey.

The resignations of the Montreal and Victoria Hockey Clubs were indicative of the status of the Athletic War in Canada near the end of the first decade of the twentieth century. Proponents of pure amateurism were gaining ground in purging those who did not subscribe to a strict definition of an amateur. Those who favoured a liberal interpretation of the definition, led by the MAAA, the Montreal Hockey Club's parent organization, had created the Amateur Athletic Federation of Canada (AAFC) in 1907. The establishment of the AAFC allowed the intermingling of amateur and professional players so that amateur athletes under its jurisdiction could participate in sports without being stigmatized as professionals by the CAAU's strict definition of an amateur. As the MAAA still commanded much respect in the Canadian sporting world, its backing of the AAFC helped to check, at least temporarily, the amateur purists' campaign. By the end of 1908, however, the AAFC and the MAAA had lost considerable public support because of a well-publicized incident in the London Olympics. Subsequently, the two rivals merged to form the Amateur Athletic Union of Canada (AAUC), which promoted the strict definition of an amateur. At the beginning of the 1908–9 hockey season, the power of the MAAA and its cause of allowing mixed amateur and paid players were waning.[2]

Elite hockey had not gone fully professional yet, but it had at last dropped the word 'amateur' from its name at the beginning of the 1908–9 season. Despite the fact that the structure and practices of the new ECHA were slowly moving it in the direction of becoming a professional organization, the Association still retained remnants of the old amateur organizational structure. One area was in the minimal separation between the administration and the members at the club level. All of its member clubs operated on the basis of membership. Several members of the Ottawa club allegedly owned stocks in the club. Theoretically speaking then, it was possible for an active player to become the president of the club and be eligible to sit on the ECHA executive board.[3]

Managing a hockey club was not an easy task. Club executives generally did not receive payment for their duties. One could only guess why they took on the posts – civic pride, sense of satisfaction, prestige. For some clubs, there might not be any club if the players did not also serve as executives. With hockey entering the play-for-pay stage, troubles in securing players led some of the volunteering executives to have second thoughts about their involvement with the clubs. Just before the start of the 1908–9 season, three executives on the defending Stanley

Cup champions' team announced that they would resign. The same apprehension occurred at the Wanderers' camp. Depending on the stories heard, there was talk that the players were planning to run the Wanderers as a joint stock company or that someone was going to buy the club. While it was true that players were under contracts, the distinction between management and players remained a grey area. At this early stage of professional hockey, players had much freedom and many options.[4]

Yet the unrestricted player movement must have disturbed those who wanted a more stable and financially profitable enterprise. Taking a page out of the OHA's rule book, the Ontario Professional Hockey League (OPHL) established a residency requirement in its first constitution to prevent players from moving to another club after February 1.[5] The OPHL hoped the measure would avoid the kind of free-for-all for which the Stanley Cup trustees had chided the ECAHA the previous year.[6] The ECHA's executives had also discussed the possibility of binding a player to his team from the previous season. During the discussion of the motion, the clubs agreed to add a rider that permitted 'bona fide change of residence.' For over an hour, the debate turned to whether a deadline should be inserted into the rider. While the Shamrocks and the Wanderers wanted a team's roster to be set by November, Ottawa vehemently objected to the deadline, claiming that the short hockey season prohibited such a restriction. Players, even paid players, had other jobs during the off-season. Thus, a player might maintain a home in one place, work in another, and play for a team in a third city. As the Ottawa representative saw it, a deadline before the season started simply did not make sense. Everyone in the meeting agreed that the motion was a good economic move to prevent players from jumping their contracts at the last minute should another club offer them bigger salaries. But suspicion held sway and no agreement could be reached regarding a deadline on legitimate change of residence. A final attempt at compromise failed when the Ottawa club rejected a Wanderers' offer to bind the clubs to a non-raiding agreement.[7]

Thus, the raiding of players went on. Being instrumental in defeating the reserve motion, the Ottawa club, not surprisingly, had the most success in signing new players.[8] As for the players, most of them took advantage of the bidding among clubs. Art Ross asked his old team, the Stanley Cup Champion Wanderers, for $1600.[9] In the previous season, the entire payroll of the Montreal Hockey Club was only $2004.35.[10] With two new clubs admitted into the league, the OPHL was offering 'a weekly salary ranging from $25 to $50 per man. In addition good occupations are being added as inducements.'[11] Didier Pitre, who had signed with Montreal before it resigned from the ECHA, went to Edmonton for an alleged salary of $1200.[12] With the average annual earning for a supervisory and office employee being $994 per annum in 1910 and players' contracts only calling for approximately three months' service, some of the players were making over four times as much.[13] As late as the first practice, the Ottawa goaltender, Percy Lesueur refused to 'get in nets, saying he had not been *invited* [emphasis added] to play.'[14]

Without any agreements to control labour, players moved freely in the marketplace. This freedom manifested itself most vividly perhaps when the Edmonton club played the Wanderers for the Stanley Cup on December 28 and 30 that year. Of the seven Edmonton starting players, only one, Fred Whitcroft, had played in any of the Edmonton's regular-schedule games. And immediately after the series was over, two players, Bert Lindsay and Didier Pitre, joined the Renfrew club in the Ottawa Valley Hockey League, which was supported by mining profits. The spare, Hal McNamara, jumped to Toronto of the OPHL, and Lester Patrick, the one-time star of McGill University, Brandon (1904), Westmount (1905), and the Wanderers (1906–7), returned to his father's lumber business in British Columbia.[15]

With mounting evidence that hockey had strayed far from the amateur code, the most glaring example that it had entered into the professional realm came when the Wanderer club was sold to a different party during the season. For the first time, buying and selling in elite-level hockey extended beyond the player market. Still, whether it was legitimate or not, player movement was a fact of life in a country that was trying to populate its vast landscape. In the United States the frontier was supposedly closed after 1890. By contrast, Canadians and newly arrived immigrants were still moving en masse to the west and the north in search of land and opportunity after the turn of the century. Yet hockey clubs had always been run on the basis of local membership, with elected executives to guide their operations. During the 1908–9 season, however, the executives of the Wanderers, under a burden of debt accumulated by the bidding war, sold the club to Fred Strachan, who was in turn financed by P.J. Doran, the owner of the Jubilee rink, located at the predominantly francophone east end of Montreal. Doran allegedly paid $750 for the Wanderers and another $3200 towards players' salaries in the previous season.[16]

For Doran, the purchase was an economic move to benefit his rink, where he wanted to move the Wanderers at the beginning of the 1909–10 season.[17] Since the ECHA played all its matches at the Arena, on Wood Avenue, Doran's proposed move immediately drew protests from the rest of the Association because the Jubilee rink seated only 3250, compared to the 7000 seating capacity of the Arena. Ottawa, winner of the ECHA championship the previous year, was looking to pull itself out of debt. Its rivalry with the Wanderers had always drawn large crowds during the regular-season schedule. Besides the Ottawa club, the Shamrock Hockey Club had also fallen onto hard times, both in the competitive standings and in its finances. Its parent organization had to take over the management of the operation of the hockey club; and there was talk that the Shamrocks might return to the amateur ranks to cut its expenses. As for Quebec, the other old club from the AHAC days, rumours of its demise occurred just about every season. Moving the Wanderers to the smaller Jubilee rink would certainly impact the revenues of the entire Association. Amidst the protests of the ECHA clubs, the old Wanderers' executives, for whatever reasons, had a change of heart and asked to get back into the Association. With its economic well-being in question, the ECHA obviously sided with the ex-Wanderers group. A potentially explosive situation was developing as the Ottawa representative questioned the legitimacy of the transfer of ownership and, in the tradition of member-based clubs, asked, 'Does one man comprise a club?'[18]

What followed demonstrated the players' power to control their own destiny in the early stages of professionalizing hockey. Unlike professional baseball's practice at the time, hockey contracts did not have the iron-clad reserve clause that prevented players from leaving clubs. Not until the previous season had the ECHA even put in a residence rule. When the dispute over the Wanderers' ownership came up, the players had their opinions. Some wanted to go with the new ownership, while the others, led by Wanderers Captain Art Ross, sided with the old faction. Although the by-laws of the ECHA allowed the clubs to hold their players from the previous season until January 15, the contracts that Ross and some others had signed released them at the end of the season, and thus they were free to seek new pastures. Ross proceeded to organize a new club, the All-Montreal Hockey Club, on November 15 with some of the Wanderer players. Since the ECHA was sympathetic to the old faction and the Ottawa club strongly opposed to having more than one English club in Montreal, the All-Montreal club hoped to replace the Wanderers in the ECHA.[19]

Despite some last-minute negotiations, the ECHA re-enacted the AHAC-to-CAHL routine: a number of clubs withdrew from the existing organization and formed a new one in order to exclude undesirable clubs. On November 25 the ECHA ceased to exist a few minutes after its annual meeting began. Ottawa, the Shamrocks, Quebec, and the Wanderers resigned from the Association in that order. In its place, the first three clubs formed the Canadian Hockey Association (CHA). From the proceedings reported in the newspapers, it would have been hard to surmise that the Wanderers knew anything about the dissolution of the ECHA. The new organization began at once reviewing applications. It rejected applications from Renfrew and Cornwall. Debate then centred on the Wanderers' application. While both the Quebec and Shamrock clubs had some sympathy for their old colleagues, Ottawa insisted that the Arena be the only venue for all CHA games played in Montreal. The Wanderer representative explained that the team did not have to play in the Jubilee rink but it did want better terms from the Arena, which stood at a sixty-forty split between the rink and the club at the time. Both the National and the All-Montreal clubs agreed to have all their games played at the Arena when their applications came up. Perhaps heeding the lesson of the 1905 split between the CAHL and the FAHL, when Ottawa left the CAHL with the Stanley Cup, the power of the Stanley Cup holder triumphed. By midnight, the CHA admitted two new members, the French-Canadian National club and the All-Montreal club; all clubs were to pay an initiation fee of thirty dollars and an annual assessment of twenty-five dollars.[20]

Immediately after this development, newspapermen were comparing the whole incident with the CAHL-FAHL split and predicting that the rejected applicants might form a new league. This did happen on December 2 at a meeting in which the National Hockey Association (NHA) came into existence. Two excluded applicants of the CHA, the Wanderers and the Renfrew club, and two other clubs from the silver-mining region of Ontario formed the new organization. In contrast to all hockey meetings held before, the NHA avoided publicity and chose to meet in a downtown business office instead of the Windsor Hotel. The meeting featured a gathering of Canada's resource-industry interests and included James Ambrose O'Brien, J.G. Barnett, Thomas Hare, and Noah Timmons. Together with the Wanderers' representative, they elected Eddie McCafferty, of the Montreal Baseball Club in the professional Eastern League, to hold the important post of secretary-treasurer. McCafferty also represented a Toronto application with a proposed new arena that featured an artificial-ice-making capability.[21]

Two stark, contrasting conditions stood out between the CHA and the NHA. As compared to the CHA's territory, the geographical distances between the NHA franchises were much greater. With travelling expenses added to the costs of the inevitable bidding war for players against the CHA, the new league's financial arrangements seemed overwhelming indeed. This made the second contrast so much more important.

Financially, the NHA's backers were notable businessmen in major North American industries compared to those in the CHA. Besides managing their vast lumber business, the Barnets were also in the banking industry. The main driving force behind the NHA was the O'Briens, who owned a vast empire of transportation, mining, and energy-resource companies in Canada and the United States. Furthermore, Michael J. O'Brien, the patriarch of the family, was well connected politically. It was true that businessmen supported the CHA teams, but they were not in the same league as the O'Briens, the Barnets, and the Timmonses.[22]

Perhaps anticipating the high costs of starting the NHA, the backers took care in setting up league policies to ensure the league's survival. They vowed to cut down expenses 'by an introduction of the business principles applied to baseball.' Because of the required travel, the league executives planned to schedule a team to play a series of games when it was on the road, instead of the traditional practice of the visiting team playing one game and returning home the same night. This in effect restricted a common practice of players holding other jobs while on contract to play hockey, unless, of course, the employer did not really care if the hockey player showed up for work. In an attempt to stabilize the franchises, the NHA required each club to put up a $1000 bond 'in token of good faith' and instituted a by-law whereby 'no club may sell its franchise for the first year; after that a two-third vote of the league will be necessary before any franchise can be transferred.'[23] This practice set a precedent in the control of the distribution of hockey games by the governing body.

In the absence of a monopsony, specialized, skilled players thrived because they were free to sell their services to the highest bidder. As the two rival leagues proceeded to draw up their respective schedules, the bidding for players became even more frantic than in the previous year. Player salaries skyrocketed. Bitter about being excluded from the CHA, Renfrew especially went after the players that Ottawa wanted to sign. Renfrew had signed the travelling Lester Patrick for $3000 a season and paid $2000 for his brother, Frank. But the biggest signing of all was Fred 'Cyclone' Taylor's, for the unheard-of sum of $5250 for one season. Comparison had been made to the contemporary baseball star Ty Cobb, of the Detroit Tigers, who commanded a salary of $6500 for a seven-month season of 154 games. Taylor's season consisted of twelve games over two months.[24]

With a bevy of established players, the NHA employed a confrontational strategy against the CHA in marketing its product. By raiding the Stanley Cup champion's roster, the NHA let it be known that it was going to face what the FAHL had tried to avoid when it was formed, namely, a head-to-head confrontation. Since Montreal was the only city that had franchises in both leagues, it immediately became the centre of the battleground. With the two leagues Montreal once again was overcrowded, with five hockey clubs. The Shamrocks, the All-Montreals, and the Nationals represented the CHA; the Wanderers and a new French-Canadian club, Les Canadiens, created especially to counter the Nationals, represented the NHA. Moreover, the NHA Cobalt owner put up the league bond for the new Canadien franchise, secured the highly popular Québécois hockey star Jack Laviolette as its manager, and gave the club $5000 in cash to sign players.

Fearing that the other side might gain an advantage, both leagues became secretive. The dates and the match-ups in the league schedules had potential revenue consequences. Montreal would now have a total of forty-seven games of professional and amateur hockey, compared to twenty-four the previous year.

Some of the games could suffer at the gate because of the increase in league games. With both leagues committed to an ugly confrontation, neither released its schedule early enough for the other side to be able to adjust its own.

In this highly charged atmosphere, brand recognition and customer loyalty became priorities. Being fairly close to the Ottawa market, the Renfrew club announced that it would run excursion charters: from Ottawa to Renfrew for all its home games, as well as to Montreal for its road games. Rumours from Ottawa suggested that there were plenty of requests for Renfrew season tickets from Ottawa hockey fans.[25] With the addition of the Canadiens, the NHA had also effectively extended the competition for fan support to the French-Canadian market sector. Since 'there is no National Commission to stop raids of the one league on players of the other ... [t]he Ottawa-Renfrew business shows what all the clubs must expect – survival of the fittest.'[26]

In the showdown between the NHA and the CHA, there was really no contest; the one with the most money won. The NHA won the pursuit of talent hands down. While the Ottawa club still had a respectable team, the rest of the CHA clubs only had mediocre talent, with a sprinkling of good hockey players among them. Perhaps the salaries might give some indication as to the difference between the two leagues. Renfrew paid Taylor over $5000, while the National club's player salaries totalled $4530.[27]

The attendance at and competitive nature of each league's contests, especially those played in Montreal, also portended which league would eventually come out on top. When the CHA finally released its schedule to the press, there were four dates when clubs in both leagues played in Montreal. The first clash would come on Saturday, January 8, 1910, when Ottawa played the Nationals at the Arena and Cobalt played the Wanderers at the Jubilee rink.

The season opener for both leagues foretold their fortunes. For the CHA, the All-Montreals crushed the Nationals on December 30 by the score of seven to two; the pre-game analysis noted that only four of the fourteen players had played in the elite league.[28] By contrast, the first NHA game between Cobalt and the Canadiens was a close contest, with the French host winning it in sudden-death overtime. Most importantly, the match drew almost a full house. A post-game report suggested that the game attracted the targeted French-Canadian population, but a large number of fans from the anglophone west end also turned up. The report did, however, criticize the inexperienced Jubilee rink for poor crowd management.[29]

In marketing, one prefers a smaller, packed house over a half-empty large arena, even if both have the same number of patrons. When the long-awaited first clash between the two leagues came, the postscript from the press might as well have been the beginning of the obituary of the CHA. For the NHA game between Cobalt and the Wanderers, the *Gazette* reported a packed house of 3000 even though the Canadiens were not playing. It also commended the Jubilee rink for keeping the venue free from the smoke that had obscured the spectators' view in the opening game.[30] As for the CHA game between the Ottawas, the defending Stanley Cup champions, and the Nationals, the *Gazette* painted a somewhat gloomy picture of an empty arena with about 1000 patrons, the majority of whom came to root for the French team.[31] While the NHA match was a relatively close game, with the Wanderers winning it ten to six, the CHA one was a sorry mismatch. Ottawa routed the Nationals fourteen to four. A further interesting note was the coverage that appeared in the *Gazette*. For this period at least, the newspaper had traditionally set aside page two for its sports news. While it devoted 2½ columns to the NHA game, the CHA game received less than one column, even with the Ottawas playing; and the report appeared on page nine.

With the start of the season going poorly for the CHA, some players began to worry about their future in the league. A day after the leagues clashed in Montreal, the *Montreal Gazette* reported that Paddy Moran, one of the two star players on the All-Montreal club, was going to play for the Haileybury club of the NHA. The other star player and organizer of the club, Art Ross, admitted that Haileybury had also approached him, but denied that he was leaving the club.[32] Two days after the initial league games in Montreal, another CHA game, in which the Nationals lost to the Shamrocks seventeen to eight, drew about eight hundred fans. The Montreal press wondered about the viability of the CHA given the poor attendance, and blamed some of the CHA clubs for not spending the necessary money to recruit skilled players.[33] This trend of poor attendance and uneven match-ups continued for the CHA, and the inevitable began to occur.

For a professional league, the bottom line almost always dictates its future. With the CHA's poor showing at the gate, informal discussions about a possible amalgamation of the two leagues began to surface in the press. Recognizing that the CHA was hopelessly talent-poor, the top two clubs, Ottawa and the Shamrocks, contemplated leaving the league. News leaked out that three NHA clubs – Renfrew, the Wanderers, and the Canadiens – and three CHA clubs – Ottawa, the Shamrocks, and All-Montreal – favoured a merger. The NHA clubs, however, had signed a pact and posted a large bond that discouraged any proposed merger without approval by the league. If the proposed merger included the rest of the NHA clubs, there would be, at a minimum, eight clubs in the new circuit, and its very size would add considerably to the clubs' travelling expenses.[34]

For the Ottawa club at least, this option still seemed far better than staying with the CHA. It was counting on a fairly competitive CHA regular schedule and the extra Stanley Cup series gate receipts to finance its payroll. So far, the regular season had been a disaster financially. And in its first Stanley Cup defence against Galt, the champions of the 1909 OPHL, which the *Gazette* described as a joke, only about three hundred even bothered to show up for the second game. The total gate receipts were about $1200 for the first game and $400 for the second. Incidentally, Ottawa won by a combined score of fifteen to four.[35] When the NHA proposed to absorb the Ottawa and Shamrock clubs as well as offering the Canadiens' franchise to the Nationals, Ottawa and the Shamrocks jumped at the chance.

When the Ottawa and Shamrock clubs formally applied to join the NHA on January 16, with the NHA dictating all the terms, the re-formed NHA represented almost a clean break from the first organizers of hockey back in the 1890s. With Quebec being left out, Ottawa was the only remaining club from the days of the AHAC. Club owners of the NHA had few ties to the upper-class fraternal roots of the early hockey organizations. Instead, powerful businessmen ran the organization.[36] The only consolation, if one could call it that, was the election of the CHA secretary-treasurer, Emmett Quinn, as joint secretary-treasurer of the NHA. Quinn, an insurance businessman and long-time supporter of hockey, had apparently earned himself a reputation as an impartial and capable secretary. The remade NHA also delegated to Quinn the important post of overseeing the board of officials.[37]

As a defeated adversary, Ottawa sent a diplomatic group of delegates to the January 16 meeting. The humiliation suffered by the Stanley Cup champion must have been hard to swallow. In the past, the Ottawa club had sometimes instigated the changes, but it always came out on the winning side. As the Stanley Cup champion, it carried certain power, as evidenced in the FAHL-CAHL battle. For the moment, its delegates had to wait outside the meeting room while the team's fate was being debated by the people whom it had driven away. The hold of the old guard, whose lineage traced back to the beginning of the AHAC, had been broken. Perhaps it was fitting that when the Ottawa representative suggested to Quinn that he would be able to recommend some fine recruits for the referee board, the Haileybury representative shot back, 'And let me add that we have a classy lot in the silver country.'[38]

At the same time as the supremacy of the NHA was being established, the Athletic War was also drawing to a close. The amateur purists had gotten what they wanted – the professionals were flushed out into the open. With this accomplished, the amateur leaders reasoned that they could exile them to suit their own avaricious purposes. What they overlooked was the fact that the exiles also included some of the most talented athletes in the sports world. As hockey had become firmly entrenched in the Canadian culture, its symbolic representation of a community and its entertainment value came to surpass the importance of the amateur ideology. Amateurism was fine so long as the games could generate enough interest to sustain the ideology financially. When professional hockey entered the marketplace, it already had a following based not on sports ideology but on success and achievement.

Professional hockey was more than capturing its market share of customers. Elite-level hockey had shifted further away from its amateur roots and moved toward professionalization during the first decade of the twentieth century. This shift included a reorientation of decision-making power and was especially marked between the CHA and the NHA. The All-Montreals of the CHA was the last club run by elite-level players in the Montreal region. It was true that an old club such as Ottawa still operated on a membership basis, and its player-members could, theoretically, run for office. Even as some of them were vocal in club policies, however, no active player ever had. The All-Montreal club was an aberration in a trend towards separating administrators and players in elite-level hockey, and the days of players participating in the decision-making process were slowly passing. Professional hockey might have taken a different form if the player-run All-Montreals had succeeded and served as a model of operation. For the NHA, the dividing line between club executives and players was much sharper. The travel and player costs required substantial investments from the original NHA promoters. Whereas club directors in previous organizations mostly volunteered their services, investors such as the O'Briens and Barnets had heavy financial stakes in their clubs and, not surprisingly, wanted the decision-making power to rest in their hands. Hence, the relationship between club executives and players increasingly resembled one of employers and employees – the kind that the O'Briens and Barnets were so familiar with in their businesses.

While executives on some clubs had excluded the players from the decision-making process, players were not powerless to voice their concerns. The demand for their skills gave them some degree of power. Even with the residency rule and, later, the reserve clause, the professional hockey industry was hardly a monopoly. Although the Montreal-based professional circuit was the premier organization and the prestige of competing in the league was alluring, there were other leagues that welcomed talented players who were dissatisfied with their clubs. Without any agreements among the various professional leagues, players were free to offer their services across leagues. Thus, the power of the management was not absolute.

The establishment of the NHA did not, however, signal the completion of the professionalization of hockey. Player control remained a work in progress, as was the issue of franchise membership. Disputes on membership had already destroyed at least six hockey governing bodies in the Montreal region between 1900 and 1909. These quarrels and their ultimate resolution usually depended on two related issues, the calibre of the clubs and their potential revenues. Before senior hockey in Montreal turned professional, excluded clubs could still participate in a lower division. In professional hockey, there was no ready alternative for any excluded club to continue operation or to recoup any of its investments unless it could induce other investors to start a rival league. By entering professional hockey, the clubs in effect had burned their bridges and gambled that the venture would be a success.

Chapter 5

In Search of Hockey Order

In the early twentieth century, professional hockey went through the beginning stages of a new industry where a number of firms competed in the marketplace and the barrier to entry in that marketplace was relatively low. New firms appeared and, just as quickly, disappeared. The National Hockey Association (NHA) was by no means the only professional league that claimed major-league status. Others, such as the Ontario Professional Hockey League (OPHL), the Pacific Coast Hockey Association (PCHA), and the Maritime Professional Hockey League (MPHL), were also operating at the time. While they did not intrude into each other's consumer market, the leagues did compete for players and the Stanley Cup, which, by now, legitimized a club and its league's status as a provider of top-notched hockey. In addition to these professional organizations, amateur leagues continued to attract skilled players. In this competitive market, skilled players could move freely among the leagues as clubs vied for their services. For the leagues, then, one of the objectives was to seek some sort of order.

Searching for order, the NHA pursued a number of measures that aimed to resolve internal and external problems and opportunities. Internally, the NHA moved to centralize authority. Between the 1910s and the early 1920s, ownership began to change hands more frequently. Wealthy tycoons such as the O'Briens left the business, and middle-class entrepreneurs returned. Although these new owners had ties with the sports industry, some of them did not have ties to elite-level hockey in Montreal. The office of NHA president became increasingly important for maintaining the continuity of the organization. Distrust among the owners and efforts to deal with other rival leagues also made the position of the president a necessity. The president increasingly shouldered more responsibility, if not more power, and assumed 'a fiduciary relationship to [the] stakeholders.'[1]

In the first full season after the dismantling of the CHA, 1910–11, the NHA decided to reorganize in a more business-like manner. The distrust and harsh feelings among some member clubs dictated that the decision-making process regarding the organization's affairs must not appear to favour one or the other. Furthermore, high player salaries that resulted from the bidding war between the CHA and the NHA could not be maintained if the NHA was going to be a sound business venture. Externally, the league wanted to eliminate the stigma of professional sports – in which money corrupted its integrity; in particular, money caused players to resort to unsportsmanlike tactics, including rough play, to win; conversely, money could also tempt players to lose a match. The last two concerns, player salaries and player conduct, drove the NHA to establish an internal control mechanism for players.

With the collapse of the CHA, the NHA executives turned inward and worked to improve its organization. The constitutions and by-laws of the various elite-level hockey organizations could be traced back to the early days of amateur hockey. For a budding professional organization, the NHA's constitution in the first year was 'a patchwork adapted neither to amateur nor professional hockey.'[2] Realizing the operational differences between an amateur and a professional sport organization, the NHA executives sought to institute polices and procedures that addressed the concerns of their particular business.

The outcome of the executives' efforts was a new NHA constitution, an impressive document covering in detail the responsibilities and power of the two paid offices of president and secretary-treasurer, as well as those of the board of directors and the clubs. To ensure the public's support of and confidence in the NHA games, the constitution also provided for penalties for, among other things, unprofessional conduct such as defaults, violation of contractual agreement, and player misconduct. Unlike the amateur clubs, who relied on the residence rule to control player movement, the NHA utilized reserve and waiver clauses instead to bind players to their teams. The *Montreal Gazette* noted these changes with approval. It also noticed the passing of a practice from the amateur days when hockey association meetings were open to the media. In an attempt to control the league's image, the owners designated the league president as the only person who could release league information. The close ties between the press and some of the owners, however, made a restriction of information flow difficult to achieve. Still, professional hockey was moving towards controlling information for marketing and publicity purposes.[3]

The immediate problem facing the NHA was to control costs. The Haileybury, Cobalt, and Shamrock clubs all fell victim to high operating costs and folded in short order.[4] Hence, the league moved to reduce the huge payroll that each club had incurred the previous season. Under section twenty-one of the new NHA constitution (see appendix C), the league limited each club's spending on player salaries to $5000 and, to prevent clubs from trying to work around the salary cap, banned the payment of bonuses. This, of course, immediately drew protests from players, among whom the Ottawa players were particularly militant. Their captain, Bruce Stuart, vowed that he would not accept a cut in his pay and would undertake to organize a new league.[5]

A different conception of the players' place in professional hockey stood behind their protest. While the salary limit treated them as an expenditure item to be held down, the players saw themselves as revenue generators whose services should be fairly compensated. With the short hockey season, all players still held other jobs and business interests, even if they devoted the winter months exclusively to playing hockey. In leaving their other careers for three months, the players demanded that their hockey salaries should, at the minimum, match the potential earnings from their other jobs. They were also aware that they were the best in their profession and wanted to be remunerated as such.[6] Reaction from the league and owners to the players' protest ranged from the dismissive to the confrontational. Since Ottawa players were leading the protest movement, an Ottawa official declared that his club would abandon professional hockey instead of allowing 'dictation from the players.'[7]

On this one issue of player salary, the clubs banded together, at least for the moment. During a meeting on November 26, the clubs did not even discuss a possible compromise or devise strategies against a possible player revolt. Instead, the league set up the schedule for the coming season, and each club paid the $500 assessment as an indication of its commitment to the league and the new constitution.[8] An attempt to form a players' league came to naught when the Montreal Arena announced that there would be no dates available to any new organization. Without the backing of the Arena, players gradually signed with their respective clubs.[9]

The lure of gate receipts and prestige from assembling a winning team, however, quickly eroded the owners' unity. As in the amateur days, NHA clubs made arrangements with players on the side to bypass the league's guidelines, and at times the owners were not subtle at all in doing so. Given the demand for skilled players, star players especially had a lot of bargaining power. Fred Taylor, arguably the most famous player of his time, threatened to hold out. He demanded that the Renfrew club president deposit $5000 into his bank account as a salary guarantee. Taylor's salary from the previous season was over $5000. It would be hard to imagine a substantial cut in Taylor's pay that required a $5000 collateral guarantee from the club.[10] In the midst of a tight race during the season, Ottawa offered its former captain, and the instigator of the players' revolt, Bruce Stuart, the set amount under the salary cap plus a bonus, which was forbidden by the constitution, if the club finished in first place. The two parties consummated the deal in less than five minutes in the Ottawa dressing room between the second and third periods of a game.[11] In a more innovative twist to bypassing the salary limit, the

Ottawa and the Wanderer clubs arranged a post-season exhibition series in New York City, with a $1000 purse to be divided among the players.[12] Hence, the salary limit did not really achieve its intended purpose – to reduce payroll. Highly skilled players could still demand and receive a high salary.

A second test for the NHA as a professional organization came in the struggle between club autonomy and league authority. Given the distrust among member clubs, the NHA granted its president power to oversee league operations and punish those who were 'guilty of conduct prejudicial to the National Hockey Association or of the welfare of hockey, regardless of whether the same occurred on or off the playing rink.'[13] Yet older clubs such as Ottawa continued to fight for the club autonomy it had enjoyed previously in the amateur associations. In reality, then, an important part of the president's job resembled that of an arbiter employed to coax the owners to abide by league decisions. The owners entrusted this delicate job to Emmett Quinn, who presided over the NHA during most of its existence.

As president of a new organization, Quinn walked a fine line in balancing the interests of the various stakeholders. Since professional hockey was a new enterprise, arguments over the policies and directions of hockey occurred frequently among club owners. The issue of referee appointments gives a glimpse of the contentious nature of the NHA. From time to time, clubs complained about biases and incompetency among the officials. George Kennedy, the new Canadiens owner, was particularly vocal. After one contest, he charged that the referee had lost the game for his team and demanded that a French-Canadian referee be appointed alongside an English one for all the Canadiens games.[14] In a later game against the Wanderers, the Canadiens threatened not to go on the ice because they were unhappy with the president's appointed officials. In reply, Quinn threatened to resign 'rather than consent to let clubs choose officials.'[15] The Canadiens backed down.

The referee question revealed the different factions in the eastern professional hockey circle. Besides ethnicity, geography divided the clubs. Montreal had been the centre of elite-level hockey from the beginning. Over the years, there had been resentment and perhaps jealousy towards Montreal's position in the hockey world. Clubs outside the city were often leery about decisions coming from Montreal. One complaint was the predominance of Montreal-based referees, whose decisions, some owners charged, favoured the city's clubs. After losing five straight games, with the last loss being on home ice, the Quebec club complained about the use of Montreal referees at Quebec's home games.[16] Attempting to appease the non-Montreal-based clubs, president Quinn tried hard to get non-Montreal referees.[17]

Although the NHA clubs continued their complaints about officiating, they knew that referees were an integral part of professional hockey and that good ones were hard to find. A referee's decisions during a game could enhance the product on the ice or, conversely, generate criticism against the league. A referee's decisions could also influence the outcome of a game, especially when the calibre of the clubs was similar. Since a successful club generally drew a bigger paying audience and betting on game results was common, a referee's decisions sometimes added fuel to the emotions of the participants during and after the game and, in turn, drew the ire of fans, players, and club officials alike. Under constant abuse from the Canadiens during the 1911–12 season, referee Bob Meldrum had had enough, and announced his retirement after a game between the Canadiens and the Wanderers. This would not be the last time that referees complained about their treatment.[18]

The emotional and monetary stakes of the game sometimes made the referee's job nightmarish, and rough play especially became a concern of the NHA. The amateurs had long contended that rough play was an inherent characteristic of professional hockey. A man who was paid to win would win at all costs. Financial rewards tied to first place and to winning the Stanley Cup certainly did not help to change many people's perception in associating professionalism with rough play. For the club owners, however, rough play could also mean damaged assets. Given the small pool of professional players, incapacitation resulting from injuries by rough play could hurt a team's standing and gate receipts. Moreover, many referees came from amateur hockey and still held the amateur ideal of gentlemanly conduct. Thus, the referees found themselves caught amid conflicting demands: to allow the players to do their job, protect the league's assets, and, at the same time, maintain some semblance of gentlemanly conduct.[19]

To improve the professional hockey brand image, the hockey governing body sought to demonstrate its willingness to deal with the problem of violence – as today. The McSorley suspension and the Bertuzzi case in the early twenty-first century have merely continued a long tradition of warding off impositions into the affairs of hockey by outside sources. Rough play occupied the NHA for several seasons and the league experimented with different penalty systems. This experimentation also highlighted the owners' dilemma on this issue. On the one hand, the owners wanted to rein in rough play or at least fend off criticism. On the other, rough play could be a winning tactic for which the owners did not want their own players punished. For the 1911–12 season, the NHA imposed a five-dollar fine and expulsion from the match for any player committing a major foul. It further added a $200 penalty to any club found paying the fine for the penalized player. If this seemed a fairly severe deterrent against rough play, the NHA reversed its policy from the previous year by allowing a substitution for any player expelled from the match. Thus, teams might lose the services of the offenders for rough play, but they would never play short-handed and have their chances of winning the game lessened.[20]

While the NHA hailed the amended penalty system as a step towards improving the game, not all the clubs approved of experimentation. Ottawa, in particular, objected to the changes made in the game. Together with the new penalty
system, the NHA also reduced the number of players on the ice from seven to six
in the 1911–12 season. Financially, the reduction of players could conceivably
decrease payrolls and the fines under the new penalty system could benefit the
league treasury. From a product packaging point of view, the reduced number of
players on ice and the penalty system opened up more space for players, thus
giving speedy players an advantage. Yet Ottawa had relied on combination play
that stressed passing among the forwards. Its system of play depended heavily on
the rover position, which was dropped by the league. Early in the season, as they
found adapting to six-man hockey difficult, Ottawa players complained about
the new rules. The Ottawa president said that he would ask the league to
immediately reverse course. No reversal, however, occurred.[21]

Six-man hockey might not have survived if the clubs, at least a majority of
them, did not benefit from the changes financially. At the end of the 1911–12
season the Ottawa club finished in second place, with nine wins and nine losses,
which did not compare favourably with its previous year's standing of first place
in the league, with thirteen wins and three losses. Losing prestige as the Stanley
Cup holder and the concomitant playoff revenues, the Ottawa club proposed an
amendment to return to seven-man hockey before the 1912–13 season. Given
the financial success of the past season for the league as a whole, only two clubs,
Ottawa and one of the two new Toronto franchises, the Tecumsehs, voted in
favour of reverting to a seven-man team. Thus ended the era of seven-man
hockey, a style that had prevailed since the early days of organized hockey.[22]

Still, bad feelings rose once again among the NHA clubs. In losing its bid to
return to seven-man hockey, Ottawa accused the other new Toronto entry, the
Torontos, of a double-cross. Apparently, the Ottawa club had made some sort of
agreement with the Torontos that Ottawa would give up the right to one of its
players, Bruce Ridpath, to the Torontos in return for the Torontos' vote. Subsequently, the Ottawa club demanded that the Torontos pay $500 for Ridpath's
right, but Toronto refused, stating that Ridpath would only act as the manager of
the team.[23] Disputes involving a Toronto team did not end in the 1912–13
season, and would eventually break up the NHA. For the moment, however, no
NHA club was contemplating derailing the league since the clubs had been
doing well financially since its founding.[24] Occasional internal bickering seemed
minor when a challenge to the NHA appeared from afar.

Professional hockey in Canada experienced a boom at the end of the first decade
of the twentieth century. With the parting of ways between amateur purists and
liberals, some hockey promoters, besides those in the Montreal region, decided to

take their chances in professional hockey leagues. Like the NHA, these were regional organizations that catered to the local entertainment markets. All projected themselves as the local premium hockey entertainment. In order to strengthen this product position, clubs in these leagues had to recruit skilled players and devise other strategies to attract customers. Hence, the leagues competed in the player market even though they did not intrude into each other's territories. The competition for players as well as the honour to become the holder of the Stanley Cup, the symbol of hockey supremacy, created conflicts between the leagues. Unlike the NHA, however, few of them had a population base that could generate enough revenue to sustain a top-flight hockey league for long. Hence, most were relatively short-lived and unstable, and lacked the quality of play of the NHA. One, the Pacific Coast Hockey Association (PCHA), however, stood out among the new professional hockey organizations.[25]

With franchises along the Pacific coast, the PCHA had a different organizational arrangement than the NHA. A brainchild of the brothers Lester and Frank Patrick, the PCHA was the only professional hockey league that rivalled the NHA from 1911 to the early 1920s. Unlike the NHA's diverse ownerships, the Patrick family ran the league from the beginning. While the PCHA elected W.P. Irving, a long-time OHA executive, as president during the first season, Frank Patrick held that post from 1913 until the league's dissolution in 1923. The Patrick brothers oversaw almost everything in the PCHA. Besides running the league, they also managed the two British Columbia franchises, with Lester operating the Victoria club and Frank guiding the flagship Vancouver club. Both played on their respective clubs, as other owners in the league took on the role of investors. Moreover, the league, rather than the clubs, assembled the players and then distributed them to the various clubs in its initial season. This practice led to cries of syndicate hockey, especially from the eastern hockey establishment. Their biographer called the brothers 'two self-assigned benevolent dictators.'[26]

As far as professional hockey was concerned, the Pacific Northwest was virgin territory. In part, the mild coastal climate could not maintain any natural-ice arena, and without such facilities, hockey was not on the local winter sports calendar. To overcome the facility problem, the Patricks built an arena in both Vancouver and Victoria with their father's lumber-industry profits. The new arenas used artificial ice-making plants to maintain the ice surface. With a seating capacity of 10,500, the Vancouver Arena was definitely the crown jewel in the Patricks' enterprise. The Victoria rink had a capacity of 4000. Projected costs for the two arenas were $320,000. But cost overruns ballooned to more than $400,000, excluding operating costs. Given their heavy investment, it was not surprising that the Patricks wanted full control of the league.[27]

The Patricks' venture into the hockey business coincided with developments in western Canada that boosted its economy and population. As an inducement for British Columbia to join the Dominion, the federal government had completed the Canadian Pacific Railway to the west coast in 1885. During the early 1900s, a second rail line linking the west coast to the east began construction. The railroad system both fuelled and was fuelled by economic prosperity and increased immigration as Canada experienced a period of economic and demographic growth at the beginning of the twentieth century. Making the best out of the announcement of the closing of the frontier in the United States, the Canadian government advertised free land for homesteaders in 1896. By the turn of the century, immigration into Canada outstripped emigration. While central Canada began a period of industrialization, western Canada attracted immigrant farmers whose products required an adequate transportation system. It was also in the interest of the industrial East to ensure reliable transport to acquire the resources it needed and to carry its products to both domestic and overseas markets. British Columbia, in particular, experienced a surge in population during the first two decades of the twentieth century. Although population growth on the Canadian west coast did not witness the same kind of explosion as in the east, the port of Vancouver experienced a boom of over 310 per cent between 1901 and 1911 and overtook Victoria as the economic centre of the province. Victoria, still a quaint city, also saw its population increased by over 50 per cent in the same period. These growing cities represented untapped markets for professional hockey.[28]

Entrepreneurs with ideas and drive thrived in the business climate in Canada during the early 1900s. Except during the war period of 1914–18, the Canadian government accepted the primacy of private-enterprise initiatives. Despite the introduction of the income tax in 1917, Canada's tax policies rarely impinged on excess business profits. Even as the United States took on the big trusts such as Standard Oil, Canadian anti-trust legislation was weak and ineffective. Indeed, capitalization of Canadian industries grew steadily between 1900 and 1912 and mergers and consolidations of Canadian corporations peaked at the end of the first decade of the twentieth century. Turn-of-the-century Canada provided a haven for entrepreneurs such as Lester and Frank Patrick, who had been helping their father run the family lumber business in British Columbia. In this favourable business climate, the Patricks decided to apply their expertise as businessmen and hockey experts when they formed the PCHA.[29]

The PCHA was unique among the various professional hockey leagues at the time. Unlike the others, the PCHA did not have any amateur hockey organizations to provide competition in the hockey entertainment business. Furthermore, the Patricks controlled the league as well as the facilities. These advantages allowed the PCHA to be the sole provider in the hockey business, but there were two important disadvantages to the situation. In the absence of an established amateur hockey market, the Patricks had to cultivate consumer demand for their product – hockey as an entertainment alternative. At the opening of the Victoria rink on December 25, the Patricks, as a publicity and promotional stunt, held a skating party that featured a brass band from the Canadian navy. In attendance with the Patricks were the lieutenant-governor of British Columbia and other dignitaries. Perhaps this first experience should have forewarned the Patricks about the 'foreignness' of their product to many patrons on the West Coast and hinted at the lack of market research by the Patricks. A local reporter commented, on this first look at the Patricks' enterprise, that 'you could tell who the Easterners were. They were the ones standing up.'[30] Related to this hurdle of cultivating consumer demand was the total lack of resource suppliers who were in close proximity, and the most important resource of all in the hockey business was players. Without any quality amateurs anywhere near the West Coast, the Patricks had to look elsewhere. In doing so, they took the demand and supply problems and tried to solve them in one stroke. They raided the NHA.

Player supply became a bone of contention among competing professional leagues in the early 1910s. While the OHA was slowly building up a strong senior amateur hockey circuit, the NHA remained the organization with the top talent. Since the Patricks had already invested heavily in their new venture, they were not going to cut corners when wooing NHA players. Sixteen out of the twenty-three players whom they signed hailed from the NHA and many, such as Newsy Lalonde, Harry Hyland, and Don Smith, were stars of the NHA. In signing these star players, the Patricks hoped to give instant credibility to the new organization and generate enthusiasm in the PCHA's markets.[31]

Initially, the Patricks' raiding did not elicit great concern in the NHA. For one thing, the dissolution of the Renfrew club in the fall of 1911 made its players available to the rest of the NHA clubs. Although Renfrew had lost some members from its high-profiled 1909–10 team, the club still had two of the top five scorers from the previous season as well as the much sought-after Fred Taylor under contract from the disbanded club. Second, the remoteness of the PCHA made some players hesitant to go to the West Coast even if the Patricks were offering much better wages than the NHA.[32] Especially for players who had business ties in the East, the opportunity cost of leaving home, business, and an established league for a new, unproven league was not enticing. In early November 1911, Eddie McCafferty, one of the owners of the Wanderers, boasted that his club could get along without some of the players who had reportedly jumped to the PCHA. Moreover, he pointed out, all but one player on the Wanderers squad had a reserve clause in their contracts.[33] Adding another obstacle to those players who were wavering, the NHA promised to ban for life any player jumping his

contract and to bar any NHA club from competing with any other club employing such players.[34] As late as the end of November and early December 1911,
however, NHA clubs remained nonchalant about players jumping to the PCHA.[35]

Despite the bravado shown by the NHA, not everything was going well. By
December 1911, the construction of the home arena for the two new Toronto
NHA expansion clubs was well behind schedule.[36] In mid-December the NHA
dropped the two Toronto clubs for the season, but allowed them to hold on to
their franchises for one year. Without the two new clubs, the NHA had a larger
pool of players, as the four remaining NHA clubs could secure the use of the
Toronto clubs' players. Yet neither Toronto club had any player of note that the
other NHA clubs might want to sign. Thus, the availability of the Toronto players
did not materially affect any club's strength.[37]

The war to sign players between the PCHA and the NHA might have been
even more intense if not for a couple of factors. Both Patricks were knowledge-
able hockey men who knew talent. Having played elite-level hockey in the
Montreal region, the Patricks were familiar with the NHA players. Thus, they
had some idea of the personnel they needed in order to make their new league a
success. The Patricks also ran a tight ship when signing players because of their
heavy initial capital outlay in the construction of the two arenas. While they were
more generous – and they had to be in order to lure players west – than the NHA
in their salary offers, the Patricks signed a minimal number of players. Unlike the
NHA, the PCHA played seven-man hockey, and the entire roster of the PCHA
consisted of only twenty-three players – seven for each of the three franchises and
two spares in case of injuries to any of the teams. Even so, the appearance of a
willing bidder led some players to demand higher salaries from the NHA clubs.
This was especially so with Ottawa, whose players had been militant leaders
against the NHA salary cap a year earlier. By late December, however, both
leagues had their players signed and ready to begin the season.[38]

There was one more instance in which the NHA and the PCHA competed
against one another – the Stanley Cup. As evident in the CAHL/FAHL split, the
Stanley Cup was an important possession not only for the legitimation of a
league but also for the extra revenues it brought clubs involved in the competition. Hence, the PCHA applied to challenge for the trophy. Yet there was no
Stanley Cup series for the PCHA. Besides the NHA's objection that the PCHA
was harbouring contract jumpers, its season did not end until March 19 and the
natural-ice arenas in the East simply could not guarantee any ice at late dates. The
PCHA's shot at the Stanley Cup would have to wait for another two seasons.[39]

Relations between the NHA and the PCHA deteriorated in the following
season even as the two leagues discussed forming a national commission to
oversee professional hockey. At the centre of the controversy was the signing of

players under contract. A number of PCHA players wanted to return east and had signed with NHA clubs. As a condition to the proposed national commission, Frank Patrick demanded that all contract jumpers from the PCHA be banned from organized hockey. Since the PCHA had had no qualms about signing NHA players under contract in the previous year, the NHA directors could not agree to his demand. Thus, the war between the two leagues intensified.[40]

Unlike the previous year's approach, the PCHA raided the NHA strategically in the 1912–13 season. Instead of securing the NHA's best players, the PCHA concentrated on two clubs, Ottawa and Quebec, the top two finishers from the past season. Since the Canadiens did not have, and were not expected to have, a very strong team, this tactic effectively left the NHA with one strong team, the Wanderers. This, the Patricks reasoned, would make NHA games uninteresting. The situation got so desperate for the NHA that the Ottawa press hinted a truce might be in the works.[41]

Aside from this strategy, the Patricks also landed the marquee player Fred Taylor, whom the PCHA had wanted all along. Taylor had sat out of hockey the previous season because he refused to report to the Wanderers, who had received Taylor's rights in the Renfrew dispersal draft. The Patricks' biographer credits Taylor as the key catalyst in generating enthusiasm for the PCHA. Whereas only half of the seats were filled in both the Vancouver and Victoria home openers and the PCHA lost $9000 in its first year of operation, the two arenas had their first sell-outs the year Taylor arrived in Vancouver.[42]

The success of the PCHA as a viable business was due to more than its ability to lure skilled players away from the NHA. Lester and Frank Patrick were also two of the most innovative hockey minds of their time, and their control of the PCHA afforded a venue for experimentation with their ideas. In order to attract customers, the Patricks began adding innovations, such as forward passing, to make their product more appealing. Many of the Patricks' innovations eventually appeared in rival leagues, and some even crossed over to other sports.[43]

Perhaps one of the most important innovations that directly affected the bottom line of the league came when the PCHA added a post-season playoff in 1918 to determine the title of the league.[44] Previously, the winner of any league became the champion, and in the major senior or later professional leagues, the champion earned the right to challenge for the Stanley Cup. With a post-season playoff format, however, clubs other than the winner of the league now stood a second chance at winning the Stanley Cup. The move certainly kept supporters' hopes up and gave the clubs another chance for more revenue. Given the erratic gate receipts and small number of clubs operating in the PCHA, the post-season playoff gate receipts provided much-needed revenue.[45] One year after the PCHA instituted the playoff system, Frank Patrick boasted that it had 'worked out better than we ever expected it would. The Professional baseball league, two of the amateur baseball leagues and several junior lacrosse and baseball leagues have adopted it ... [and] not a single fan found fault with the playoff system.'[46] It was this kind of innovative thinking, as well as product differentiation, the PCHA relied on to attract consumers.

The high cost of the bidding for players finally forced the two leagues to come to an agreement in 1913. Among other things, the two leagues agreed on a series of player controls, including the recognition of each other's reserve clauses, player suspensions, and the division of the labour market. More importantly, the Stanley Cup ceased to be a challenge trophy after this point. It became a championship series between the PCHA and the NHA. When Vancouver won the Stanley Cup in the 1914–15 season, hockey culture in general and professional hockey in particular finally became a national phenomenon.[47]

The PCHA's contribution to professional hockey extended beyond Canada. It added two American franchises, Portland (1914) and Seattle (1915). While the short-lived IHL had franchises in Canada and the United States, it had never achieved the status and prestige of an elite-level league. Thus, the PCHA represented the first successful effort to export major league hockey from Canada into the United States.[48] When Seattle won the trophy in 1917, a sizable crowd of 12,000 paid to attend the four-game series.[49] By crossing the border, the PCHA had also forced the Stanley Cup trustees to break with the original purpose of the trophy – to determine 'the championship Hockey Club of the Dominion.' Instead, it was now the symbol of the 'world' championship.

The NHA and PCHA presented two different possibilities for organizing the professional hockey network. Whereas the NHA had more ownership diversity, the PCHA remained under the firm control of the Patrick family, which had initially organized and promoted the league. The diverse nature of NHA ownership meant greater potential for internal conflict and left the league much more vulnerable to external threats, especially when they were well engineered by an organized and informed foe. This difference in the administrative structure of the two organizations revealed itself during the various wars between the two leagues and would eventually culminate in the resignation of the NHA president, Emmett Quinn.

Even though the Patricks served as owners, promoters, facility providers, and players, the distinction between players and management was becoming sharper. After the Patricks, no player, with the exception of Mario Lemieux in 1999, would become the owner of the team on which he was also a player. For one thing, no hockey player could muster enough capital if his entire income was based on his hockey salary. Furthermore, contracts with reserve and waiver

clauses now bound players to one team. An interleague agreement only reinforced management mechanisms to control players, although greed and ego at
times reduced the effectiveness of these controls.

For the first time in the development of elite-level hockey in Canada, the
PCHA represented a sustained challenge to the entrenched hockey establishment
in the Montreal region. The NHA, and its later descendant the National Hockey
League (NHL), had to share the player market with the western upstart. Although
their relationship was not always amicable, the NHA-NHL and the PCHA
coexisted through an inter-league agreement that made the affairs between the
two more manageable. Even as the PCHA presented an alternative for the players,
it at least did not compete for the NHA's consumer markets nor any of the
potential markets within the NHA's territory. Hence, the inter-league agreement
took on great significance as an instrument regulating the only potential source
of conflict, the competition for players, between the two leagues. By recognizing
each league's territories and player rights, the inter-league agreement brought a
degree of order, no matter how tenuous, into professional hockey. This instrument of order for the two rivals would serve the NHA well when the Montreal
hockey establishment went through another metamorphosis in 1917.

Chapter 6

An Inglorious End and
an Inauspicious Beginning

Professional hockey went through a reorganization in 1917 that had its origin in the expansion of the NHA beyond the Montreal region earlier in the decade. The NHA had decided to grant franchises in Toronto, the second largest city in Canada, in the 1911–12 season. Toronto was a logical choice for expansion. Besides its large population base, Toronto had been an important amateur hockey centre since the formation of the OHA in 1890. Yet the NHA's expansion to Toronto carried an ironic twist. While the PCHA was an established rival to the NHA, it was the desire of the NHA directors to exclude an objectionable Toronto club owner, Edward J. Livingstone, in 1917 that led to the demise of the NHA and the birth of a new ruling body in professional hockey.

Like some of the directors in the pre-NHA era, the Toronto hockey entrepreneurs consisted of people with connections to amateur hockey who saw professional hockey as a viable business opportunity. However, some of these Toronto men did not come from the same network of hockey entrepreneurs as those involved in the NHA and its predecessors. This created tension and divisiveness within the NHA. One outcome was the creation of the National Hockey League (NHL) along the familiar lines of hockey's past method of reorganizing – the abandonment of an old league to exclude certain people. The establishment of the NHL also helped to bring together those who were committed to professional hockey and weed out those who were less committed. In addition, the new league owners' dislike of Livingstone unified them and helped to alleviate some of the distrust among them. In order to prevent the Toronto owner from entering professional hockey, the NHL owners were willing to vest their trust in the League president to that end. By the beginning of the 1920s, the NHL was a small regional business. Yet it had built a fairly unified culture without which the next phase of its development would not be possible.

Edward James Livingstone did not venture blindly into the professional hockey business. He had been an OHA club director as well as manager of hockey and football activities of the Toronto Rugby and Athletic Association (TRAA).[1] His TRAA hockey team had some of the best amateur talent in the OHA and was the champion of the senior division in 1914. When Livingstone bought the NHA Ontarios, he was probably counting on his connections in Toronto amateur hockey to stock his professional club.[2]

Despite Livingstone's skill as an amateur hockey manager, his venture in professional hockey did not go smoothly. His team did not fare well in the standings. Trying to change his luck, Livingstone renamed his team the Shamrocks the following season. But the luck of the Irish did not smile on him either. The First World War further confounded Livingstone's efforts to assemble a competitive club. The Great War began during his first year in the NHA, when some athletes, including amateur hockey players, had joined the armed forces. That did not materially affect the NHA or Livingstone for that season, but he must have known that mostly anglophone Ontario would supply more than its share of men to the war and that many amateur athletes would answer the call. Indeed, Ontario led all of Canada in voluntary enlistments. Between August 1914 and October 1917, 191,632 from Ontario volunteered. By contrast, Quebec, Canada's other populous province, had 48,934 enlistments. Since Livingstone had frequently tried out amateur players frequently in an effort to strengthen the club throughout his first season, he undoubtedly realized what the war could do to the supply of players. During the annual meeting for the 1915–16 season, the NHA owners held serious discussions regarding whether to continue operation as the European conflict escalated.[3]

If Livingstone wondered about the potential drain of manpower due to the war, a more immediate trouble in the labour market occurred shortly after the annual meeting. The PCHA once again declared war against the NHA. PCHA president Frank Patrick accused the NHA of reneging on the inter-league agreement and refused to do business with the NHA as long as its president, T. Emmett Quinn, remained in office. Although Livingstone's Shamrocks did not have anyone of quality that the PCHA might want, the PCHA signed the Torontos' top two scorers and another player jumped to the coast league. With the Torontos depleted, the Shamrocks could expect competition for amateur players in Toronto that would conceivably drive up the prices for their services.[4] To counter the player-shortage situation and to solve the woeful performance of his squad, Livingstone purchased the Torontos with the intention of combining the best of both squads into one team. Worried about public outcry over fixed games now that the two Toronto teams were owned by the same person, other NHA owners demanded Livingstone sell the Shamrocks by November 20, 1915. When Livingstone failed to comply, the League took over the disposition of the Shamrocks.[5]

Livingstone's troubles only increased when the NHA gave a military unit, the 228th battalion, the defunct Shamrock franchise before the 1916–17 season. Almost immediately, Livingstone got into an argument about players with the new team. Besides the 228th, he was feuding with just about every club in the league as well as the facility provider, the Toronto Arena Gardens Company.[6] When the league met on February 11, 1917 to discuss the withdrawal of the 228th, which had been ordered to depart for Europe, the owners decided to drop the Torontos for the remainder of the schedule. For unknown reasons, Livingstone was not at the meeting, but he sent a telegram asking the NHA to carry on with a five-club, double schedule for the remainder of the season. The NHA had not done well financially with an odd-numbered circuit in the previous season and the other owners refused his request. Moreover, the owners were all too eager to reinforce their own clubs by holding a draft for the Toronto players given the tight player market. Hence, president Frank Robinson announced the suspension of the Toronto club 'for transgressions of the rule' and put the Toronto players in a lottery for the other clubs, with a stipulation that these players would be returned to the Torontos when the club was reinstated.[7]

The NHA owners' distaste for Livingstone was such that rumours of excluding Toronto indefinitely began to fly shortly after the suspension of the Toronto club.[8] Livingstone did not help his cause when he accused the NHA of ignoring irregularities in some league games. He then demanded that Robinson expel the Wanderers for tampering with the Torontos' players.[9] Perhaps the last straw for the owners occurred when Livingstone issued writs against the NHA and its member clubs for unstated damages in dropping the Toronto club. To forestall the next possible NHA move, Livingstone also filed for an injunction 'restraining the defendants from releasing, disposing of or otherwise dealing with the Ottawa, Canadien, Wanderer and Quebec clubs which would permit them to form an independent association.'[10]

Authors Holzman and Nieforth have argued that the other NHA owners banded together in order to oust Livingstone, but it was more complicated than a simple conspiracy.[11] While it was true that the other owners disliked Livingstone, the abandonment of the Torontos did not occur simply because Livingstone, the newcomer, challenged the established authority. As the Great War progressed, Canadian recruits had been steadily declining after the initial enthusiasm for the war ebbed. Enlistments had dropped from just over nine thousand in January

1917 to under sixty-five hundred in June. Yet the Canadian government wanted to send an extra infantry division to bolster the existing four Canadian divisions already in France. On June 11, 1917 Prime Minister Robert Borden introduced the Compulsory Service Act despite vocal opposition from organized labour, farmers, and many francophones. It became law at the end of August, to come into effect in the new year. Conscription affected the male population between the ages of twenty and thirty-five, which fell in the range of most if not all hockey players. For professional hockey, this demand would further tighten the player market. Yet the Arena Company in Montreal threatened to lock out the NHA if the league could not produce quality teams.[12] Furthermore, a majority of the NHA owners did not want a five-club schedule because 'one team was always idle and to give them all a show three matches had to be played every week.'[13] A third factor in abandoning the Torontos involved the resignation of the NHA president, Frank Robinson, who, by the fall of 1917, was president in name only. Frank Calder, the secretary-treasurer, had been running the daily operations and one of Livingstone's nemeses, Sam Lichtenhein, assumed the duty of investigating the Toronto situation. It became clear before the 1917 NHA annual meeting that the league wanted only four clubs and Toronto was not on the list. Sure enough, the NHA announced the suspension of operation during its annual meeting because '1. it was unfeasible to operate a 5-team league and 2. The scarcity of talents due to the war.'[14]

The suspension of the NHA was really a ruse by the rest of the clubs to exclude Livingstone from professional hockey. In dispensing with an unwanted element, the other NHA clubs chose to follow the method employed by their various predecessors in elite-level hockey – to reorganize themselves into a new body. On November 22 four NHA clubs – Ottawa, Quebec, Canadiens, and the Wanderers – met and formed the National Hockey League (NHL) at the Windsor Hotel in Montreal. At that meeting, M.J. Quinn of the Quebec club moved, seconded by George Kennedy of the Canadiens, that the new league adopt the NHA constitution. Unlike the case of past reorganizations, however, these clubs did not bother to resign from the NHA, at least not initially. Thus, the NHA still existed technically, but with only one member, the Torontos. In reporting the launching of the NHL, the *Montreal Gazette* noted that the new league had the same constitution and reserve lists as the now defunct NHA. It concluded that the NHL 'was apparently a move to bring about a change in the ownership and management of the Toronto Club more than anything else.'[15] As the Ottawa representative at the meeting remarked, 'Livingstone was always arguing. Without him we can get down to the business of making money.'[16]

The formation of the NHL represented a shift of the power structure in the administration of professional hockey. Whereas previous elite-level hockey organizations had been rife with power struggles among the various clubs, the NHL was moving towards consolidating decision-making power in the hands of its president. Self-interest among the clubs still existed. But the persistence of Livingstone to return to professional hockey united the NHL clubs against a common enemy because, unlike the PCHA, Livingstone operated within the NHL's territories. In dealing with Livingstone's lawsuits and other schemes, the owners entrusted to and empowered Calder to defend their interests. Calder's successful handling of Livingstone and other internal problems earned him the owners' trust as well as more power and responsibilities.

Calder's attempt to establish the power of the president came during the initial meeting of the NHL. When the owners elected Frank Calder as president of the NHL at a salary of $800, they also agreed to his demand that 'there could be no appeal from his decisions.'[17] This concession by the NHL owners was no small feat in the consolidation of administrative power in professional hockey. As the sport editor of the *Montreal Herald* and the NHA's secretary-treasurer in the Emmett Quinn regime, Calder had seen how the self-interests and bickering among the owners overshadowed the president's decisions. Given the weakened state of professional hockey during the First World War and the troubles with Livingstone, Calder was wise to seize the moment and insisted on placing the president as the ultimate arbiter in professional hockey. And sure enough, troubles began as soon as the NHL was formed.

Despite their dislike of Livingstone, the NHL owners were not blind to the market potential of Toronto. At the NHL inaugural meeting, the Quebec Bulldogs informed the others that they would suspend operations. M.J. (Mike) Quinn, the long-time manager of the Quebec club who had managed the club to two consecutive Stanley Cup victories, had retired due to ill health. Unable to find someone to replace Quinn, the other directors of the Quebec club opted to suspend operation of the club for the inaugural season.[18] With the demands on the league's resources because of the upcoming Livingstone lawsuits, the NHL acceded to Quebec's request and allowed the club to retain its franchise. This withdrawal, however, opened up a spot for a fourth club. Represented by William Northey, the Toronto Arena company applied and received the Toronto franchise. Thus, the NHL's inaugural season began with the Montreal Canadiens, the Montreal Wanderers, the Ottawa Senators, and the Toronto Arenas. By aligning with the Toronto rink management, the League momentarily, at least, stopped the potential threat of a rival league from Livingstone.[19]

Even the best-laid plans, however, could not anticipate all contingencies. The NHL's plan for a four-team schedule came to an abrupt end shortly after the 1917–18 season began. On January 2, 1918 the Montreal Arena, where both the Wanderers and Canadiens played, burned down. While the Canadiens regrouped and moved into the Jubilee rink, the Wanderers declared their intention to withdraw from league play during a January 3 emergency meeting. Calder and the other owners, however, did not want a three-club circuit if they could help it. Thus, they tabled the Wanderer's request.[20]

Having sustained losses since 1914, Sam Lichtenhein, promoter of wrestling, boxing, and horse racing and owner of the Wanderers, was not going to let parliamentary procedure change his mind. The Wanderers' season opener on December 19 drew only 700 fans. It was time to stop the bleeding. Lichtenhein announced that he would disband his club after January 5.[21] When the Wanderers did not show up for their January 5 game at Toronto, the other owners passed a resolution stripping the Wanderers of their membership and imposed a fine of $500 on the club during the next League meeting.[22] Thus, the NHL limped along with three clubs. Not until the 1919–20 season, when M.J. Quinn reactivated the Quebec club, did the NHL return to a four-club schedule.

As the NHL struggled to survive, Livingstone continued his efforts to place his team in a league. His lawsuit against the NHA did not result in a favourable ruling. The court tried and dismissed his case in February 1918. Livingstone appealed the ruling and the Supreme Court of Canada dismissed his appeal in November 1919. After losing his battles in the courts, he switched strategies by trying to destroy the NHL from within and without. Livingstone allied himself with Percy Quinn, a director of the original Torontos and brother of former NHA president Emmett Quinn. Percy Quinn had purchased the Quebec franchise in the summer of 1918, but he was non-committal about reactivating it. After repeated efforts to get an answer from Quinn, Calder declared the Quebec franchise under suspension on November 16.[23]

In order for Livingstone to continue on in professional hockey, he needed to have three elements in place: players, ice time, and a league. He was able to retain his players via an arrangement with the Toronto Arena Gardens when the Gardens entered a team in the inaugural NHL season. Essentially this arrangement allowed Livingstone's Torontos to operate in the NHL, and he had the last word on player transactions.[24]

Livingstone knew that securing ice time and a place in the NHL would be problematic. Through Percy Quinn, an insider, he tried to eliminate these obstacles. Acting as Quebec's new owner, Quinn was able to get options on ice time with the Ottawa and Jubilee rinks, at which NHL games had been held the previous season.[25] This move effectively gave the Livingstone faction control of ice times in two of the three NHL cities. Moreover, Livingstone filed suit against the Toronto Arena Gardens for breach of contract when the Gardens refused to return his players after the 1917–18 season. He asked for $20,000 in damages; the amount could potentially be a bargaining chip for ice time in Toronto.[26]

Finding a league for Livingstone's club was a more formidable challenge because the NHL directors would never allow him into their fold. Getting options on ice time, however, was a step towards solving this problem. Livingstone then proceeded to announce the creation of a new hockey league, the Canadian Hockey Association (CHA) in late October.[27] In so doing, he placed the acquisition of ice time as the main goal in his struggles with the NHL. As the established league, the NHL was able to compel the rinks in its franchise cities to fall in line. Perhaps because of Livingstone's demands in his lawsuits against the rink management in Toronto, the Arena Gardens was the first to affirm its loyalty to the NHL. One of its directors informed Calder that Quinn pretended 'to ask for [ice] privileges for the Shamrocks, not stating in which league they expected to play ... so that they could switch to C.H.A. after they obtained them,' and asked 'if we cannot as a whole cook Mr. Quinn's goose good and plenty.'[28]

The showdown between the Livingstone-Quinn coalition and the NHL came shortly thereafter. After Toronto refused to give ice time to the CHA, Dey's rink in Ottawa also announced that it would go with the NHL.[29] This effectively ended any hope of starting a new league. Even at this late date, however, Calder still wanted to include Quinn in order to isolate Livingstone.[30] But when Quinn and Livingstone elicited the aide of Tom Wall, the owner of the defunct Ontarios, to force a vote to revive the NHA, Calder decided to call their bluff. In December the suspended NHA held a meeting with all the original six teams represented. While Livingstone had three votes in his favour to revive the league, there were also three opposing votes. Somehow, Livingstone found out that the Canadiens' owner, Kennedy, had sold twelve of his shares to A.A. Barbeau of the Brunswick-Balke-Collender Company and insisted that the Canadiens' vote was invalid.[31] To Livingstone's dismay, however, Barbeau voted to retain the Canadiens' right to vote. Furthermore, Calder outmanoeuvred Livingstone by reminding him that none of the clubs in the Livingstone coalition had paid the league assessment, and thus they had defaulted their rights in the NHA.[32] When Quinn, as chair of the meeting, denied a motion to adjourn, some owners questioned his authority and asked for his credentials as the Quebec representative. Quinn refused and the Canadiens owner, Kennedy, walked up to the chair and said to him: 'You are afraid to read your agreement with the Quebec Club, and you cannot produce your credentials; you lie and you know you lie.'[33] Afterward, the NHL clubs walked out of the meeting, and the NHA never operated again.

With the saga of the NHA coming to an end, the NHL had eliminated one of the avenues for Livingstone's return to professional hockey. Livingstone, however, continued to be an annoyance after the 1918–19 season. Despite the dismissal of his case against the NHA, Livingstone's suit against the Toronto Arena Gardens dragged on for several more years, and he continued scheming to return to professional hockey via other routes. Livingstone was nonetheless off the NHL's back for the moment, even though the outcome of the Toronto Arena Gardens lawsuit would undoubtedly affect the League in some way. His belligerence helped to unite the remaining clubs; at least momentarily they left their usual bickering behind. In the middle of the Livingstone lawsuit against the NHA, the remaining three NHL clubs agreed for the first time to share equally in the playoff gate receipts.[34] Disagreements among the owners and between the owners and the president continued, for greed and self-interest still drove the owners. In the face of a more deadly enemy, however, Calder was successful in demanding more authority from the owners and justified it by defeating the Livingstone faction.

Calder's power also came from his successful handling of the internal affairs of the NHL. With three clubs operating in the 1918–19 season and Livingstone's influence active in the Toronto market, Calder worked hard to add another club to the league, which in part explained his patience with Percy Quinn over the latter's controversial purchase of the Quebec club. Since the club had been operating in senior hockey for a long time, it was Calder's first choice to restore the NHL to a four-team league. As early as February 1918, Calder realized that a three-club league could not continue indefinitely. In order to justify a playoff, the NHL followed the old NHA practice that divided the season into two halves. The winner of the first half would engage the winner of the second in the post-season playoff. The Canadiens had won the first half and Calder worried that the team would lose playoff revenues if it won the second half as well.[35] In March 1919, Calder asked Mike Quinn if he would operate the Quebec franchise again.[36] Quinn, the former principal operator of the Quebec franchise, was unhappy with Percy Quinn, to whom he had sold the franchise. Percy Quinn had not paid him in full and had conspired with Livingstone against the NHL. In May 1919, Mike Quinn asked Calder to see if Percy Quinn would return the Quebec franchise.[37] Late in the fall that year Percy Quinn relented and released his claim to the Quebec franchise. Calder then suggested to Mike Quinn that he organize a club under a different name and apply for membership in the NHL. In a special meeting held on December 2, the NHL directors formally approved the application of the Quebec Athletic Club after they had cancelled Percy Quinn's Quebec Hockey Club franchise because of his failure to operate the club in the 1918–19 season. To avoid another debacle, the directors attached a condition to their approval of Quinn's application – 'that in the event of his discontinuing or losing control of his franchise rights in any manner said rights revert to the National Hockey League without any recompense.'[38]

Quebec's return to professional hockey was not going to be a happy experience. Besides its problems in assembling a competitive team, the Quebec club had also become the sacrificial lamb for another Livingstone-Quinn threat after the end of the season.[39] As part of the settlement for Livingstone's lawsuit against the Toronto Arena Gardens, Percy Quinn had assumed the managing directorship of the facility in June 1920. His appointment immediately brought the prospect that the NHL's Toronto franchise, now renamed the St Patricks, was in danger of not getting ice time in the coming season. Furthermore, Livingstone and Quinn might start a new league or restart the NHA if they could convince the Hamilton rink interest to join them. In mid-July, Fred Hambly, the St Patricks' owner, proposed to Calder that the NHL should consider including Hamilton in order to ward off Livingstone. Hamilton could also be the Toronto club's home arena should Percy Quinn refuse to grant the club ice time.[40] Calder agreed with Hambly and began actively pursuing Hamilton's rink owner, Percy Thompson.[41] Together with Tom Gorman, the Ottawa owner, and Hambly, Calder met with Thompson in late July.[42]

It was not clear how much of the Hamilton affair Mike Quinn of Quebec knew about. Calder, however, had considered the Quebec situation as early as August. In a letter to Gorman, Calder worried that Mike Quinn might join Livingstone 'with the prospect of losing their NHL franchise.'[43] Of the four NHL clubs, the Quebec club, at the eastern end of the NHL circuit, was the weakest. Unlike Toronto, which was at the western end, Quebec had a much smaller population base from which to draw its customers. Since the League frowned upon an odd-numbered club circuit, Quebec seemed the logical choice to be excluded in order to accommodate the Hamilton entry. By late August, a former Toronto owner warned Calder that Livingstone and Percy Quinn had met with Thompson to discuss the start of a new league, and he suggested that the NHL should grant a franchise to Hamilton as quickly as possible.[44] Calder got busy in the early fall; Hamilton agreed to pay $5000 for a NHL franchise.[45] Despite a Quebec deputation expressing their desire to continue operations, the NHL officially granted Hamilton a franchise and tabled the Quebec request during the NHL's annual meeting in November.[46] In breaking up Livingstone's attempt to ally with Hamilton, Calder further earned the trust of the owners in his ability as a chief executive officer. During the same meeting, the owners gave Calder the power to oversee the league's finances, including acquiring credits, issuing debt instruments, and entering into 'any business he may think fit.'[47]

While the NHL was successful in derailing Livingstone's plans to return to professional hockey, it was not doing so well in controlling players. Despite the reserve and waiver clauses, the players still commanded leverage in determining where they wanted to apply their hockey skills. One reason was that professional hockey was still a part-time commitment in a player's work year. Another had to do with the small pool of professional players available. Since the AAUC adhered to a strict definition of an amateur, many amateur players were reluctant to turn professional. Besides, '[t]he good amateurs in spite of the O.H.A. regulations and in spite of an attempt in this part of the country to make the amateurs toe the mark seem to be able to command more money than our own players.'[48]

For clubs that tried to improve their strength, there were several solutions to solving the problem of a relatively small player market. One was to try the amateur player market. Another alternative was to trade with other clubs. A trade, of course, demanded the clubs involved give up something valuable. Weak clubs were hardly in any position to improve their lot via this method.

A third alternative illustrated the owners' recognition of the peculiar nature of their business, which required some degree of cooperation. This solution called for the loaning of players to bolster another club's strength. While clubs competed against each other, they also realized that the business could not exist without each of them succeeding. Moreover, clubs such as Ottawa that successfully attracted and retained skilled players realized that a non-competitive league was bad for business. Hence, they endeavoured to help the weaker clubs to make the competition more evenly matched.

Even though the other clubs were willing to help, there was no guarantee that the loaned players would report for duty. Since players had other jobs, some were unwilling to move to a different city, especially in the middle of the season, when it was difficult to make arrangements with their other employers. When Ottawa loaned out two players, one to Hamilton and the other to Toronto, during the 1920–1 season, both players refused to report to their respective clubs. There were two avenues open to the Hamilton and Toronto clubs. They could either ask the League to suspend the players, as Hamilton did, or try to induce them with more financial rewards, which the St Patricks attempted.[49] The St Patricks' owner, Percy Hambly, tried in vain to lure Sprague Cleghorn, the loaned Ottawa player, to report to Toronto. Cleghorn turned down Hambly's eventual offer of $1750 for the remaining ten weeks of the season and 'an all the year round job with Percy McBride Sporting Goods Co.'[50] Calder assured Hambly that Cleghorn would not be permitted to play anywhere else, and he subsequently suspended Cleghorn. In the end, Cleghorn did play for Toronto under an agreement that involved a trade between the Canadiens and the St Patricks.[51]

Despite the problems with acquiring players, the NHL began a relatively stable period in the early 1920s. It maintained friendly relations with the other major professional leagues in Canada, the PCHA and, later, the Western Canada Hockey League (WCHL). Unlike the case in the early days, the competition for the Stanley Cup had now become the exclusive domain of the professional leagues.

This fact and the league playoffs that led up to the 'World Championship' helped to maintain both the NHL's stature and its bottom line. In 1922, for example, each NHL club received $1750 plus reimbursement of their travelling expenses for the playoffs.[52] For the 1922–3 Stanley Cup playoffs, the NHL's share of the gate was $683.72.[53] Between 1917 and 1921, the NHL net profits increased from $36.56 to $1105.46.[54] Thus, the NHL had established itself as a small but profitable business in the commercialized hockey industry.

Along with its financial gains, the NHL increasingly centralized its operation and granted its president more power to manage the league. Livingstone certainly provided the NHL owners with a reason to unite. To thwart this enemy, they were willing to delegate more and more power to Calder. Representing the NHL in the lawsuits that Livingstone filed against the NHL owners, Calder succeeded in protecting the owners' interests and further justified the need for his position, as well as increasing the scope of his authority. At the end of the 1920–1 season, the owners gave Calder $500 as a bonus for his work.[55] Before the start of the 1921–2 season, the owners voted to increase his salary to $1200, in part because of their appreciation of his management of the league's affairs and, perhaps, their recognition of Calder's expanded duties.[56] In 1922 the owners authorized Calder to attend a meeting in the West with the PCHA and a new western professional league, the Western Hockey League, and gave him 'a free hand to carry on negotiations on behalf of the National Hockey League.'[57] The NHL owners would require more of Calder's administrative and negotiating skills soon thereafter as the League took a bold step in expanding its operations.

Chapter 7

Going South, Part 1

The years between 1923 and 1927 were crucial for the development of the NHL as a professional sports organization because they were the formative years in the expansion of the NHL's sphere of influence. Beginning around 1923, the NHL experienced a period of rapid growth, increasing its number of franchises from four to ten. Within three short years, the NHL had become an international business that included Canadian and American franchises in the Northeast and the Great Lakes regions. The initiative to expand, however, did not come from the NHL. Rather, middle-class entrepreneurs who had been denied access to the NHL started the process. Ironically, the NHL expansion gradually displaced these hockey promoters, who had been the chief organizers in early major-league professional hockey. By the end of this period, wealthy individuals and corporations located in major metropolitan areas dominated professional hockey. Backed by wealthy owners, the new franchises contributed to the rising costs of operating a competitive club. Middle-class entrepreneurs increasingly found staying in the league difficult, and the NHL moved towards becoming an exclusive organization for wealthy owners. In essence, the expanded NHL erected a barrier to entry into major-league professional hockey by raising the costs of owning a franchise.

For such an important phase in its development, the initiative behind the NHL's expansion into the United States surprisingly did not come from the League. During a league meeting in January 1923, Leo Dandurand, the Montreal Canadiens owner, introduced Tom Duggan to those at the meeting. For some there Duggan required little introduction. He had tried unsuccessfully to acquire a second franchise in Montreal four years earlier, even though the league had only three active franchises at the time. It was quite possible that the then Canadiens owner, George Kennedy, did not want another competitor in the same market. This time, however, Duggan was not seeking a franchise in a Canadian city; he was trying to convince the owners to grant him options to franchises in the United States. After listening to his proposal, the owners unanimously agreed to authorize the league president, Frank Calder, to handle the negotiations with Duggan.[1]

Given the close trading relationship between the United States and Canada, Duggan's proposal represented the latest in a long series of cross-border hockey exchanges.[2] At the turn of the twentieth century, American hockey promoters had begun using Canadian hockey players as drawing cards in their winter sports calendar. Canadian players stocked the short-lived International Hockey League that operated around the Michigan/Ontario border. Before 1923, rink owners in the United States often invited Canadian teams to play exhibition series. Especially in New York and Boston, these post-season exhibitions were usually financially successful affairs for the participating clubs.[3] Yet they were more than sporting novelties for the American audience, since promoters often touted Canada as the home of skilled hockey players. At least in the northeastern states, hockey promoters and fans equated Canadian hockey players with excellence in the sport. In 1911, the exhibition tour of the Ottawa and Wanderer teams was so successful that there was talk of forming an American section of the NHA. Nothing came of this particular idea, but Boston promoters began recruiting Canadian players to man a local amateur league the following season.[4]

The eastern professional hockey establishment had deserted its plan for expansion into the United States after 1911. Internal troubles from the Toronto franchises and external battles with the PCHA occupied its energy and time through much of the 1910s. The First World War had also decimated professional teams' rosters to the point that the NHA almost folded. Immediately after the war, the continuing saga with Eddie Livingstone limited the NHL's focus within Canada and, more specifically, southern Ontario. By the early 1920s, the NHL was beginning to show signs of financial recovery from the lean war years. Despite a deep economic recession in Canada at the time, the NHL did not suffer as much as other industries. Under Calder's leadership, the NHL had actually increased its net profits between 1917 and 1921. The league's healthy financial status attracted entrepreneurs. Yet the NHL's preoccupation with Livingstone dictated a strategy aimed at thwarting his return to professional hockey. The admission of the Hamilton franchise was a prime example.[5]

In its battles against Livingstone, the NHL mostly reacted to his schemes. Hamilton received an NHL franchise precisely because Livingstone was planning on starting a league that included Hamilton. Excluded from the NHL, Livingstone tried to form a new league with franchises in Toronto, Hamilton, and Cleveland in 1920. Livingstone conceded that the Montreal-Ottawa-Quebec region was NHL's stronghold. Instead of establishing franchises there, he wanted to create

another regional organization that covered southern Ontario and, more importantly, the United States. Not only did Livingstone's scheme include Cleveland,
where he had made contacts in his NHA days, he had also approached New York.
Percy Hambly, the Toronto owner, alerted Calder that Livingstone had held talks
with Tex Rickard of Madison Square Garden. Calder predicted that nothing
would come out of Livingstone's meeting with Rickard. Even so, the NHL
warded off Livingstone's latest effort in part by granting the Hamilton Arena
owner, Percy Thompson, a franchise. By including Hamilton, the NHL was able
to stop Livingstone's scheme for the time being.[6]

After a court decision to throw out his case against the NHA and the NHL,
Livingstone's next attempt to organize a league came two years later. On 23
October 1923 a Toronto court found the Toronto Arena Gardens 'in breach of
contract' and awarded $100,000 to Livingstone.[7] Potentially, this judgment could
bankrupt the rink. A more probable scenario would have the Arena Gardens
negotiate a settlement with Livingstone, most likely giving Livingstone control
of the facility. This control could conceivably force the NHL to admit Livingstone,
or worse, would allow him to set up a rival league in the NHL's own backyard.
Shortly after the award of damages from the lawsuit, Livingstone announced that
he would resurrect the idea of an international hockey league. By this time, the
NHL had extended Duggan's options to branch out into the United States.

While the NHL executives worried about Livingstone's schemes, they had
also, albeit inadvertently, recognized the rising value of an NHL franchise. When
the NHL was wooing Hamilton as part of its counter-action against Livingstone's
new league, in 1920, Duggan had also offered to purchase the Quebec franchise
for $5000 if the League allowed him to move the franchise to Montreal. In part to
ensure the inclusion of Hamilton, Calder countered with a $7500 price tag for
the Quebec franchise, which Duggan declined.[8] Seventy-five hundred dollars
was cheap when compared to the sale of the Canadiens franchise a year later.
When the Canadiens' owner George Kennedy passed away in 1921, Duggan
submitted a $10,000 bid for the franchise, but was turned down. While Calder
thought Duggan's bid was much too high, the Leo Dandurand group eventually
had to pay $11,000 for the franchise.[9]

Although a bonanza for the NHL treasury, the rising value of an NHL
franchise also served to restrict ownership to those who could afford the price
and location to heavily populated cities. Duggan lost his bid for the Canadiens in
part because Calder thought Duggan did not really have that kind of cash up
front. Calder's assessment of Duggan was probably correct, because Duggan did
not apply for a franchise again. Instead, he acted as an NHL franchise salesman
and hoped to negotiate a deal in which he would be given stock in one of the
new franchises. Duggan also knew that the likelihood of another NHL franchise

in a Canadian city was slim. NHL franchises already occupied Canadian cities that had the requisite population base and financial backing, and their owners frowned on having another competitor in their respective markets. Moreover, Canada was still in an economic recession, whereas the economy was booming south of the border. Hence, large cities in the northeastern United States were logical places for Duggan to peddle his franchise options.

An emerging mass consumer culture, energized by an economic boom at the beginning of the 1920s, made the industrialized northeastern United States a potential market for professional hockey. Since the last quarter of the nineteenth century, the United States had been shifting from a customer society towards a consumer culture. Instead of 'purchasing the objects of daily life from familiar craftspeople and storekeepers,' Americans, especially those who lived in the urban areas, 'bought and used mass-produced goods as participants in a national market.'[10] Among other things, changes in technology, work habits, and economy fuelled this process. The development and refinement of mass production techniques made goods more plentiful and less expensive. An emergent advertising profession promoted these goods in print and, soon, in a new public medium, the radio, which became widely available due to technological advances. Especially for many middle-class Americans, increased earnings and credit buying afforded them inroads into this consumer culture.[11]

The changing nature of work also contributed to the mass consumer culture. By the early twentieth century, more and more middle-class Americans had become salaried employees. These mostly white-collar workers toiled in large corporations in which bureacratization, division of labour, and mechanization reduced the significance of the individual and his opportunities for achievement and recognition. For these workers, the American dream of success via rugged individualism had become untenable. Luck seemed more important to achievement than hard work and talent in twentieth-century corporate America. Taking advantage of shorter working hours and rising prosperity, many middle-class Americans turned to commercial entertainment in what Jackson Lears has called the 'quests for psychic satisfaction through high-style consumption.'[12] In movies and in commercialized sports Americans found heroes who defied a regimented corporate world, and who proved that individual success through hard work and skill was still possible. Babe Ruth and Jack Dempsey, alongside Douglas Fairbanks and Charlie Chaplin, became idols whose lives and exploits were followed by millions. Spectator sport expenditures rose from $30 million in 1921 to $46 million in 1923.[13] Weekly movie ticket sales increased from 40 million in 1922 to 100 million in 1930.[14] In populated industrial and commercial cities in the northeastern United States, opportunities awaited those entrepreneurs who could deliver the high drama of sports competition to an adoring public.[15]

External opportunities and threats drove the NHL's American expansion. As economic prosperity in the 1920s contributed to the blossoming of sporting spectacles in the United States, hockey entrepreneurs such as Tom Duggan and Eddie Livingstone wanted to exploit the opportunity by selling hockey as an entertainment commodity. Given the presence of the Canadiens in Montreal, Duggan probably realized that the prospect of another NHL franchise in Montreal would be slim. His failed attempts to acquire an NHL franchise were testaments to that reality. Livingstone, on the other hand, was still fuming about being excluded from professional hockey. He also must have realized that it was unlikely the NHL would ever welcome him back into the fold. Using the sizable settlement from his lawsuit against the Arena Gardens to establish an international league was a more probable option for his return into professional hockey. An international league would not only bypass fierce territorial battles with the more established NHL franchises, it would also give Livingstone's scheme many more large markets than the NHL had. Recognizing the potential damage to themselves if Livingstone were to establish himself in the American markets first, the NHL owners decided to grant Duggan the options and task of expansion. Thus, Duggan and Livingstone, both dissatisfied entrepreneurs, were two important figures in the NHL's southward expansion.

In his bid to profit from selling NHL franchises, Duggan targeted the two largest industrial and commercial centres in the northeastern United States, Boston and New York. As major metropolitan markets on the East Coast, these cities were logical economic choices for expansion. Calder reported at an NHL meeting in March 1923 that Duggan was working to set up franchises in Boston and New York or Brooklyn, and the governors approved giving Duggan an option until June 1.[16] In the following meeting, Duggan asked and received approval for an extension on the option for 'any two of Brooklyn, New York and Boston.'[17] When it seemed unlikely that any of the three cities was ready to join the NHL for the upcoming season, Calder consented to let Duggan keep his options for another year.

Unlike today's much ballyhooed sport-league expansion, Duggan's effort was met with a lukewarm response at best. Duggan's problems in New York were twofold. He needed a willing investor as well as a suitable facility. Duggan tried to solve the two problems through the person of George L. (Tex) Rickard, who could provide solutions to both. Tex Rickard had arguably become the most famous fight promoter by the 1920s. Although he had made and lost fortunes, Rickard had never included hockey promotion in his varied and colourful career, and he was not interested in an NHL franchise when Duggan came calling. Rickard, however, had access to a major facility that the NHL viewed as an important criterion in granting a franchise. In 1920, Rickard had obtained a ten-year lease on Madison Square Garden with the backing of John Ringling of circus fame. In between boxing matches, Rickard filled the Garden with wrestling matches, six-day bicycle races, basketball games, Sunday night dances, and other activities. Despite his knack for promotion, Rickard did not see hockey as a viable activity for the Garden. After much persuasion from his friend and right-hand man at the Garden, Colonel John Hammond, Rickard at last consented to add professional hockey as part of the venue's winter sports calendar. In February 1924 Duggan was finally able to get a verbal agreement with Rickard to put a professional hockey team in Madison Square Garden for the following season.[18]

Whereas Rickard controlled the facility, it was William V. Dwyer who eventually bought the new hockey franchise. Like Rickard, Dwyer had no connection with the game before his purchase of the NHL option. Dwyer made his fortune in bootlegging when Prohibition became law in the 1920s. Big Bill, as he was generally known, associated with gang bosses such as Legs Diamond, Dutch Schultz, and Owney Madden rather than with athletes. Yet he had capital. At the time he ventured into professional hockey, Dwyer owned businesses in transportation, warehouses, night clubs, and casinos. Under the urging of a newspaper friend, Dwyer purchased Duggan's option for the New York franchise, and allegedly paid $80,000 for the Hamilton players in 1925 when the new Madison Square Garden was built to house his professional hockey club.[19]

Besides New York, Calder considered Boston a key to controlling professional hockey in the East because of its vibrant hockey culture.[20] Amateur games in Boston often drew large crowds. Yet amateur hockey in the United States was in turmoil in 1924. Amateur hockey clubs in Boston such as the Boston Athletic Association team and the Boston Hockey Club played in the eastern section of the United States Amateur Hockey Association (USAHA). In early 1924 charges of professionalism flew against the western power house, the Pittsburgh Yellow Jackets team, which denied and was cleared of these charges.[21] What galled the Bostonians was that the USAHA secretary-treasurer, Roy D. Schooley, also managed the Pittsburgh team. When the Pittsburgh team led by Canadian star Lionel Conacher beat the New Haven club by a score of eight to three, the *Boston Globe* sarcastically reported that the 'Pittsburg [*sic*] *Canadian* hockey team easily overwhelmed the light New Haven *Canadian* hockey team.'[22]

Nor was Pittsburgh the only USAHA club that enticed Canadian players with money and jobs. Boston amateur clubs were not 'simon-pure' themselves. John J. Hallahan of the *Boston Globe* charged that '[l]ocal players ... might not bear having the calcium directed at them, when it comes to the true definition of the word amateur.'[23] Boston hockey fans, by contrast, did not seem to object to the presence of Canadians or paid players on American amateur teams as long as the competition was entertaining. Indeed, an editorial complained that fans often had to buy their tickets from scalpers when there was an important game.[24] Disgusted with 'shamateurism' and prompted by civic boosterism, Charles Adams, a sport enthusiast who made his millions in the grocery business, threw his lot in with the professional game.[25]

The new Boston franchise, however, faced facility problems. Although he had purchased a franchise option from Duggan, Adams was unable to secure the use of the Boston Arena as the new club's home ice. Unlike Rickard, who more or less controlled Madison Square Garden, Adams was merely one of the directors of the Boston Arena, and in Boston not everyone favoured the professional game. George Brown, the Boston Arena manager, was afraid that professional hockey could hurt the local amateur game's gate receipts. In 1922, for example, Brown decided against a proposed exhibition series between two pro teams in favour of a challenge series between the Canadian and the American amateur champions.[26] When the directors of the Boston Arena were considering Adams's proposal of adding a professional franchise in 1924, gate receipts from the amateur games for that season had totalled $300,000.[27] They voted against the professional franchise for the 1924–5 season. A dejected Adams commented, 'My chief regret is that other United States cities will be first in the professional hockey field, and I always am happiest when Boston is in front.'[28] Without a playing facility, Adams owned a $15,000 franchise with no tangible assets.

The NHL's American expansion plan began to fall apart after the 1923–4 season came to a close. Lack of suitable facilities was undermining Duggan's efforts. Besides Boston, it also became apparent by late summer that Madison Square Garden would not be ready to accommodate the new New York franchise. The Garden did not have an ice rink. As part of the conditions to admit the New York franchise, Madison Square Garden was to alter its seating capacity and instal an artificial ice plant. The work did not proceed as planned, however. After the League meeting on August 31, it seemed unlikely that there would be any American clubs in the upcoming season.[29]

While the southern expansion plan was sputtering, the prospects for expansion had prompted others to jump into the fray. The Toronto Granites, Olympic champions, and the Soo Greyhounds, Canadian amateur champions, were both rumoured to be joining the NHL.[30] A Montreal group headed by Senator Donat Raymond and William Northey formed the Canadian Arena Company and started construction of a new arena, the Forum. A professional hockey club would be the cornerstone for this project.[31] Livingstone also announced that he would organize an international league with teams based in 'Toronto, Ottawa, Buffalo, New York and Brooklyn and Pittsburgh and Boston are also likely.'[32] Even Duggan, perhaps afraid that the Boston and New York franchises might not materialize, applied for a franchise for Philadelphia in July.[33]

In this frenzy, the Forum group had the most solid financial backing. By July 24 it had already raised $403,000 from the political and economic elite of Canada.[34] Sensing that the planned expansion into New York had stalled, NHL officials began to look seriously to the Forum group, even though the Canadiens did not like the idea of competition in the same market.[35] The Canadiens finally consented to a second franchise in Montreal when the League voted to pay the club $10,000 out of the $15,000 franchise fee 'for the splitting of their exclusive territory.'[36] Billed as the English Montreal team, the Montreal Maroons replaced the New York entry in the 1924–5 season.

With various groups expressing interest in professional hockey and rumours of the formation of rival leagues, the four existing clubs wanted to ensure the viability of the NHL. Certainly old members such as Ottawa, the Canadiens, and Toronto remembered the desertions of the past, and the 'feeling ... was that those who had carried professional hockey through its darker days should stick together.'[37] In July, NHL member clubs entered into an agreement binding themselves together for ten years. Among other things, the agreement prohibited members from conducting business with any outside agency 'without the full knowledge and consent' of the others. Unlike the case in the past, the agreement also raised the stakes for desertion. It imposed a $20,000 bond as a guarantee that a club would remain in the League.[38] Together with the distribution of new franchise fees to existing clubs, this monetary penalty increased the opportunity cost for any club contemplating defection.

Amateurism, ironically, became the catalyst in reviving the expansion drive of professional hockey in Boston. On September 26 the Amateur Athletic Union of Canada announced that it would ban any amateur player who changed 'his residence to the United States for competitive purposes.'[39] This ruling had a large impact on many 'amateur' hockey teams in the United States and perhaps, in part, helped Adams's cause in Boston. A few days after the report, the Boston Arena manager, George Brown, in an apparent change of heart, announced that Boston would be home to a professional hockey team in the upcoming season. To protect the lucrative commercialized amateur hockey market in Boston, Brown acquiesced to the inclusion of professional hockey in the Boston Arena if the new NHL franchise would promise not to tamper with local amateur players. Art Ross, the manager of the new NHL Boston franchise, reassured the public that 'he and his players will spend their leisure time here assisting in the development of amateur players.'[40] The Boston Bruins and the Montreal Maroons officially joined the NHL for $15,000 per club at the November annual league meeting.

With the addition of the Bruins and Maroons, the NHL began the 1924–5 season with six clubs, one of which was in the United States. In the first phase of this development, the lack of facilities almost made the expansion impossible. Even in Canada, the construction of the Forum demonstrated the dependence on facilities of franchise owners. This dependence gradually led to a trend of ownership of both the franchise and the facility. While this had been true with the Hamilton franchise before expansion began, the newer facilities would be grander in scale and more expensive to build, which, in effect, contributed to the rising costs of owning an NHL franchise and excluded those who could not afford the increased financial requirement.

The 1924–5 season was also significant in the shifting composition of NHL ownership. The Montreal Maroons was the last Canadian franchise to be admitted into the NHL. Not until the 1970s did the NHL grant another franchise to a Canadian city. Boston, by contrast, represented the first of a series of American franchises admitted into the league within the next two years. Pittsburgh and New York joined the NHL in the next season, when the League granted the Townsend brothers, the Duquesne Garden rink owners, a franchise in Pittsburgh and Dwyer's New York Americans commenced playing in the new Madison Square Garden. The inclusion of Pittsburgh and New York reconstituted the executive board into a slim Canadian majority, with four of the seven teams based in Canada. American expansion reached a feverish pitch in the spring of 1926 when New York sought a second franchise, Chicago and Detroit also presented their applications for league membership during the governors' meeting in January. Two other groups, from Detroit and Chicago, submitted their requests for a franchise in the NHL as well. This flood of interest from American promoters could potentially make them the majority in the NHL.[41]

There is no proof that bloc voting based on nationality ever occurred in the NHL. Still, nationalistic sentiments emerged in Canada in light of the entry of American franchises. One expression of a fear of American dominance in Canada's national winter pastime appeared in 1926. During the Stanley Cup series in April, representatives from five different groups in Detroit and two different groups in Chicago made their franchise applications to the governors. Overwhelmed by the number of applicants, the NHL governors tabled the requests and appointed a committee to investigate the merits of each application.[42] When the governors reconvened to discuss the applications on May 1, the meeting lasted two days as the governors disagreed on whom they would grant the franchises to. As a further complication, the NHL constitution required a unanimous vote for the admittance of a new member. Even as the governors toyed with compromises, the issue remained deadlocked. Sensing the meeting was going nowhere, Charles Adams advised the governors that Boston and the Maroons would ask for a special meeting to change the constitutional requirement of unanimous assent to a two-thirds majority for granting a franchise.[43] That meeting took place on May 15. On a motion by Ottawa, seconded by Boston, the NHL amended its constitution and changed the requirement for admission to a two-thirds majority. On the same day, the governors granted a Chicago franchise to the Huntingtion R. Hardwick group and a Detroit franchise to the Townsend-Seyburn group.[44] A *Montreal Star* editorial lamented before the May 15 meeting: '[No] Canadian pro hockey enthusiast [can] close his or her eyes to the two-third vote which is to rule future National Hockey League affairs in a body which, as things look now, will consist of six United States and four Canadian clubs.'[45]

There were costs associated with the NHL expansion. American dominance of the NHL, however, was not one of them, as the *Star* editorial implied. It would not be until the late twentieth century that traditionalists in Canada could point to a series of American-born NHL presidents governing the league's affairs in New York as convincing evidence that Canada had lost control of professional hockey. For the time being, nationalistic sentiments precipitated only some of the internal disagreements. As owners of professional hockey franchises, the American like the Canadian owners were capitalists whose main interest was the profitability of their franchises. Their common interest in profit, however, did not necessarily ensure harmonious relationships among them. With the high franchise prices and increased costs for operating an NHL team, the owners argued over many issues concerning the policies of the League and rules of the game that could potentially affect the bottom line. Nevertheless, this period of expansion was a significant milestone in the history of professional hockey, because it did not affect the NHL alone. Southern expansion by the NHL also significantly changed the professional hockey network as a whole.

Chapter 8

Going South, Part 2

As an unplanned business project, the NHL expansion in the middle third of the 1920s was a bonanza beyond the league officials' wildest dreams. While they did not initiate the project, league directors were quick to seize the opportunity once they realized the potential benefits of expansion. Since the league directors had not developed a business plan for the expansion, they never fully considered the consequences associated with an expanded league.

One consequence was the positioning of the NHL as the exclusive governing body in major-league professional hockey. As the NHL expanded southward and westward, it unexpectedly triggered the demise of other major professional organizations. Although several professional minor leagues appeared at the same time, the NHL was the only major professional hockey league in North America. Without a rival major league competing in the professional hockey labour market, the NHL became the sole employer in elite-level professional hockey by 1927.

Expansion brought benefits as well as problems to the NHL, however. Besides increasing the NHL's capitalization through the admission of wealthy owners, the NHL expansion also staked the league's claim to the largely untapped American consumer market.[1] For the older clubs, the expansion brought an unexpected windfall by way of increasingly large franchise fees. Yet internal conflicts also accompanied the good times. With an international membership, nationalistic sentiments constituted the basis for some of these conflicts, and civic and regional antagonisms increased with an expanded league territory. Personality and ego clashes also fuelled these internal quarrels. Thus, the president's role became even more crucial as arbitrator and peace-maker. To hold such a diverse group together, he often had to tread a fine line in exercising the power of his office. The trust and unity that existed within the NHL in the early 1920s, however, had been eroded.

In terms of benefits to the NHL, the expansion into the United States achieved what league officials had anticipated: it stopped Livingstone from starting an international league. With the NHL capturing all the important industrial and commercial centres in the Great Lakes region, the northeastern United States, and central Canada, Livingstone could not break into those markets as a major-league operator. Potential investors in these markets were more likely to follow an established organization than an entrepreneur who might receive a large sum of money from a pending verdict in a lawsuit.

Expansion also brought the NHL a period of prosperity unparalleled in its previous history. Fees paid by eager franchise applicants provided a windfall for existing league members. During a meeting in April of 1925, the NHL governors passed a motion to affirm that only the Canadiens, Hamilton, St Patricks, and Ottawa clubs were eligible for access to the $41,000 franchise account that contained money paid by new franchises. Boston and the Montreal Maroons, however, shared the $3171.16 surplus in the working account with the other four teams.[2] In 1926, the four pre-expansion clubs demanded and received the sum of $3701.76 as a portion of the revenues from the sale of franchises.[3] By 1927, when the League had ten clubs, the franchise account had increased to $77,731.37, with $10,797.93 in the working account.[4] Increases in the working account, which included league revenues other than franchise fees, pointed to the general success of professional hockey in the expanded league.

Yet problems accompanied these years of prosperity. When the NHL added the two new franchises in the 1924–5 season, a corresponding increase in the demand for players occurred. This facet of the expansion – the availability of quality players – was clearly evident with the Boston Bruins and the Montreal Maroons in their debut season. With the inter-league agreement still in place, both clubs could look forward to building their rosters through two avenues: purchasing players from the other professional clubs and leagues, and signing amateur players. No professional club in its right mind would part with its quality players without substantial compensation. Thus, these new clubs could only get players who were considered dispensable by their old clubs. To acquire new talent, then, the new entries to the NHL turned to the amateurs. Under Art Ross, the Boston team was particularly aggressive. Ross was able to sign players from the USAHA with the help of Roy Schooley, the USAHA secretary. Through his long-time association with the Patricks of the PCHA Ross also obtained the services of players in the Western League. Nonetheless, the Bruins and the Maroons finished at the bottom of the standings at the end of the season.[5]

Some players took advantage of this new demand in the labour market. Player union and agents, as powerful forces in contract negotiations, did not exist yet; but the Ottawa manager, Tommy Gorman, complained that two of his players had hired lawyers to draw up their own contracts instead of using the standard NHL ones.[6] Amateurs also seized the opportunity and used the increase in demand as leverage. Some amateur players insisted on deleting clause 7 in the standard NHL contract, which granted the club the right to terminate the contract arbitrarily and unilaterally with just one day's notice.[7]

The stir in the labour market was not the only problem associated with expansion. Since the addition of the Boston franchise, Canadian clubs had become apprehensive about the increase in travel costs. With the addition of Pittsburgh and the New York Americans in 1925, there was going to be even more travel. When a flood of franchise applications from American cities and the admission of a second New York franchise at the beginning of 1926 occurred, the Canadian club owners became quite alarmed at the potential increase in travel costs. The Canadian club owners reasoned that franchises in big American cities, with their larger population base, could more readily absorb the increased costs of an expanded league than those located in the smaller Canadian cities. Even though the League had already approved New York's application for a second franchise during a November meeting in 1924, the Canadian owners added new terms to the original agreement in 1926. Specifically, they wanted to include some form of financial compensation for the increased travel to New York now that the city had two franchises. Thus, on February 14, 1926 Leo Dandurand of the Canadiens and Frank Ahearn of Ottawa put forth a motion authorizing Calder to interview Colonel Hammond of Madison Square Garden 'to renew the application ... at a price of $15,000 with the provisions that clubs visiting Madison Square Garden ... should receive 5% of the gross receipts.'[8] The NHL directors assured Hammond that the renewal of his application would be accepted at the next meeting if Hammond agreed to the 5 per cent 'travel tax.'

Besides their concern to recover additional travel expenses, there were other reasons why the NHL directors wanted to renegotiate Hammond's application for a second New York franchise instead of rejecting it outright. As the major metropolitan centre in the United States, New York held the key to establishing the NHL in the American market. Although the NHL already had a franchise in New York – Dwyer's Americans – the current Madison Square Garden application for a second franchise was far more important. Besides the fact that Dwyer had been arrested in a police investigation of bootlegging and bribery eleven days before his team opened in the new Madison Square Garden on 25 December 1925, Tex Rickard was now behind the second application.[9] Whereas Dwyer was only a tenant, Rickard was the landlord. Given facility problems in the past, embracing Rickard's application would consolidate New York as NHL territory and would deal Livingstone's international hockey league scheme a heavy blow. Thus, Calder arrived in New York on February 22 and met with the Madison Square Garden interests, who were also eager to 'consider any proposition which will lighten the burden for clubs with a smaller earning power in additional trips to New York' so long as it 'be made to apply equitably to other cities as well.'[10]

Hoping to minimize his own club's travel costs, Adams, the Boston owner, also tried to bring about a satisfactory settlement. When Hammond complained to Adams about the NHL reneging on the Garden's application for a second New York franchise, Adams explained that the addition of the New York Americans had helped the Boston club by lowering travel expenses in the previous season; 'but ... clearly ... it hurts associate interest in Canada.' Furthermore, he did not feel 'that any of the present Canadian teams should be forced into a position that makes their operations less profitable ... [Y]ou expressed your willingness to readjust ... the conditions so that the Canadian teams would be fairly treated. This is all I ask and I am sure it is all they ask.'[11] In the end, all sides agreed to a gate split of 3.5 per cent of the gross receipts to the visiting team for all league games.[12]

Based on their handling of the second New York franchise application, the NHL governors clearly had not fully appreciated the potential consequences of their expansion plans beforehand. Another unintended outcome of the NHL expansion was the demise of major-league hockey in the West. The Patricks' hockey empire was in decline during the early 1920s. They had been shifting franchises to new cities in hope of sustaining western professional hockey. In the early spring of 1923, the situation looked gloomy for the PCHA. Attendance had not improved, and the league had been operating with just three teams. As far as prestige was concerned, the PCHA was no longer the sole major-league organization in the West. Its regular-season champion had to compete against the champion of the new Western Canada Hockey League (WCHL) for the right to challenge for the Stanley Cup. With the Seattle team dropping out in 1924, the Patricks disbanded the PCHA and brought the Vancouver and Victoria teams, both owned by their family, into the WCHL. This, however, was a last-ditch effort on their part to keep professional hockey on the West Coast.[13]

The importance of skilled players in professional hockey was abundantly evident in the demise of western major-league hockey, which began to crumble in the spring of 1926 as expansion fever reached a high pitch in the East. Representatives from the NHL, the WCHL (now renamed the Western Hockey League, WHL), and a proposed minor league, the American Hockey League, met in Montreal. Supposedly, this informal assembly of hockey magnates was to discuss matters of unifying playing rules and minor-league affiliations. But rumours had spread that the WHL Edmonton and Saskatoon franchises were seeking to move east or, at the very least, affiliate with the NHL.[14] At the governors' meeting on 17 April the NHL officially awarded the second New York franchise to Colonel John Hammond of Madison Square Garden. With a second New York franchise approved and at least two more potential additions for the 1926–7 season, there could conceivably be three more clubs searching for players. To complicate matters further, some of the applicants vowed that they would start a new professional league if they could not get into the NHL.[15] This spurt of interest in professional hockey would undoubtedly increase the demand for skilled players. On the other hand, it could also provide an opportunity for an entrepreneurial businessman who had a hot commodity for any new franchises – established professional players.

As the NHL investigated the potential franchise owners, the Patricks began to inquire about selling their players. Except for the Saskatoon club, they convinced the other WHL clubs to share in the sale of the players. In May, Frank Patrick submitted a proposal to the NHL board of governors to dispose of the WHL players. Reporters had gotten wind of some of the details in the proposal. Charles Adams, the Boston Bruins owner, was to underwrite the entire Western League for $300,000, but the plan 'was dropped when opposition was voiced that [with] Mr. Adams at the head of the syndicate, his club would be in position to secure the "cream" of the western players.'[16]

The media only had part of the story right. The entrepreneurial drive of the Patricks and Art Ross played an important role in the destruction of the WHL. With the help of Ross, Lester's boyhood friend and now manager of the Boston Bruins, Frank Patrick had been negotiating with two of the potential owners.[17] On May 2 Frank Patrick signed an agreement with Huntington (Tack) Hardwick, one of the Chicago applicants, selling fourteen western players, most of them from the Portland club, for $100,000. Charles Adams acted as the guarantor for this transaction as well as two others, one to Detroit and one to Boston.[18] The next day, Patrick signed another agreement with Paul R. Bierer of Detroit, selling another fourteen players, most from the Victoria club, for $100,000. Bierer paid Patrick $25,000 on the spot, with the remaining $75,000 due on June 1.[19] Interestingly, neither Hardwick nor Bierer had received their franchises at the time of the purchases. The local newspaper in Vancouver lamented the next day that 'the breaking up of the Western Hockey League is obvious.'[20] When Frank Patrick returned to Vancouver, he announced that there would be no professional hockey for the upcoming season and that Lester Patrick, guardian of the Victoria club, would be heading east to coach hockey. The death knell had sounded for western major-league professional hockey.

In general, entrepreneurs are go-getters. For them, rules and regulations are fine so long as they do not interfere with their missions. In disposing of the WHL players, the Patricks disregarded inter-league agreement procedures governing the sale of the players. Sensing his and his family's investments slipping away, Frank Patrick tried to salvage what he could. Besides his share in the player transaction, he also tried to arrange something extra for himself and his brother.

Calder disapproved and thought that Patrick had attempted to '"shake us down" plentifully' by first selling to 'the Eastern clubs players with no guarantee of their reporting and at a price which I think was excessive, when averaged up … [S]econdly, he attempted to extort $25,000 for himself "for his valuable services in securing a franchise in the National Hockey League for the Friedberg group."'[21] Mostly, Calder objected to the fact that Patrick never asked for waivers for these players who, of course, would have been swept up by the eastern clubs. In addition, Patrick also secured an agreement from the Friedberg/Bierer group to hire Lester Patrick as coach of the new franchise for a salary of $10,000, to buy an ice plant for $13,000, and to pay his expenses, totalling $20,000. When the Townsend/Seybourne group instead of the Friedberg/Bierer group received the Detroit franchise, Patrick then tried to sell the same players to the new franchise owners. They refused to pay Patrick's price, however. After negotiations with the new Detroit owners failed, Patrick threatened that the Friedberg group might take their players and start a rival league if the NHL rejected their application.[22]

Frank Patrick's threat turned out to be idle. He apparently was in desperate need of capital for repairs to the Vancouver Arena, which had been condemned as unsafe by Vancouver authorities.[23] Moreover, the NHL practically controlled the ice time in all the cities where it had a franchise. Even as rumours of a new league formed by rejected applicants in Detroit and Chicago continued, Calder worked to bring the Patricks under control.[24] Friedberg was having difficulties meeting his payment for the player deal to the Patricks. In late August he attempted to sell the players to the Detroit franchise owners, but was rebuffed for asking too high a price. Sensing that the Patrick-Friedberg coalition might break, Townsend of Detroit asked Calder to help him get into direct negotiation with Frank Patrick.[25] By October, the negotiations between Detroit and Patrick finally came to fruition when the Townsend group took over the players whom Frank Patrick had originally sold to Friedberg but had not paid for in full. The destruction of the WHL was finally complete.[26]

Thus, the NHL stood alone in the major professional hockey market by the beginning of the 1926–7 season. Its franchises covered important population centres in the northeastern and midwestern United States as well as central Canada. While several minor professional hockey leagues also came into existence (see chapter 9), the NHL now was the sole producer of elite-level hockey matches. Whereas the western professional leagues, notably the PCHA, promoted a different style of hockey with different playing rules, with the demise of the WHL there was now only the NHL brand.[27] The collapse of the WHL also meant there was a concentration of elite-level players in the NHL when Frank Patrick sold the WHL's most valuable assets to the league. Only the top western players, however, found employment in a shrunken player market. Others either had to find employment in the minor leagues or left professional hockey altogether. The NHL had now become the only employer of elite-level hockey players.

At the start of the 1926–7 season, the NHL monopolized major-league hockey because no other major league existed. The demand for an NHL team in 1926 helped to drive up the price of a franchise and raise the requirements for admission into the League. Applicants had to show financial accountability. To ensure favourable action on their applications, applicants also promised the construction of large, modern arenas. New league members spared no expense in assembling competitive teams to attract customers. Hence, the expanded NHL raised the barrier for entry into major-league professional hockey, since heavy financial requirements limited NHL membership to the wealthy.

With the heavy investments required to operate in the expanded league, owners were particularly watchful of the returns on their investments. Before the 1925–6 season, all teams shared equally in the playoff profits after the deduction of expenses, even for those who did not participate in the playoffs. The season when Duggan first presented his expansion proposal the four clubs shared $6400 from the playoff receipts equally.[28] This mentality of equal revenue sharing changed with the addition of wealthy owners. In 1926 the League adopted a sliding scale for playoff revenues that was relative to the success of the teams involved. Under the new format, the winner took 20 per cent of the pooled receipts, while 17 and 13 per cent went to the second- and third-place finishers, respectively. The League retained the rest in a working account.[29] The $21,611.21 playoff profit from that season, an increase of over $13,000 from the previous season, proved to be a bonanza to the six clubs participating in the playoffs.[30] From this point on, playoff non-participants did not receive a share of the playoff receipts.

While the NHL cornered the market in producing top-flight professional hockey games, it found controlling the labour market rather more difficult. In part, elite-level amateur leagues, in which some clubs paid their players under the table and provided them with year-round employment, still offered an attractive alternative to many players. Monopsony, whereby the NHL was the sole buyer of talent, was still years in the future. Hence, NHL clubs jealously guarded players on their rosters and the competition for promising amateur players was fierce. In 1925 the League amended its constitution to limit a club's roster to twelve active and two inactive players, with a $35,000 salary limit. Its definition of inactivity included players who refused to report and those who would not honour their contracts. The governors further passed a motion to reserve any amateur player agreeing to a tryout. These measures effectively lessened the bargaining power of the players by preventing other clubs from negotiating with malcontents. While the governors unanimously voted for limiting roster size and expanding the reservation list, the New York Americans (via John Hammond) objected to the salary limit, even though New York and Pittsburgh, both new entries for that season, had a salary cap of $45,000, $10,000 higher than that of the other clubs, for the next two seasons.[31]

The New York Americans' objection to the salary cap demonstrated the difficulty in controlling labour costs in the expanded NHL. As clubs tried to control these costs, they were also continuously searching to improve their rosters. With the Forum and the new Madison Square Garden seating over 10,000 each, and new arenas in the works for Boston, Detroit, and Chicago, the potential of large gate receipts awaited those who could present competitive teams to the paying customers. Thus, the expansion magnified what had been the case in the past – conflicting concerns between controlling player salaries and the need to put a competitive team on the ice. Moreover, the change in the NHL's playoff revenue scheme in 1926 further increased the importance of assembling a competitive team. Not surprisingly, arguments about the ownership of players dominated the league meetings in the fall of 1926.

Perhaps the most acrimonious dispute centred on Boston's acquisition of seven WHL players. Both Chicago and Detroit had bought their players from Frank Patrick for $100,000 apiece. Given the demand from the League for these new entries to assemble competitive teams, there was little grumbling about the spending spree. Yet many owners objected that Adams, through his manager Art Ross, underwrote the sale and in the process purchased seven highly touted players. This, they felt, gave Boston an unfair advantage because the inter-league agreement was still in force when the deal was made. All the teams would have had a chance at these players had they been waived as required by the inter-league agreement. During a stormy meeting in September, the League passed a resolution to annul the player deal between Boston and the WHL. With Boston and Chicago abstaining, seven clubs voted to rescind Boston's claim on the players and appointed a committee, headed by Calder and the two Montreal club owners, to dispose of the players. The lone objection came from Ottawa.[32]

Controlling labour cost and players had been objectives of professional hockey from the beginning. The Boston affair, however, also demonstrated a return to the power struggles between owners and the league president. Since the establishment of the NHL, Calder had been successful in running the affairs of the league with few objections from the owners. In part, the Livingstone affair had turned the league office into a central information-gathering and operational command post, with Calder at its helm. Calder's attention to details and his success in thwarting Livingstone at every turn garnered the owners' trust in his ability as the chief operating officer. Moreover, Calder represented a constant when the NHL was going through changing ownership during the early days. The owners of the new clubs, however, had not gone through the battles against Livingstone and they were not at all hesitant to question Calder's motives and methods in running the league. Since Boston's admission into the NHL, the relationship between Adams and Calder had steadily deteriorated. It began with Adams's complaints about officiating.

Complaints against the referees had been with hockey even before the organization of professional leagues. Distrust among clubs in past organizations led to the delegation of the appointment of referees to the president. This was not new. The twist in Adams's complaint lay in its nationalistic tone. Shortly after Boston began its first season, Adams complained that his team did not get any breaks from the referees, who were 'altogether too *national* in spirit for the best interests of the *international* game,' and 'in every case of doubt their decisions are in favor of the Canadian team in our games.'[33]

Despite Calder's assurances, Adams's suspicion continued. After a Boston game played at Toronto in the following season, Adams complained about both police intimidation and referee bias. He then suggested the hiring of American referees in proportion to the composition of the NHL clubs, claiming the current officiating crew was pro-Canadian if not anti-American.[34] Calder defended the referees and pointed out that the players 'virtually are all Canadians, and I cannot imagine ... a Montreal or Toronto man refereeing in a New York–Ottawa game giving the edge to the Ottawa Club because it was Canadian.'[35] Calder's explanations apparently fell on deaf ears, and his constant defence of the referees only drew further suspicion. Since Montreal was the league's headquarters, Adams suspected the Canadian owners, especially those in Montreal, had much more influence on Calder and the league's policies than did the American clubs.

After the rancourous September meeting when the League nullified Boston's purchase of the seven WHL players, Adams again expressed his bitterness over the decision and hinted that Calder might lose his support in future league endeavours. Thus far Calder had been patient with Adams's complaints. The latest threat, however, drew his ire. He pointed out that he had ruled in favour of Adams's rights over the seven players before the directors voted against Adams. Moreover, Calder rejected 'the support of any man in anything that I do ... if that support is given merely for the sake of possible future benefits by himself.'[36]

There was no explanation given, but the NHL governors rescinded the resolution that nullified Boston's purchase of the WHL players during the next meeting. It was quite possible that player controversies involving the other clubs led to some manoeuvring and compromises. Seven clubs claimed and counter-claimed players before their fellow governors during the October 16 meetings. Two of the members appointed to the committee overseeing the dispersal of the seven Boston players were themselves parties to these proceedings. Despite this victory keeping the seven players, Adams's relationship with Calder did not improve, and it culminated in his resignation as Boston's governor in 1933.[37]

Besides Adams of Boston, Major Frederick McLaughlin, owner of the Chicago Blackhawks, was also constantly challenging Calder's position as NHL president. Like Adams, McLaughlin was ferocious in protecting his interests in the Chicago club. Unlike Adams, however, McLaughlin was new to the hockey business. McLaughlin's lack of connections and knowledge of hockey accounted for his defensiveness over Calder's decisions as well as his suspicions of other fellow owners in league affairs. McLaughlin first challenged Calder's power as the league's chief executive over Chicago's territorial rights, and the relationship between the two resembled a roller-coaster ride thereafter.

In the hectic days of expansion, the NHL was having difficulties deciding among competing groups for franchises in Detroit and Chicago. Besides changing the requirements for approval of admitting a new franchise, the governors hoped to placate the rejected applicants by further agreeing to grant a second franchise in Detroit and Chicago in the future. This, of course, violated the NHL constitution, which forbade the granting of a second franchise in a city without the consent of the existing franchise. Thus, the Huntington Hardwick group from Chicago and the John Townsend group from Detroit had to sign a consent for a future second franchise in their respective cities as a condition for receiving their franchises.[38]

If Adams's nationalistic sentiments played a part in his struggle with Calder, the eccentric and hard-nosed Chicago owner Major Frederick McLaughlin presented a different challenge. McLaughlin was a millionaire who had made his fortune from the coffee business. In sporting circles McLaughlin was a renowned polo player, but he knew nothing about hockey. While Huntington R. Hardwick led one of the two Chicago syndicates in acquiring a NHL franchise, McLaughlin was the major financial backer and soon assumed control of the new Chicago franchise. A veteran of the First World War, he named the team after the nickname of his 333rd Machine-Gun Battalion, the 86th (Blackhawk) Division. His wife, Irene Castle, designed the team logo.[39]

It is not clear why McLaughlin ventured into a business in which he had no experience. Civic pride probably played a part in his association with the NHL. Like civic boosters in other major metropolises, McLaughlin linked the reputation of his city with the success of its sports teams. Although the Chicago franchise had bought the Portland club from the WHL, critics in Chicago told

McLaughlin that the team would finish no higher than fourth place in the five-team American division. A worried McLaughlin expressed his fear for the team's fortunes once the initial enthusiasm ebbed.[40]

While McLaughlin was cordial at the beginning, he was soon battling with Calder over several issues. His suspicion of the eastern establishment attempting to dominate league affairs first flared up in the local arena situation. For its first season, Chicago played in the Chicago Coliseum as it awaited Madison Square Garden's plan to build a new arena in Chicago. The League approved the scheme so long as Madison Square Garden had no interest in the Chicago franchise. By November, a rift emerged between McLaughlin and Madison Square Garden. McLaughlin did not like the idea that his club had 'to play in their building if and when they build one ... without regard to our opinion as to the reasonableness of the rent they might ask ... [A]nd because of your very close relation with them,' he told Calder, 'I am wondering if you are lending a sympathetic ear to their argument.'[41] In the same letter, McLaughlin also hinted that the NHL had been ignoring Chicago, as his request for information on developments between the NHL and the American Hockey Association (AHA) had gone unanswered.

A much more provoking dispute involving the Blackhawks' NHL constitutional rights, however, soon engulfed McLaughlin and Calder. In December McLaughlin wrote Calder about the issue of granting a second NHL franchise in Chicago. By that time the AHA had established a franchise in Chicago run by none other than E.J. Livingstone. Livingstone's AHA club also played in the same building as McLaughlin's Blackhawks. And, further, the status of the AHA was ambiguous. It neither admitted to being a minor league nor claimed to be a major league.[42] McLaughlin certainly did not want another franchise in Chicago. Citing the league constitution, which forbade a second franchise without the consent of the existing holder, McLaughlin argued that the agreement extracted from Hardwick when he tried to gain a franchise in the NHL did not supersede a member's constitutional rights.[43]

The relationship between McLaughlin and Calder deteriorated in the new year. McLaughlin's suspicion of the eastern establishment, and perhaps his inferiority complex in hockey matters, skewed his opinions on Calder's actions. In January Calder wrote McLaughlin soliciting his views on changing the offside system in the game. McLaughlin replied, 'I can't help but wonder the identity of the influential league member from whose mouth the very suggestion that I uselessly made to you carried so much weight. It must have been someone who you didn't regard as you did me – a greenhorn influenced by Western propaganda.'[44] He then went on to request a vote to use two referees for all league games, and sarcastically asked, 'or do you think this idea is suggested to me by Western propaganda?'[45]

After McLaughlin received Calder's reply affirming the League's right to grant a second franchise in Chicago, he proceeded to seek legal advice that would back his claim. Resenting Calder's ruling on the franchise issue, McLaughlin lectured Calder about the president's power: 'You quite honestly and frankly admit that in spite of the present autocratic nature of your job, it should be made even more so. I am equally frank to admit that to have it as autocratic as it is now is, from a business point of view, absurd.'[46] McLaughlin then reminded Calder that it was the governors who paid his salary, and 'so long as I continue to represent a quarter of a million dollars invested ... in hockey in Chicago, you may rest assured that I will not accept your decisions as final or not to be questioned.'[47]

Despite McLaughlin's ire over the question of the second franchise, he nevertheless recognized Calder' abilities as a capable executive. When Calder intimated that he would fight on regardless of McLaughlin's objection, McLaughlin explained his views on the NHL corporate structure. He acknowledged Calder's capabilities and granted that 'it would be a sorry and deplorable loss to the League' should Calder decide to resign. On the other hand, '[t]he people who are putting up their money and risking their capital for the sake of developing hockey are the ones who should decide all questions of policy, and this kaiser, or czar, attitude should surely by now be recognized as out of date.'[48]

In this struggle, the different personalities and management styles of the two antagonists clashed. Both McLaughlin and Calder were obstinate about the correctness of their positions in the matter. While McLaughlin was curt and hard-nosed, Calder tried to accomplish his league duties via cajoling and alliance-making. Hoping that group pressure might work against McLaughlin's objection to a second franchise in Chicago, Calder pointed out to McLaughlin that it was the 'wish of the Governors themselves,' rather than Calder's personal desire, to grant another franchise in Chicago.[49] This, however, did not convince the Chicago owner. Calder then bypassed McLaughlin and wrote to Hardwick, asking if the agreement consenting to a second franchise in Chicago 'was made a part of the assets of the Chicago National Hockey Team Incorporated, and [whether] the Chicago National Hockey Team Incorporated assumes your responsibility under that agreement.'[50] But Hardwick could not help, and told Calder that McLaughlin had full control of the Chicago club. Hardwick did try to get a copy of the agreement, but came away empty-handed.[51]

McLaughlin was furious because Calder had gone behind his back. Besides asking Hardwick for the agreement, Calder had also approached LaFlamme, the lawyer who sided with McLaughlin, for a copy of the legal opinion. McLaughlin chastised Calder for having 'some code of ethics of your own which justifies you in proceedings of this nature ... [Y]ou will receive no copies of anything from this organization unless you ask for them through me, and then only if they exist, and if I think you should have them.'[52]

In this test of wills between the league president and a club owner, Calder's diplomatic and networking techniques failed him. Thus, he resorted to his power as the league's administrator to solve the problem. Calder believed that he represented the NHL and as such had entered into an agreement with the original Chicago applicant, Hardwick. Since Hardwick was responsible for Chicago's entry into the NHL, Calder wrote him demanding that the Chicago club 'accept the terms of the agreement between the National Hockey League and Huntingdon R. Hardwick, May 28th, 1926 ... [or] we will without delay take steps to erase your name from the League and cancel any association with you.'[53] Paddy Harmon, a rejected applicant for a Chicago franchise, had perhaps gotten wind of the spat and wired Calder stating that he was ready to receive the second franchise in Chicago.[54] Calder's tactic to bypass McLaughlin made the Chicago owner even more suspicious of Calder's intentions.[55]

While internal power struggles were part of the NHL intrigue, external threats to the organization usually mitigated the internal quarrels as members closed ranks to confront their common enemy. There had been rumbles from the AHA that it was unhappy with its arrangements with the NHL. Moreover, the AHA had placed a franchise in Chicago with Livingstone as the owner. Livingstone then filed suit against McLaughlin for tampering with Livingstone's players and McLaughlin mused, 'It looks pretty certain now as if I were to have the honor of being a lodge member of yours, as apparently I am to be made a member of the sued-by-Livingstone lodge.'[56] During the February NHL meeting, governors voted to rescind the consents by Chicago and Detroit to waive their rights should the NHL decide to grant a second franchise in their cities. Moreover, they stroked McLaughlin's ego by appointing him and Calder to negotiate with the AHA. For someone who felt humiliated because of his inexperience in hockey matters, the negotiation committee post must have given him a feeling of belonging. Indeed, McLaughlin's relationship with Calder improved as the two worked to bring the AHA in line with the NHL.[57]

Besides Calder's conflicts with Adams and McLaughlin, other tensions existed within the NHL executive board. With the demise of the WHL and the movement of other professional leagues to seek minor-league affiliation with the NHL, external threats from rival leagues became more and more remote. Competition now came chiefly from other NHL owners. The controversies over the players from the disbanded WHL constituted an initial bone of contention among the owners. Another concerned each club's competitive standing.

Some of the new owners, especially those who prided themselves as sportsmen, began complaining about rough play used as a means to winning. They apparently did not anticipate the level of violence on the ice. Adams, long connected with amateur hockey in Boston, became alarmed about rough play in the NHL even though amateur hockey was not immune to rough play. In Boston's first season he told Calder that he had warned the Boston players about 'the foolishness of *vicious* play.'[58]

The question of rough play and the president's power to intercede over such tactics came to a head during the last game of the 1926–7 Stanley Cup final between Boston and Ottawa. Near the end of the game, several fights erupted. One Boston player, Billy Couture, assaulted both officials, who were on their way to the dressing room. Calder was present at the game and witnessed the whole ruckus. He immediately fined five players. Of the five, Calder suspended Hooley Smith of Ottawa for a month in the following season and expelled Couture from the League. He then announced that the NHL governors would decide in a meeting if there would be further action against other players and the Boston manager, Art Ross, for their part in the melee. Anticipating lobbying efforts from the Ottawa and Boston clubs to revoke the suspension and expulsion, Calder took the opportunity to bring up the subject of executive power with McLaughlin. Calder predicted that his authority as president would be usurped because 'every string will be pulled in certain quarters to have my ruling set aside ... [I]nternal politics can be used to overcome what should be considered an earnest endeavour to keep the game within bounds.'[59]

Astute as Calder was in the internal dynamics of the NHL, he saw an opportunity to convert owners like McLaughlin who questioned the necessity of broad presidential power. In this particular incident, McLaughlin agreed that Calder's action with the players was fair and contended, if the governors did not support Calder: 'I will not only admit that the President of the League should have *all* the power, but I will further admit that as a League it is a dismal failure and should be done away with.'[60]

McLaughlin did not have to name the ones who might oppose Calder's decision, but it was clear that he intensely disliked Adams and Ross. McLaughlin had previously complained about the Boston team's roughhouse tactics, which they had 'been allowed to indulge in all season [and] will both have a serious sporting and financial effect on the future of professional hockey.'[61] In a later matter concerning Art Ross signing an amateur who also happened to sign with the AHA, McLaughlin admitted that 'had anyone other than Bostons [*sic*] gotten Couture my feelings in the matter would be far less strong. I do hate to see that Boston outfit constantly get away with murder, and hope some day ... to stage a little private murder of my own.'[62] Acting as a peace-maker, Calder counselled that '[f]or public consumption the "murder" idea may have its points but within the family circle I am not so stuck on it.'[63] Yet Calder should have known from his dealings with McLaughlin over the granting of the second franchise in Chicago that the major was as hard-headed a person as Calder had ever dealt with. Calder's advice fell on deaf ears, for McLaughlin vowed that he was 'pretty certain to always be in the opposite direction to [Adams].'[64]

As the NHL halted its expansion after the 1926–7 season, it stood alone in the major professional hockey business and had begun the first steps towards monopolizing the commercialized hockey industry. With the demise of the other major leagues, the NHL alone ruled major-league hockey and had substantially raised the barrier for entry into the industry. In the process, professional hockey had ceased to be the domain of middle-class entrepreneurs. Ownership of a franchise now rested with men of substantial wealth. Along with new capital came strong egos that clashed over the protection of their self-interest. The internal fighting between McLaughlin and Adams was by no means the only tension on the executive board. More was to come with the sale of the St Patrick's Hockey club to Conn Smythe, whose battles with Art Ross were legendary. McLaughlin also added another enemy to his list when James Norris bought the Detroit franchise in the early 1930s. In these tests of will and wits, Calder's position became even more crucial. Whether the owners liked it or not, the position of the president became critical for the League to survive among its conflicting factions.[65]

Yet internal bickering alone did not enhance the importance of the league president. The demise of the WHL eliminated one headache for both Calder and the League, but several hockey organizations sprang up to apply for affiliation with the NHL as minor leagues. Their different locations across the continent meant that Calder had to spend more time on his occasional trips to visit these leagues beyond his tour of the NHL cities. In other words, the NHL did not just manage its own affairs – it ruled over the professional sector of the commercialized hockey industry. Since many of the new owners had to attend to their multimillion-dollar business empires, it was not surprising that they were willing to empower Calder to deal with these organizations. Thus Calder's responsibilities increased as the NHL became the only major professional league. While he still had to report to the NHL board of directors, most, if not all, of the NHL owners accepted Calder as their representative when it came to dealing with affiliates and external agencies.

Chapter 9

Birth of the Minor-League System

During the middle third of the twenties, the NHL had taken a major step towards becoming a powerful sports organization. Besides gaining increased economic power through its expansion into the United States, the NHL had also extended the control of professional hockey via the creation of a minor-league system. In the spring of 1926, applications for NHL franchises from American cities poured in, even as the league increased the franchise fees from $15,000 to $50,000.[1] Entrepreneurs who could not afford the increased operating costs in the NHL formed minor leagues that catered mainly to markets ignored by the NHL. Fearing the economic power of the expanded NHL, these minor leagues affiliated with the NHL. Through formal agreements, the minor leagues acknowledged the NHL as the major governing body in professional hockey. In return, the minor leagues hoped for some degree of order in the marketplace via the establishment of protocols in inter-league affairs. Since minor leagues existed from coast to coast, they constituted a network of organizations that promoted professional hockey, with the NHL at the head.

The minor-league network extended the NHL's control of the professional-hockey marketplace. Through negotiated agreements with the minor leagues, the NHL established an alliance of professional hockey promoters in North America. This alliance of professional hockey leagues sought to control systematically the distribution of hockey games and the labour market. Conflicting interests between the major and minor leagues, however, put stress on the system of controls. Although the NHL was the established brand in professional hockey, it nevertheless recognized the importance of the minor leagues as training centres and warehouses of talent as well as strategic defenders against hostile hockey promoters. Hence, the NHL had to make concessions in the inter-league agreements in order to maintain the alliance. Still, the NHL was able to include provisions into the agreements that effectively utilized the minor leagues as a buffer zone to absorb some of the business risks involved in the operation of a major league. In that sense, the minor-league system was indispensable in the hegemony of the NHL in commercialized hockey.

Five groups, spanning the continent from coast to coast, formed the initial minor-league system in professional hockey in the mid-twenties. Three stood out in the development of professional hockey and the NHL's control of the marketplace: the American Hockey Association, the Canadian-American Professional Hockey League, and the Canadian Professional Hockey League.[2] These organizations all operated either near or in NHL territories. The circumstances that led to each league's existence were different, but their promoters recognized the opportunities in the professional-hockey marketplace during the frantic days of the NHL's expansion in 1926. Most of the minor-league clubs carved their market niches in smaller urban centres that the NHL ignored. Many organizers in these minor leagues also owned the local arenas in which their clubs played. Recognizing the large difference in economic power between themselves and the NHL, these hockey-club owners chose a strategy of cooperation, instead of confrontation, with the NHL. Adapting the model operating in professional baseball, they positioned themselves as providers and trainers of talents for the NHL.

The American Hockey Association (AHA) had already been in operation as the Central Hockey Association (CHA) prior to 1926 and, before that, as the western section of the United States Amateur Hockey Association (USAHA). The AHA's status, before it joined the professional rank, resembled the Eastern Canadian Amateur Hockey Association of the early 1900s. While it maintained itself as an amateur league, many of its players received payment and/or jobs in exchange for their hockey skills. When Pittsburgh left the western USAHA and joined the NHL in the 1925–6 season, it reserved the entire Pittsburgh Yellow Jackets and Hornets rosters. The remaining member clubs of the section then formed the CHA, which still maintained its amateur standing.

By April 1926, some of the CHA clubs were contemplating deserting their amateur status and turning professional. In part, a raid by the NHL Pittsburgh club and Colonel John Hammond, who was trying to man his new Rangers franchise, prompted the decision. Three clubs in the CHA – Minneapolis, Duluth, and Winnipeg – had substantial investments and felt the raid by the NHL clubs threatened the viability of their organizations. By negotiating an affiliation agreement with the NHL, the CHA directors hoped to avert any further player losses by an NHL raid. They appointed Frank Patrick to act on their behalf.[3]

As an established organization, the CHA had some leverage over the other proposed minor leagues. Its top teams had enough skilled players to provide quality competition. The Pittsburgh club, for example, finished third in its first season in the NHL with essentially the same players who had played in the CHA the year before. When the Montreal Maroons won the Stanley Cup in their second year of operation, their leading scorer, and the league's most valuable player, was Nelson Stewart, who had played on the CHA's Cleveland club the previous season. In early May, Patrick and Calder worked out an agreement whereby among other things, both the NHL and the renamed AHA consented to have the Stanley Cup trustee, William Foran, settle any disputes. This, of course, had been the arrangement in the inter-league agreement between the NHL and the defunct WHL. Furthermore, the agreement stipulated that only the AHA was eligible for a world series with the NHL, should there be one.[4] By September, the AHA formally signed the agreement with the NHL. Perhaps with the insistence of the AHA, the agreement did not specifically label the AHA a minor league. There would be, however, no world series for the AHA to justify its position as, at least, a non-minor league.[5]

Whereas fear of a player raid drove the AHA to affiliate with the NHL, supplying talent to the NHL was the purpose in the creation of the Canadian-American (Can-Am) Hockey League. After the May 1926 NHL meeting, when it became apparent that the WHL would no longer survive, Albert Geiger Jr of Boston proposed to Calder a new league with franchises in the cities of Boston, Providence, Springfield, and New Haven. He assured Calder that the new league would not be a rival, but one in which the NHL teams could 'place some of ... [their] reserve players with one of these teams' and be allowed to 'draw one or two players' each year from this reserve.[6] Geiger told Calder that Adams and Hammond both favoured the proposal. Adams had also agreed to sponsor a Can-Am club 'on a percentage basis ... and ... he would have the right at the end of any playing season of taking one man from this team to strengthen his own.'[7]

In setting up the Can-Am, Geiger's group recognized the Canadian origin of the game and the drawing power of Canadian clubs. Besides the four proposed American franchises, the Can-Am also actively pursued Canadian entries. Given the long history of Canadian teams playing exhibition matches in New England, Can-Am directors hoped to generate public interest by including Canadian franchises in their circuit. Yet the organization of an all-Canadian minor league in southern Ontario hampered Geiger's effort to recruit Canadian entries. Originally, Geiger wanted Calder's help in enlisting some of the OHA senior clubs that were rumoured to be leaving the amateur ranks. Since those OHA clubs were relatively close to each other geographically, it would be hard to convince any one of them to leave the group because of the resulting increase in travel costs.[8] Calder suggested that a team from Quebec would be much more feasible. A Quebec City club joined the rest of the four American cities in 1926. By mid-

August, Charles Clapp, the newly elected Can-Am president, informed Calder of the official formation of the league. The Can-Am directors adopted the NHL constitution, playing rules, and, with minor changes, the NHL's standard player contract, and authorized its Quebec City member to draw up an affiliation agreement with the NHL.[9]

Like the AHA, the Canadian Professional (Can-Pro) Hockey League came from amateur hockey. Unlike the AHA, however, all the Can-Pro clubs had played in the OHA, the bastion of pure amateur sports, the previous season. What had occurred twenty years earlier with senior amateur hockey in the Montreal region now took place in southern Ontario. Top senior clubs, under the pressure of assembling and maintaining a winning team, succumbed to the financial realities of commercialized amateur hockey. These clubs often recruited players from other locales to strengthen their rosters.[10] The symbolic representational status of a city's senior hockey club also fuelled the demand for a successful season. Peterborough's city council, for example, postponed a council meeting in order to attend a playoff match between Peterborough and London. Its local newspaper averred that nothing could awaken 'a spirit of civic pride so quickly' as 'the success of a team representing the home city ... [in] the final series for the OHA championship.'[11]

Noting the increased financial requirements of and public demand for a top-flight senior OHA club, some club directors began to contemplate alternative strategies. By early 1926, several top OHA clubs in southern Ontario were openly discussing the formation of a professional circuit, and the London club president, Jack A. Anderson, asked to meet with Calder.[12] Not surprisingly, amateur purists in Toronto criticized the idea. A second proposal then appeared in the press advocating that six senior clubs form a separate amateur circuit within the OHA. In order to qualify for admission, all clubs had to play on artificial ice, which of course eliminated dependence on cold weather for maintaining a playing surface and could thus extend the length of the hockey season.[13] Given the predominance of the amateur ideal in Ontario, at least in its sport governing bodies such as the OHA, AAUC, and CAHA, the proposal for establishing another level in the club hierarchy would be a far more acceptable alternative than turning professional. And it might have turned out that way if not for other developments within the OHA and professional hockey.[14]

The landscape of the player market changed dramatically as news of further expansion by the NHL appeared regularly in the press in 1926. Since the NHL did not announce the limit of its expansion, the number of applicants vying for an NHL franchise undoubtedly alarmed the elite OHA clubs. Most of these applications came from large American population centres, such as Detroit, Chicago, Cleveland, Philadelphia, and Buffalo, which could draw greater resources than many OHA cities with the possible exception of Toronto. Promises of constructing a large, modern arena often accompanied these applications. In this atmosphere, it seemed very probable that the demand for players would swell. Indeed, the player grab started in earnest by the time the Canadian senior amateur championship, for the Allan Cup, began in late March. Four players from the champion Port Arthur (now Thunder Bay) Bearcats revealed to the press that they had each been offered a professional contract of $5000 and a $1500 signing bonus. Another report hinted that some of the best players from the Port Arthur team might be heading to eastern OHA clubs.[15] Since there was no arrangement between the professional and the amateur leagues, OHA clubs did not have any protection against professional clubs signing their top players. As top OHA clubs had already engaged in their own recruiting war, it seemed futile to try to convince skilled players to stay in the amateur ranks now that there were so many more opportunities available. For the OHA clubs to compete in the player market, they had to try harder to sweeten the deal with their star players.

Indeed, the desire by some of the top OHA clubs to protect their player assets drove them into the arms of professional hockey because their governing body, the OHA, decimated their rosters. In an attempt to maintain the amateur ideal, the OHA decided to crack down on players who changed residences for the sole purpose of playing hockey. In mid-May, OHA secretary William A. Hewitt warned several Hamilton recruits that the OHA would not certify them as amateurs if they moved to Hamilton. This reignited the desire of Hamilton, Niagara Falls, Windsor, and Toronto to break away from the OHA. Frederick Wilson of the *Toronto Globe* chided these clubs and suggested that they should leave the OHA 'without whining about it.'[16] The Windsor press retorted that the 'corpulent executive of the Ontario Hockey Association' had refused 'playing permits to a host of stars, even although the latter have fulfilled all the requirements of the OHA regulations.'[17] Given the tension between OHA executives and the clubs, Calder asked Anderson if the OHA clubs were going ahead with the proposed minor league.[18]

When the press published the results of the OHA's player certification in mid-June, the full force of the OHA struck the five clubs that were going to form an elite league hard. Hamilton lost three players. The OHA refused certification to three London players and suspended one more. Windsor lost eight players and Stratford lost five, with one more waiting to be considered. Only Niagara Falls went unscathed.[19] The Stratford club announced the next day that it would not be able to compete in the OHA, as it was relying on the players who were refused certification. As a matter of fact, Stratford could not even compete in the OHA's intermediate series, since it had only four players returning from the previous year, and one of them had an injured knee that prevented him from playing hockey.[20]

Decimated by the OHA's refusal to certify many of their players, seven clubs met in Hamilton on June 27 to organize a minor professional league, and elected a committee to meet with Calder to discuss affiliation.[21] Of the seven, Brantford was the first to cast doubt on the feasibility of joining a minor league. It objected to the proposed team salary set at $17,000 and the $5000 bond. Since Brantford played in a small rink that seated only 3000, it would have to raise ticket prices to an almost unreasonable level in order to break even. Moreover, the club did not own the rink and had to pay 50 per cent of the gate receipts for the use of the facility. It estimated the total cost to play in the proposed league to be close to $30,000.[22]

When the clubs met again on August 4, Brantford decided against turning professional. Six clubs formed the Can-Pro, electing Charles King of the Windsor club as president. The owners proposed to organize each club as a farm club for an NHL parent club. A newspaper report described the owners as optimistic about their venture. King informed Calder the next day of the league's formation and requested permission to use the printer who produced the NHL standard contract. Although a framework of systemic control had been set, the relationship between the NHL and the minor leagues was by no means smooth.[23]

An important feature of the NHL's influence in the marketplace was the control of the distribution of its games. Under the NHL constitution, an NHL owner held the territorial rights of a franchise without competition from another member of the league unless he so consented. This exclusivity in the local market established the NHL as the sole producer of professional hockey and allowed clubs to monopolize their local markets, but only, of course, if there were no rival leagues vying for the same area. Calder and the owners of the older clubs certainly did not want a repeat of the days when the NHA and the CHA competed in the Montreal market. While most of the minor-league clubs operated in cities that did not have an NHL franchise, the minor leagues were nevertheless producers of professional hockey and could conceivably declare themselves major leagues. Hence, the NHL insisted in the affiliation agreement that a minor league must obtain consent from a major-league club if it wanted to establish a franchise in the same city. As Calder stated cogently, 'We are willing to co-operate with minor league clubs, but will not consent to entertain them as competitor.'[24] The proposed Can-Am Montreal franchise illustrates the apprehension of the NHL owners regarding the intentions of the minor leagues.

NHL owners were often fearful of potential competition within their market territory. When the Can-Am directors contemplated adding a Canadian franchise, their first choice was Montreal. They invited the Canadiens' owner Leo Dandurand to enter a French-Canadian team in the league, but he was reluctant.

3168—HOCKEY MATCH, VICTORIA RINK, MONTREAL.

An artist's impression of a hockey match at the Victoria rink in Montreal. Notice that the spectators were all standing and there are no side-boards. Early rinks were not built for hockey specifically, but entrepreneurs quickly seized on the hockey craze and added the game to their rinks' schedule. (Notman and Son/Hockey Hall of Fame)

Hockey match at McGill University, 1884. Upper-class institutions such as universities played a major role in promoting hockey. McGill was instrumental in developing hockey's modern form. Many early rinks were outdoor rinks. (Notman and Son/National Archives of Canada/C-081683)

James George Aylwin Creighton, a Haligonian studying in McGill, is generally acknowledged as the father of modern hockey. He was instrumental in organizing the first reported modern ice hockey match, which was held at the Victoria rink in Montreal in 1875, and published the first set of hockey rules in 1877. Creighton later went to Ottawa and helped to promote his version of hockey there. (Hockey Hall of Fame)

Spurred on by 'the interest that hockey matches now elicit, and the importance of having the games fairly played,' Frederick Arthur Stanley, Baron Stanley of Preston, Earl of Derby, Governor General of Canada, donated the Dominion Hockey Challenge Cup in the 1892–3 season to be 'held from year to year by the leading hockey club in Canada.' His deed helped to institutionalize and commercialize elite-level amateur hockey as teams and leagues pursued the prestigious trophy, popularly known as the Stanley Cup. (Hockey Hall of Fame)

The 1893 Montreal Hockey Club was the first recipient of the Stanley Cup (front and centre in this photo), which propelled its governing body, the Amateur Hockey Association of Canada, into prominence. (Hockey Hall of Fame)

Organized hockey began spreading beyond the elite anglophone communities in the Montreal area near the end of the nineteenth century. French Canadians started forming hockey clubs such as the Montagnard Club. Early francophone clubs were never really competitive at the senior level. (Hockey Hall of Fame)

Irish Canadians were another group that tried to break into elite-level amateur hockey. The Montreal Shamrock Hockey Club was especially successful, and not only at the rink. Most early hockey organizations relied heavily on former players to serve as executives. Harry Trihey (seated second from the left), who was scoring leader during the 1898–9 season, went on to serve as president of the Canadian Amateur Hockey League. (Hockey Hall of Fame)

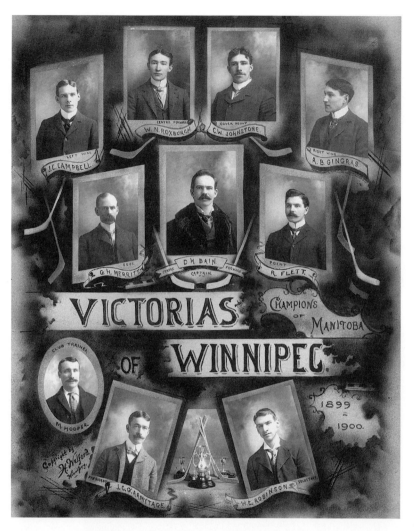

Organized hockey also spread geographically. By the end of the nineteenth century, Winnipeg clubs were quite successful in challenging Montreal's dominance of the game, and the Winnipeg Victorias won the Stanley Cup in 1896. The 1899–1900 version of the same club, shown here, was involved in an infamous challenge series against the Montreal Victorias. The incident, which involved the referee's refusing to continue because he felt he was insulted, indicated the importance of winning and the erosion of the amateur ideal of sportsmanship in elite-level competition. (Henry Welford/Hockey Hall of Fame)

Until the end of the first decade of the twentieth century, small towns such as Kenora, Ontario, could muster a team and issue a challenge for the Stanley Cup. Although the 1905–6 Kenora Thistles in the photograph did not succeed, the 1906–7 team captured the Cup from the Montreal Wanderers in January, only to lose it back to them in March. Increasing costs in maintaining a top-flight squad eventually relegated small-town teams to lower tiers of competition. (J.G. Banks/National Archives of Canada/C-001597

The Montreal Wanderers posed with some of their fans during the Stanley Cup challenge in Winnipeg in 1907. Accusations of hiring hockey players, rough play, and bickering about gate receipts, location, and referees, in the two Stanley Cup series that year between the Wanderers and the Kenora Thistles fuelled amateur purists' suspicion of commercialism in sport and their resolve to adhere to a strict definition of an amateur athlete. (Notman and Son/Hockey Hall of Fame)

Elite-level hockey in the Montreal region split into two camps, the amateurs and the professionals, in 1908. In the next year, two governing bodies appeared on the Montreal professional circuit. One organization, the National Hockey Association, was backed by wealthy investors, such as James Ambrose O'Brien (second from right, top row), in Canada's burgeoning resource industries. The resulting bidding war for players between the two leagues drove up salaries. O'Brien's team, the Renfrew Creamery Kings, became better known as the Millionaires because of the team's payroll. O'Brien quickly found that small populations could not sustain top professional hockey teams, and he abandoned this venture two years later. (Handford/Hockey Hall of Fame)

A National Hockey Association legacy is the creation of a franchise designed to appeal to the French population in Montreal. The Canadiens were first financed by the Association's backers but were later taken over by a Montreal sport entrepreneur, George Kendall, who was also known as George Kennedy. (Hockey Hall of Fame)

The Montreal circuit expanded into Canada's second largest city, Toronto, after the original wealthy backers of the National Hockey Association deserted the professional hockey business. The league granted Toronto two franchises. The Toronto Blueshirts, shown here, were competitive and won the league championship in 1914. (Hockey Hall of Fame)

Professional hockey was not limited to the Montreal region. Lester Patrick (left) togeth-er with his younger brother, Frank (right), organized the Pacific Coast Hockey Association, initially with franchises along the Pacific coast. Although the region had no history of ice hockey, the Patricks built an organization that rivaled the older, much more established, eastern hockey powers. The Patricks' enterprise, however, would col-lapse in the mid-1920s, when much wealthier American and Canadian investors from more populous cities than those in the west entered the professional hockey business. (Hockey Hall of Fame)

A major problem facing the Patricks' enterprise was the mild climate of the Pacific coast. It precluded the use of natural-ice arenas, which were prevalent in the hockey business at the time. The Patricks solved that problem by building two indoor artificial-ice arenas, one in Vancouver (shown here) and the other in Victoria, the first of their kind in Canada. Their heavy investments in these facilities reinforced the need for the Patricks' new league to be successful and, in part, drove them to be especially innovative in presenting their products to the public. (Hockey Hall of Fame)

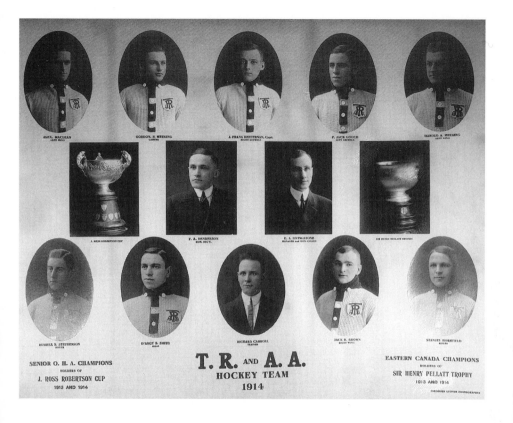

ALEX. MACLEAN
LEFT WING

GORDON. S. MEEKING
CENTRE

J. FRANK HEFFERNAN, Capt.
RIGHT DEFENCE

F. JACK GOOCH
LEFT DEFENCE

HAROLD A. MEEKING
RIGHT WING

J. ROSS ROBERTSON CUP

F. A. HENDERSON
HON. SEC'Y.

E. J. LIVINGSTONE
MANAGER and HON. COACH

SIR HENRY PELLATT TROPHY

RUSSELL S. STEPHENSON
ROVER

D'ARCY S. SMITH
GOAL

RICHARD CARROLL
TRAINER

JACK H. BROWN
RIGHT WING

STANLEY HORSFIELD
ROVER

SENIOR O. H. A. CHAMPIONS
HOLDERS OF
J. ROSS ROBERTSON CUP
1913 AND 1914

T. R. AND A. A.
HOCKEY TEAM
1914

EASTERN CANADA CHAMPIONS
HOLDERS OF
SIR HENRY PELLATT TROPHY
1913 AND 1914

FREDERICK LYONDE PHOTOGRAPHER

After the end of the Athletic War, Toronto became the power centre in amateur sports. However, some amateur hockey organizers in that city saw opportunities in the professional game. E.J. Livingstone (second from right, middle row) was a successful amateur sport organizer in hockey and football. He would enter the professional game and find himself constantly battling the other owners. The desire of rival owners to get rid of Livingstone led to the birth of the National Hockey League in 1917. After many attempts to re-enter the game, Livingstone was ultimately banished from professional hockey. (Frederick Lyonde/Hockey Hall of Fame)

About the same time that E.J. Livingstone entered professional hockey, a newspaper sports editor named Frank Calder became part of the National Hockey Association's administration. Calder assumed the presidency of the new National Hockey League in 1917 and remained at the post until his death in 1943. During his tenure as NHL president, Calder led the battle against Livingstone, witnessed the collapse of the Patricks' hockey enterprise, expanded the league into the United States, oversaw a minor league hockey network, and negotiated a favourable agreement with the Canadian amateur hockey governing body. (Hockey Hall of Fame)

In the early 1920s, an entrepreneur, Tom Duggan, initiated a movement to expand the NHL. Although he is possibly one of the most important hockey individuals in the league's history, little is known about Duggan. (Hockey Hall of Fame)

The first American NHL franchise was the Boston Bruins, owned by Charles Adams, a millionaire in the grocery business. As a director of the Boston Arena, Adams was familiar with the business potential in commercialized, elite-level amateur hockey and jumped at the chance to become part of the NHL expansion when Duggan came calling. Adams eventually had a fallout with Frank Calder and retired from active management of the Bruins. (Hockey Hall of Fame)

After its Boston debut, the NHL expanded to the American media capital, New York, in 1925 with the New York Americans. The owner, 'Big Bill' Dwyer, was arrested in a government sting operation before the new franchise's first game and is noticeably absent from this 1925 promotional flyer. Instead, Tom Duggan was listed as the team's director. (Hockey Hall of Fame)

New York Americans 1925-26

Back L-R: Ken Randall, John "Crutchy" Morrison, Joe Simpson, Cozy Dolan (Trainer), Earl "Spiff"
Campbell, Rene Boileau, Charlie Langlois.

Middle L-R: Joe Ironstone, Alex McKinnon, T.J. Duggan (Director), Tex Rickard (President), Tom
Gorman (Manager), Mickey Roach, Edmond Bouchard, Vern Forbes.

Front L-R: Wilfred "Shorty" Green, Bill Burch, Red Green.

The New York Americans were very successful in drawing spectators. Their landlord, Tex Rickard (second row, seated third from left), who built the third incarnation of the Madison Square Garden, decided that he wanted his own team and in 1926 entered the NHL as the owner of the New York Rangers. (Hockey Hall of Fame)

By 1926, the NHL expansion had reached a climax, with entrepreneurs clamouring to join the league. Besides the New York Rangers, teams in Chicago and Detroit also were admitted. The Chicago owner, Major Frederick McLaughlin, a millionaire in the coffee business, would battle Frank Calder in league affairs. McLaughlin had the additional distinction of being the only new NHL owner sued by E.J. Livingstone. (Hockey Hall of Fame)

One of the unsuccessful bids for a Chicago franchise was headed by Patrick T. (Paddy) Harmon. Instead, Harmon became a facility provider and built the Chicago Stadium in 1929. Here, he stands in front of the famous Stadium organ with his daughter, Patsy, and Mr and Mrs Ralph Waldo Emerson, who were both organists. (DN-0088167, Chicago Daily News negatives collection, Chicago Historical Society)

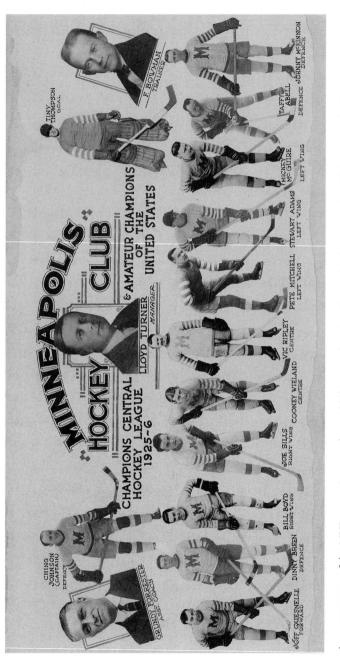

A consequence of the NHL expansion was the establishment of a minor league hockey network, which consisted of both new leagues and existing amateur clubs deserting their amateur leagues and turning professional. An example of the latter was the Central Hockey League (CHL), which became the American Hockey Association. Based in the Midwest, the CHL was a powerhouse in American amateur hockey in the mid-1920s. The manager of one of the CHL clubs, Lloyd Turner, was a former manager of the defunct Western Hockey League club the Calgary Tigers. (Glenbow Archives PB-368–15)

The Great Depression affected the NHL, especially small-market teams like the Ottawa Hockey Club. Although the Ottawa club had enjoyed a long and illustrious history in both elite-level amateur and professional hockey, its fortunes steadily declined in the late 1920s despite the efforts of its principal owner, Frank Ahearn, to save the club. The club eventually withdrew from the league in 1934, and professional hockey did not return to the city until 1992. (Hockey Hall of Fame)

As the Great Depression deepened, a minor league, the American Hockey Association (AHA) claimed major league status. Backed by James Norris Sr, one of the richest men in North America, the AHA survived for two seasons before returning to the NHL-controlled minor league network. Norris, however, was welcomed into the NHL circle and became the owner of the financially troubled Detroit franchise. (Hockey Hall of Fame)

By the mid-1930s, an upheaval in the Canadian amateur hockey circle allowed the NHL to dip into the amateur player talent-pool previously controlled by the Canadian Amateur Hockey Association (CAHA). William A. Hewitt, a long-time amateur hockey official, was a key figure in bringing the CAHA and the NHL to an agreement. (Hockey Hall of Fame)

Still, his fear of potential competition prompted him to agree to the proposal. To his relief, there would not be any Can-Am franchise in Montreal. The proposal never proceeded beyond the planning stage, probably because there were already two NHL franchises in Montreal. Instead, the Can-Am settled on a franchise in Quebec City.[25]

While the Can-Am deferred to the wishes of the NHL and refrained from placing a franchise in Montreal, the question of territorial rights soon became heated between the NHL and the minor leagues. Shortly after the 1926–7 season began, the Can-Am requested permission to expand into Brooklyn. Can-Am president Clapp argued that his league could not go on forever with only five clubs and that the NHL would benefit from a cooperating league. He also hinted that another group was planning to move into Brooklyn as well, and that that group might not be as friendly. Clapp further asserted that a minor-league club could help the local NHL club's attendance 'by increasing public interest.'[26] Calder, however, doubted that the New York NHL clubs would assent to having another club in the area. He counselled Clapp to 'go easy on discussing franchises for the purpose of promoting buildings ... As to their thrashing about looking for a new league, there is not the slightest danger. Million dollar arenas for outlaw hockey leagues simply are not being built.'[27]

In addition to his concern about the violation of the New York clubs' territorial rights, Calder also worried that the new minor leagues might decide to declare themselves major leagues. To ward off such moves, Calder was careful about allowing minor leagues into major-league markets. In dealing with Clapp's request, he asked Hammond to use his influence with the Springfield club to stop Clapp from pursuing a franchise in New York. He suggested to Hammond that 'the whole scheme ... is a step in the direction to raise the Canadian-American League to major league proportions.'[28] Hammond agreed that 'any effort to build an arena and place the Canadian-American League Club in New York City [is] an unfriendly act and detrimental to our interest.'[29] As in Montreal, the Can-Am league was not successful in its pursuit of a franchise in New York.

The Can-Am's attempt to enter the New York market also indicated the influence that the NHL had on the minor leagues. In the case of the Can-Am, the financial interest of the New York Rangers in one of the Can-Am clubs helped to thwart the proposed expansion into New York. For clubs in other leagues where NHL clubs did not have financial interests, the threat of a player raid preyed on the minds of the minor-league owners and influenced their decisions regarding to their relationship with the NHL. The final elimination of the NHL's longtime nemesis, Eddie Livingstone, demonstrated the power of the NHL in this regard.

The ex–Toronto owner had been a thorn in the side of the NHL since its creation. His various lawsuits against the league and its members diverted time and energy from their business. The ill-will towards Livingstone was such that the NHL owners fought him at every turn rather than let him back into professional hockey. In the frantic days of expansion, however, Livingstone slipped back into professional hockey via the AHA. His return to professional hockey was not due to Calder's neglect of the league's number-one enemy. Knowing Livingstone's desire to get back into professional hockey, Calder was actually alert enough to try to ward off such a move early on. Before the NHL made its decision about the new Detroit ownership, he had J.L. Woods, one of the Detroit bidders, ascertain that his arena's architect had no connection with Livingstone.[30] In turn, and perhaps knowing the NHL's determination to keep him out of hockey, Livingstone was careful about his moves. As the rumours of a new rival league emerged in August, Livingstone wrote Calder denying any connection with Frank Patrick and the proposed league.[31] What Calder and the NHL did not know was that Livingstone had managed to gain control of the Chicago franchise in the AHA.[32] At the beginning of the 1926–7 season, Livingstone pulled another coup by securing ice time at the Chicago Coliseum. Unaware that Livingstone had already secured a franchise in the AHA, Charles Hall, the Coliseum manager, under instructions from Chicago owner McLaughlin, told Livingstone that he would not get ice time unless he had a franchise in the AHA.[33] By the time Calder and McLaughlin got wind of Livingstone's manoeuvres, it was too late for the NHL to do anything. This, however, was to be Livingstone's last hurrah in professional hockey. It ended again in a series of lawsuits.

Despite knowing the NHL's disdain over the presence of Livingstone in the AHA, its president A.G. Warren tried to renegotiate a new agreement after the 1926–7 season. Still perceiving his league as superior to the other minor leagues, Warren proposed to divide professional hockey into three categories, major, intermediate, and minor, for the following season. While Warren did not provide any basis for the divisions, he clearly saw the AHA as belonging in the intermediate category, below the NHL but above the rest of the minor leagues. The NHL, however, had no intention of recognizing the AHA as anything other than a minor league.[34]

As Warren dickered about the terms of the renewal, the NHL became impatient. Since the AHA had delayed in renewing the agreement, Art Ross, ever opportunistic, signed a player away from the AHA's Winnipeg club. Given this precedent, McLaughlin asked Calder if the NHL could start signing AHA players.[35] McLaughlin thought that the League had been too patient with the AHA group, who chose 'to be very stiff-necked about coming into organized hockey ... [I]f they want to stay out it must be [at] their own risk.'[36]

By early June, dissension among the AHA owners brought the league under the same minor-league agreement as the Can-Am and Can-Pro. Warren had been holding out for better terms because his team had lost considerable money the previous season. Other owners began to worry about the possibility of an NHL raid. Duluth and Winnipeg, in particular, wanted an agreement to preempt such an event, as well as to hold down player salaries.[37] On June 20 Warren met with Calder and McLaughlin at the Old Elm Golf Club in Chicago. Over a game of golf, they patched up their differences. Incidentally, Calder was so enchanted by the result that he instituted an annual golf tournament to network with potential and current hockey stakeholders.[38] Warren more or less deferred to Calder as the sole adjudicator in any disputes between the AHA and the other leagues. In July Warren submitted a list of AHA players who were also claimed by various minor leagues and suggested that the players 'could be ... more easily disposed of after signing the agreement and your exercising the power to decide these matters vested in you in the proposed agreement.'[39]

By reining in the AHA, the NHL also finally got rid of Livingstone. After Warren submitted a proposed agreement similar to what other minor leagues had signed, Calder advised McLaughlin that the NHL should not sign it 'until they have shown us that they have officially severed connections with this lunatic [Livingstone].'[40] On August 24 the AHA passed a resolution terminating Livingstone's membership. In sending a copy of the resolution to Calder, Warren proposed, 'I hope that matters are now adjusted to your satisfaction, and that the agreement may be renewed along the lines we discussed in Chicago, and which I believe are covered to your satisfaction in the agreement submitted.'[41]

In its dealings with the minor leagues, the NHL had been fairly successful in controlling the distribution of professional hockey via various tactics. As in the cases of the Can-Am's expansion plans and the renewal of the agreement with the AHA, Calder's tactics brought results favourable to the NHL. Recognizing the benefits of the minor leagues to the NHL, Calder had a preferred approach in his dealings with the minor leagues. Seldom did he resort to threats. Instead, Calder presented himself and the NHL as allies who were eager to help the minor leagues establish themselves as going concerns. When the Can-Am was pleading its case to expand into Brooklyn, Calder advised Clapp of other potential cities within proximity of the Can-Am's exiting franchises.[42] On the other hand, the case of Livingstone also demonstrated that the NHL was not beyond using threats. Given the history of animosities between Livingstone and the other NHL owners, it should be remembered that his case was unique. Nevertheless, the control of the distribution of professional hockey illustrated the growing power of the NHL. Not only did it dictate where professional hockey franchises could be located, it also influenced decisions as to who could be associated with them.

The growing power of the NHL did not stop with its influence on the distribution of games. It also extended to the labour market. Players constituted the single most important asset for NHL clubs. Indeed, concerns about recruiting and keeping quality players had been with hockey before the existence of the NHL or even professional hockey. Since the establishment of professional hockey, various mechanisms such as the reserve clause, the waiver rule, and the option helped to control the labour market in professional hockey. The total sum of these devices bound a player to a particular club unless the club deemed it advisable to release him. In effect, they restricted the player's ability to market his skills somewhere else and thus helped to depress the potential value of his services under a free-market system. Other than the occasional player raids between rival leagues when competition for players drove up prices, these measures were fairly effective in controlling the labour market. The establishment of the minor leagues further contributed to stabilizing the player market in several ways.[43]

To ensure a ready supply of players, the NHL instituted a loan agreement in the initial affiliation agreement with the minor leagues. It allowed the NHL clubs to lend players to minor-league clubs without asking for waivers first. This effectively allowed NHL clubs to overstock players. Before the establishment of the minor-league system, player supply depended on inter-league trades and the signing of amateurs. These were not reliable sources. With the advent of the minor leagues, NHL clubs could expand beyond their roster limits and send extra players to the minors to get playing time that they might not have with their parent clubs. If the NHL club required the services of a given player, it could recall him. Since the minor-league clubs that took in the players contributed to their salaries, the system also alleviated the cost of keeping extra players.

To ensure an even more stable player supply, the agreement further instituted a clause that allowed an NHL club to draft a player from a minor-league club for $5000.[44] While the minor leagues acted as reservoirs of excess players for the NHL, they also included players who did not have an NHL contract. Thus, the draft gave the NHL clubs a chance to obtain players whom they had not previously identified as major-league material. It also shifted some of the responsibilities and hassles in the search for, as well as negotiations with, amateur players to the minor leagues. At the insistence of the minor leagues, who wanted to protect their rosters for the first year, the draft clause did not become effective until the 1927–8 season.

Without the draft clause being in effect for the 1926–7 season, minor-league clubs were free to sell players to any NHL club after they had asked for waivers within their own leagues. A draft, of course, limited the number of potential buyers to one and possibly depressed the price for the player. The minor leagues were not happy about the draft in its present form, and at least the Can-Am league attempted to eliminate it. Indeed, Clapp tried to set a precedent by allowing the NHL clubs to buy a Can-Am player without the player having to clear waivers within the league. He suggested to Calder that these arrangements 'and the clause allowing for loaning players to our League subject to certain conditions ... renders unnecessary any draft.'[45]

The minor leagues soon learned that stabilizing the player supply for the NHL meant destabilizing the personnel of their member clubs. Indeed, NHL clubs abused the loan provision during the first season the affiliation agreement was in place. Charles King complained to Calder that an NHL player had been on loan to one of the Can-Pro clubs, but that the parent club had then recalled the player a few games later and promptly sold him to another NHL club. An exasperated King proposed that the loan provision be banned and that the minor leagues 'develop amateurs to be later sold or drafted by the National Hockey League.'[46] The loan provision, as it existed in the agreement, created havoc in the staffing of the minor-league clubs and eventually led to the no-recall clause in the new agreement signed in 1927. In order to 'counteract the juggling of players which went on in some quarters last season,' the new agreement permitted NHL clubs lending their players until February 15, but the parent club could not recall the player for three weeks after the loan.[47]

The loan provision was not the only measure objected to by the minor leagues. Can-Am president Charles Clapp was also unhappy with the draft clause, even though it would not go into effect until the second year. An incident involving the Can-Pro just before the affiliation renewal meeting may have helped to convince Clapp of the draft clause's potential consequences. The NHL Detroit club had expressed interest in a Can-Pro London player, Larry Aurie. London owner Anderson asked for $10,000 for Aurie, then changed the price to $9000 plus a player. Representing the Detroit club, Percy LeSueur countered with $7500 the day before the meeting. Anderson then told LeSueur that he had promised to consult with Aurie before he would be traded, and that he would get back to LeSueur after doing so. When the newspapers detailed the agreement reached on May 17, they revealed that an NHL club could draft a player for $5000. Thus, Detroit backed out of the deal and drafted Aurie for less than what it would have had to pay. Although the Can-Pro league protested, Calder ruled in favour of the NHL club.[48]

By the end of the first season in which the affiliation agreement was in effect, the initial cordial relationship between the minor leagues and the NHL had begun to erode. This was especially true for the Can-Am league, which was perhaps the most enthusiastic supporter of the minor-league system in the beginning. While the affiliation benefited the NHL, the Can-Am found the relationship too one-sided for its liking. When its president suggested some modifications to the new affiliation agreement, Calder flatly rejected them and insisted that Clapp sign the agreement without any changes.[49] Not subtly, he asked Clapp if the Can-Am was a party to the affiliation agreement.[50] Reacting to Calder's threat, Clapp protested bitterly. He pointed out that Calder did not even have the courtesy to consider the changes Clapp had suggested and complained that the NHL was bullying the minor leagues 'because you figure that the strength of your League is sufficient to tell us what we shall do without considering the fact of co-operation.'[51]

The establishment of a minor-league system in 1926 represented another major step in the growing influence of the NHL in the professional hockey marketplace. In their willingness to affiliate with the NHL, the minor leagues essentially enlarged the sphere of influence of the NHL brand of hockey. Before 1926 there were at least three brands of hockey, as played by the CAHA, the WHL, and the NHL, each with its own playing rules. In terms of the number of participants, the CAHA had the most players under its rules. There had been attempts to unify the rules of play between the professionals and the amateurs. A Regina (Saskatchewan) CAHA delegate complained that as rinks hosted both amateur and professional league games, sometimes one after another, 'spectators are absolutely bewildered' by the different rules under the WHL and the CAHA. He suggested that if 'the NHA [*sic*] and the CAHA combined we would have 90% of registered hockey players in Canada playing under one set of rules, and I think would force the Western Canada League to adopt similar rules.'[52] Yet the NHL was able to maintain, if not promote, its style of hockey with the dissolution of the WHL, its expansion into large American cities, and the addition of the minor professional leagues. These minor leagues, especially the AHA and the Can-Pro, represented the cream of the amateur ranks and the skill level of the professionals in these leagues more than made up for the numerical superiority of the amateurs in terms of the prestige of each style of hockey. Since not all amateur players could make it into the NHL, the cumulative effect of top amateur players playing in the minor leagues devalued the commercialized amateur leagues' games.

In terms of market penetration, the minor leagues together with the expanded NHL occupied many important hockey markets. Not only did the addition of Boston, New York, Pittsburgh, Chicago, and Detroit put the NHL into major population centres in the Northeast and the Great Lakes region, the minor leagues allowed the NHL influence to extend to a secondary market without the NHL actually granting franchises to any new cities. This secondary market indirectly established the NHL's presence and served to deter others from organizing a rival league.[53] As the AHA and the Can-Am found out in the cases of Livingstone and the Brooklyn expansion respectively, the NHL could dictate to the minor leagues whom they could do business with and where they could establish their territory. Hence, the NHL was able to control the supply of professional hockey games beyond its own franchise cities.

Besides enabling strategic control in the distribution of professional hockey games, the minor leagues also acted as intermediaries in the supply of players, serving as a buffer between the NHL and the amateur leagues. Through the draft and loan provisions in the affiliation agreement, the NHL clubs decreased their business risks in the scouting and recruiting of players. Although the NHL clubs still performed these functions, the minor leagues now shared in the costs. Signing an amateur player was a gamble that might or might not bear fruit for an NHL club. The draft allowed the NHL clubs to secure players who might escape their detection, while the loan provision allowed an NHL club to send a player who did not make the grade to an affiliated minor-league club for seasoning. Since the minor-league club either paid or shared in the cost of the player's salary for the use of that player, the arrangement also reduced the cost of player inventory for the NHL clubs.

The minor leagues aided the NHL in the player market in other ways. Mechanisms to control labour in professional hockey would only be effective as long as other organizations honoured them. Thus, alliances with the minor leagues were crucial in controlling player movement. Furthermore, the establishment of the minor leagues increased employment opportunities for hockey players and the viability of a career in professional hockey.

The formation of the minor-league system was a significant development that contributed to the consolidation of the NHL's power. Scholarly works on the NHL and other professional sports governing bodies have often focused on the internal structural controls designed to stabilize the organization. Few, if any, studies have examined an organization's power base through its relationship with external contributors, such as the minor leagues. For the NHL, minor leagues were important to its power base because they helped to control the production and distribution of professional hockey games. Through the affiliation agreement, the minor leagues promised to recognize NHL territorial rights. With few exceptions, these leagues also adopted the NHL rules of play. In essence, the NHL style if not the NHL level of hockey extended beyond the eight NHL cities. As players within the minor-league system could conceivably either move up to or come from NHL clubs, this gave the NHL exposure in the markets where it did not have franchises and, thus, further promoting the NHL brand.[54]

Despite the apparent benefits to the NHL, the relationship between the major and minor leagues was often dialectic rather than dictatorial. Even with its economic superiority, the NHL had to be careful about the terms of affiliation in its agreements with the minor leagues. Without some reciprocal benefits that would make minor-league clubs profitable, a minor-league system could not exist. As trainers of talent, the minor leagues received compensation for players taken by the NHL through the draft. Moreover, the NHL president acted as an arbitrator providing an avenue for conflict resolution among the various minor leagues. This reduced the chances of inter-league battles which, without such recourse, meant expensive player raids. Conflicts did occur between the NHL and the minor leagues, however, over the terms of affiliation and their interpretation. Thus, the relationship between the minor leagues and the NHL was an uneasy one in the formative years of the minor-league system.

As the 1927–8 season began, the NHL laid claim to its supremacy in professional hockey. All of its rivals had either been subjugated or vanquished. With a ready reserve of players, the minor leagues helped to stabilize the player market. Unlike the case in the early days of hockey, when multiple senior or major leagues existed, players who traded their skills for remuneration had fewer options. Through its numerical strength, the CAHA remained the only organization that prevented a total domination of the commercial-hockey marketplace by the NHL. The brand of commercialized amateur hockey in the CAHA, however, would be severely tested during the Depression years.

Chapter 10

Decline of the Ottawa Empire

Thanks to its agreements with the minor leagues, its expansion into American markets, and the demise of the WHL, the NHL stood alone at the top of the professional hockey world by the late 1920s. On February 13, 1928 the NHL governors met at the King Edward Hotel in Toronto. President Calder reported that the gross earnings of all clubs for the season to date were $1,314,584, an increase of more than $109,000 over the previous year. Yet even with this financial windfall, there were signs of troubles with some NHL clubs. The Pittsburgh and Detroit clubs had been doing poorly both in the league standings and in attendance. Furthermore, the minor leagues complained about the inequities in the inter-league agreement.[1]

The economic slump of the 1930s exposed internal and external problems that had been momentarily covered by the general prosperity of the league after expansion. Three NHL franchises folded and the league had to take over the management of a fourth club. The NHL owners recognized that the league's survival depended on collective measures to counter the business downturn. But when it came to dealing with individual clubs, most of them believed that market forces dictated the success or failure of a business. As with the pre–New Deal attitude on relief for the downtrodden, league involvement was to be minimal and individual initiative was the road to salvation.[2] In Canada the belief was prevalent that economic hardship was 'due [in] large measure to the will or option of the individual.'[3] When a delegation of western mayors sought relief from the federal government, Prime Minister William Lyon Mackenzie King reminded them that relief was a local matter. Since the revenue structure of the NHL favoured the home club, clubs that could not generate enough interest at home, either because of a small market size, poor management, or unfavourable rink lease, faltered without some help from the League. The demise of the Ottawa franchise provided such an example.

Ottawa's case franchise demonstrated the fate of a member club that had lost its usefulness to the others. NHL members needed each other because of the uniqueness of their product – the production of a game. Without at least one other member, there is no product. Moreover, a closely contested game is economically more valuable than one that is not, because a league dominated by one strong team makes its games too one-sided and outcomes too predictable. Hence, members are economically most useful to each other if all have fairly competitive teams. Assembling a competitive team, however, requires substantial expense in recruiting and retaining skilled players. Thus, increased player and travel costs in the expanded NHL strained the financial capacity of a small-market team such as Ottawa.

The financial pressures on the Ottawa team did not necessarily mean that its demise was inevitable, even though the Depression complicated Ottawa's troubles. Alternatives to remedy the team's financial problems existed. Yet the internal dynamics of the league narrowed the choices. Self-interest, personal animosities, and differences in values and beliefs all played a part in moulding a path towards the dissolution of the Ottawa franchise.

The year 1927 was a watershed for the Ottawa club in its long and illustrious hockey history. It had just won its ninth Stanley Cup in a continuous and successful membership in senior hockey dating back to the 1890s. Of all the current NHL clubs, Ottawa remained the only member that pre-dated the establishment of professional hockey. In its transformation from a senior amateur hockey club to a member of the professional league, it had consistently been able to assemble a very competitive team. Even when player salaries rose at various times in professional hockey, the Ottawa club was able to retain most of its players with the lure of a secure civil-service position in the capital city. Moreover, the club management had cultivated a strong relationship with other local amateur hockey clubs in the Ottawa Valley region thus helping the senior club to identify and secure talent. Unlike Toronto and Montreal, the Ottawa club never had to share its market with a second professional club. Its importance, however, extended beyond the number of victories it had accumulated. In the turbulent history of elite-level hockey, when governing bodies appeared and disappeared, backing from the Ottawa club often meant the continuance of a governing body. Unbeknownst to the club, 1927 would be Ottawa's last hurrah as, arguably, the most important club in hockey history thus far. By the 1934–5 season it had moved to St Louis. The club folded in the following year.

Ottawa's troubles began as the NHL rounded out its membership with the addition of Chicago and Detroit. Despite the incompleteness of the records for the 1927–8 and 1928–9 seasons, it is clear that Ottawa's revenues had been in a steady decline since the 1927–8 season. The average receipts per game dropped from just above $4000 to below $2500. For the 1929–30 season, Ottawa's $4256.80 average per game was nearly half of Toronto's $8145.37.[4] Yet the cost of operation had escalated. In the 1927 NHL annual meeting, the governors moved to abolish the salary limit and increase the waiver price from $2500 to $5000.[5] At the end of the 1926–7 season, Ottawa had the fourth lowest attendance, even though it had won the Stanley Cup. Only Pittsburgh and the two newcomers, Detroit and Chicago, had fewer patrons.[6]

Despite its rich hockey tradition, Ottawa began to feel the strain of operating in an expanded league. At a time when the NHL allowed its members to increase spending, Ottawa's situation limited club revenues. First and foremost, the size of the Ottawa market placed limits on revenue potential. Toronto, which had more than 600,000 inhabitants, was the NHL's second smallest market, while Ottawa, according to the 1931 census, listed only 126,872.[7] Another factor affecting Ottawa's revenue was its pricing structure. As late as 1930, Ottawa charged $2.00 for its best seats, the lowest in the league, and that figure only applied to 293 seats. The scale then dropped off to $1.35 for another 150 seats. Perhaps because of its origin as an amateur club supported by membership subscription, Ottawa also had the lowest ticket prices in the league, charging as little as $0.25. It actually had five categories of seats priced below $1.00. Few other clubs had more than two price categories below that amount and only Boston had seats for as little as $0.50. In Toronto, the highest-price tickets went for $2.75.[8]

Ottawa did seek to improve its financial position. It raised ticket prices in the 1926–7 season without success. In appealing to the league for help, it listed five reasons for its revenue woes. Besides the failed attempt to increase ticket prices and the small size of the market, Ottawa governor Redmond Quain attributed the growth of skiing as a recreational activity, 'the dilution of playing strength' in an expanded league, and new teams without a hockey tradition as detriments to Ottawa's profitability. Quain argued that Ottawa had possibly reached its maximum market potential, as it drew $210,000 on the road and only $86,000 at home. He saw the $16,000 loss for the 1926–7 season as a pattern that would continue and pleaded with the governors to assist the Ottawa club because 'its hockey history and name make it a valuable asset always as a visiting team.'[9] During a governors' meeting, Quain petitioned to increase Ottawa's share of its road games from the usual 3.5 per cent to a rate not exceeding 15 per cent if Ottawa's revenues could not cover its operating expenses. Charles Adams suggested the upper limit be set at 10 per cent and McLaughlin seconded the motion. The NHL, however, was not going to come to Ottawa's aide without conditions. League governors approved the motion with an amendment from Colonel Hammond of the New York Rangers that 'a Committee, to include an accountant, be appointed by the President to settle the situation surrounding the percentage to be paid to visiting club [*sic*].'[10]

Hope for a scheme that would help weak clubs such as Ottawa quickly evaporated. The two New York clubs sponsored a motion to continue the 3.5 per cent visitors' share at the next league meeting. At the end of 1927, the committee charged with examining the proposed increase in the visitors' gate receipts for weak clubs came back with a recommendation of keeping the status quo.[11] Ottawa's owner, Frank Ahearn, expressed his disappointment to Calder and suggested that 'if all the clubs of the league are to secure financial stability, some arrangement along the lines of the baseball split is necessary.'[12] When the proposed Pittsburgh sale came up in the March meeting, Ahearn once again raised his case with Calder. If the governors did not rework the gate receipts for the visiting club, Ahearn feared that the NHL would be forced to take over a financially troubled club, which then 'would create a precedent whereby other clubs that are losing financially would have a right to expect at least equal treatment.'[13]

At the time, Pittsburgh was in a more dire situation than Ottawa and the governors' attention was on the former. During the March 12 meeting in New York, the governors voted five to three against transferring the option on the Pittsburgh franchise from Irwin Wener to Joseph P. Huhn, and further charged Calder with the responsibility of handling the disposition of the Pittsburgh franchise. No discussion, however, was on record regarding any proposal that might help either Pittsburgh or Ottawa.[14]

Without any immediate relief from the league, Ahearn had to resort to various measures to keep the Ottawa club operating. In late March, Ahearn authorized Calder to charge the $2000 league assessment against Ottawa's franchise account. Ahearn apologized for having to dip into the franchise's equity account.[15] The tailspin had begun for Ottawa. But why did the NHL ignore Ahearn's plea for revenue sharing?

The attitude of Calder perhaps provides an insight into one facet of the entrepreneurial approach to the economic crisis within the NHL – a preference for individual initiative. After Ahearn told Calder that the projected loss for Ottawa in the 1928–9 season was going to be somewhere between $20,000 and $40,000, Calder wrote McLaughlin that Ahearn's proposal would not succeed in hockey like it did in professional baseball. He opined that 'a club with a lesser constituency might sit back and lose all initiative, knowing that it would be taken care of anyhow.'[16] The richer clubs might then feel they had a right to intervene with the troubled club's operation, which would compromise the integrity of professional hockey.

While Calder was influential with some governors, Ottawa was not without its sympathizers in the league. Besides Pittsburgh, which was in the same leaking financial boat, Ottawa had a vocal supporter in McLaughlin. As a new member, his Chicago club had not been doing well financially. Since joining the league in 1926, the Blackhawks had been playing in the Chicago Coliseum. The Coliseum had a relatively small seating capacity, however, and the Blackhawks often had to share the facility with other events such as cattle shows. Moreover, hockey was a new sport in Chicago whose patrons lost their initial enthusiasm after three straight losing seasons. The club's average home gates were $4464.04 and $4230.22 for the 1927–8 and 1928–9 seasons respectively. Not until the team moved into the new, larger Chicago Stadium at the end of 1929 did the home gate receipts improve.[17] While McLaughlin could look forward to a new arena in the hope of renewing local interest, he knew first-hand the frustrations of operating a money-losing team. Thus, he disagreed with Calder's assessment of the Ottawa situation and warned that 'a chain is only as strong as its weakest link, and the present N. H. L. is beautifully designed to make weaker the weak links.'[18] McLaughlin then ridiculed the short-sightedness of the owners who refused to help Ottawa. He believed in devising a scheme to 'help them only in proportion as they help us'; because Ottawa was such a good draw 'all the way around the circuit, why should we consider it "help" to give them what they manifestly deserve?'[19] His message was clear. A 'deserving' member was one that continued to be beneficial to the other members in the organization.

McLaughlin's analysis of the Ottawa situation gives a glimpse of collectivism and individualism at work within the structure that the NHL was becoming. With the exception of a minor rebellion from the AHA between 1930 and 1932, the NHL had more or less reined in the professional circuits since the creation of the minor-league system. In this and other endeavours against external threats, the NHL governors recognized the advantage of collective support. Yet when it came to internal affairs, self-interest was the order of the day. According to the governors, individual efforts determined the failure or success of a franchise. If an owner failed in his efforts to save a troubled franchise, little support could be expected from the league. And, of course, this was decades before John Manley, the federal Industry minister, proposed to subsidize the Canadian NHL teams in 2000.[20]

Despite the corporate culture of individualism within the NHL, the League did attempt to assist Ottawa. By the beginning of 1929 Ahearn hinted that he would consider moving the team if things did not improve.[21] While Calder affirmed his support for the continued presence of Ottawa in the NHL, he advised Ahearn that Ottawa's defensive style of hockey was hurting the club and suggested that Ottawa needed new talent.[22] Ahearn agreed with Calder's assessment and vowed not to sell his star players, Kilrea, Clancy, and Finnigan. Bringing a touch of nationalistic sentiment into his argument, he warned that the Canadian teams stood to lose the most if Ottawa should disband.[23] At mid-season, Ottawa floundered at the bottom of the Canadian division with five victories, nine losses, and eight draws.

Despite its current league standing and financial woes, Ottawa's past reputation still commanded respect and market value. Queries about the possible sale of the Ottawa club began to trickle in. In late January, Leonard Cohen of the *New York Evening Post* asked Calder if the Ottawa club was moving to an American city the following season.[24] Cohen's inquiry was not without justification. Paddy Harmon of Chicago and a group in Philadelphia had expressed interest in moving the Ottawa club.[25] In spite of offers from American promoters, Ahearn informed Calder in mid-February that he had offered the Ottawa club to its landlord, the Ottawa Auditorium, for 'less than half the price it is now worth.'[26] Ahearn apparently felt it was his civic duty to keep the franchise in Ottawa, and hinted he could have sold the franchise for more.

The Auditorium management, however, could not raise enough funds. At the end of April, Ahearn agreed to extend the option to purchase the club, and Auditorium director Fred Burpee asked Calder for help. In its drive to raise private funding, the Auditorium fell short and, instead, issued $125,000 worth of 7 per cent preferred stock.[27] By August Ahearn came to an agreement with the Auditorium and relinquished his control of the team.[28]

For the Auditorium, the purchase was a gamble. Its directors knew that the Ottawa club had been losing money. Hockey, however, was the raison d'être of the Auditorium. The directors certainly did not wish to see their major tenant move out of town. They reasoned that the rent the Auditorium normally received plus the gate receipts would make the facility profitable.

To further their chances of success, the Auditorium directors decided to continue the practice of playing a few Ottawa home games in the bigger markets. For the 1929–30 season, Ottawa transferred two of its home games to Atlantic City, two to Detroit, and one to Boston. Moreover, the new club president, William Foran (also the Stanley Cup trustee), again asked the League to increase the percentage paid to visiting clubs from 3.5 to 20 per cent or more. Calder, in his attempt to influence McLaughlin's conviction about the weak clubs, characterized Foran's message as a request for 'preferential treatment.'[29] Just before the semi-annual meeting in September, Foran made his request official by circulating a letter to all member clubs outlining Ottawa's case for an increase in the visitors' percentage of the gate. Using last season's receipts, Foran detailed the drawing power of Ottawa on the road and, like his predecessor, again referred to the revenue-sharing scheme of professional baseball. He argued that 'any organization which can gross over $2,000,000 in a season becomes an important business and requires an arrangement which will make all of its members reasonably prosperous to hold it together.'[30] At the semi-annual meeting the owners tabled Foran's request for a later meeting.[31] In the December league meeting the governors appointed a committee to investigate the matter.[32]

While the Ottawa club awaited the committee's findings, its financial woes continued. Just before the season began, one of the club's directors, Redmond Quain, asked Calder to release Ottawa's share in the franchise account so that money would be available to pay the instalment due Ahearn.[33] Calder refused the request and suggested that Ahearn's demand for payment via Ottawa's equity was a 'somewhat distasteful way out of the Auditorium's difficulty.'[34] In a separate letter to Quain, Calder pointed out that Ottawa had already drawn $15,701.76 from the equity account since 1922. Based on a technicality, Calder refused to release the rest of the money, but he promised to bring the issue up at the next governors' meeting.[35]

The belief in individual responsibility for one's welfare still ruled even as the stock market crashed at the end of October 1929. For Ottawa, no additional help was forthcoming from the League when the governors met in February 1930. The 3.5 per cent visitors' share remained unchanged.[36] This should not have come as a surprise to Ottawa since three of the four members on the committee were the same governors who had recommended retention of the 3.5 per cent visitors' share in 1927. Unlike 1927, when times were still good, this time the committee recommended redistributing the 3.5 per cent visitors' share. Only 3 per cent would go to the visiting club, with the League retaining the remaining 0.5 per cent in a special bank account known as the National Hockey League Joint Relief Fund. The governors then set guidelines for withdrawals from the relief fund. A club could receive an amount equal to one-half its deficit if a majority of the NHL board of governors approved. In the spirit of Calder's fear that financial assistance from the League would lead a club to lose its will to succeed, the League adopted the committee's suggestions that the League and the governors could formally audit an applicant's operation. The governors would then decide on the projected operating budget in order to determine the amount of 'relief' given to the club.[37]

No club ever applied because none wanted to open its books to the scrutiny of the other owners, thereby revealing its strengths and weaknesses. Such a move would entail exposing its methods of operation, prospective talent, and contract negotiations. In other words, the club stood to lose its competitive advantage.

And so, ironically, for the weaker clubs such as Pittsburgh and Ottawa, the establishment of the relief fund meant losing another 0.5 per cent from their revenues.

Ottawa's situation continued to spiral downward. At the end of the 1929–30 season the Auditorium was lacking three-fifths of the payment needed to purchase the Ottawa club. In the purchase agreement, Ahearn had retained the power to dictate the sale of the club's assets, including player contracts, in case of default. To protect his assets Ahearn asked Calder to inform the governors that any sale of the assets must have Ahearn's approval.[38]

Still hoping to keep the team in the city, Fred Burpee put the Ottawa club up for sale, asking $200,000 with provisos that the potential buyer must agree to a ten-year rental agreement with the Auditorium and that the club must play at least 25 per cent of its scheduled games in Ottawa. Burpee set January 10, 1931 as the expiration date for the offer.[39] Its former owner, now turned mortgage-holder, Ahearn, expressed sadness at the state of affairs of the Ottawa club and told Calder that the Auditorium was 'at the end of their rope.' Replying to Calder's comment that someone might be interested in buying the club, he surmised that new blood might be able to turn the club's fortunes around.[40]

The urgency to salvage the Ottawa club could not have come at a more inopportune time. As Canada entered the second full year of the Depression, the commercial failure rate in the Dominion rose dramatically. In 1929, 2310 businesses, with a total value of $44,441,000, had failed. By the end of 1930, the numbers had increased to 2741 and $57,191,000.[41] Under the existing conditions, Calder thought the $200,000 price tag was too high, although he reaffirmed his wish that Ottawa continue operation. As dire economic news filled the newspaper pages, Calder wanted to keep the problems facing his League away from the media and warned Ahearn not to discuss Ottawa's financial troubles with the press.[42]

While its sale was still tentative, the Ottawa club carried on with various stopgap measures to keep itself in operation. Besides transferring some home games to bigger arenas and drawing from its franchise account to pay for the league assessments, it also received much-needed operating capital by selling some of the players. Although Ahearn had promised not to sell his star players, the desperate situation required drastic measures. Before the 1930–1 season, it sold one of its most valuable assets, Frank 'King' Clancy, to Toronto in exchange for a reported $35,000 and two players. It then sold two others to Philadelphia for an undisclosed amount.[43] Pursuing this avenue for much-needed cash was so crucial for Ottawa's solvency that Quain complained to Calder of a pact by other NHL clubs to stop buying players from Ottawa without the approval of the president. He argued that this 'conspiracy and boycott' prevented the Ottawa club from carrying on 'with funds obtained from the transfers of players' contracts.'[44] He blamed the collapse of a three-player deal with the New York Rangers on such a compact and reminded Calder that Ottawa had been the 'meal-ticket' of the NHL in the early years of expansion, when Chicago, Detroit, the Americans, Pittsburgh, Toronto, and Boston were putting in 'farcical performances.' As a sign of his frustration, Quain threatened to release his letter to the press.[45]

It was not surprising that the other governors wanted to prevent Ottawa from selling its players. They realized that their home gates depended, to a large degree, on the competitive strengths of the member clubs. The lowly Pittsburgh/Philadelphia club had not been able to draw a crowd, either at home or on the road, for a number of years. If Ottawa, with its glorious past, sold off its best players and consequently diminished its playing strength, the league would have at least two bad draws for the season.[46] Like today's Montreal Canadiens and Toronto Maple Leafs, who represent hockey's Canadian roots, the Ottawa club was a powerful national symbol in the early twentieth century and the 'Canadianness' of the sport was a major selling point in hockey, especially for the American franchises. When Chicago entered the League, for example, McLaughlin asked Calder specifically for, and received, a Canadian opponent in its home opener. For these reasons, the League wanted the presence of a traditionally competitive Canadian club, even though it denied any meaningful financial aid to Ottawa.[47]

Left to fend for itself, Ottawa soon found another alternative to its dilemma. Near the close of the 1930–1 season, a Chicago group including Paddy Harmon, the failed bidder for a Chicago franchise, Tom Shaughnessy, the ex–Chicago Blackhawks head coach, and James Norris, a multimillionaire, expressed interest in buying the Ottawa club and moving it to Chicago.[48] The problem with this proposal hinged on the willingness of the existing Chicago club owner, McLaughlin, to waive his exclusive territorial rights. In May Quain asked Calder if James Strachan of the Maroons and Leo Dandurand of the Canadiens could persuade McLaughlin to assume 'a more reasonable attitude.'[49] McLaughlin, however, did not want a second major-league team in Chicago, especially since gate attendance had improved after his club moved into the Stadium.[50] Despite his sympathy for Ottawa and his rhetoric about mutual benefit, McLaughlin was not about to sacrifice his market monopoly.

McLaughlin's antagonistic relationship with the Stadium group further handicapped the proposed sale of the Ottawa club to the Norris group. Harmon and Norris were behind the construction of the Chicago Stadium, where the Blackhawks now played. Besides the fact that bad blood existed between McLaughlin and Harmon over the bid for the Chicago franchise, negotiations for the lease (between the Blackhawks and the Stadium) did not ease any tension between the two factions. Replying to Quain's plea for intervention by Dandurand

and Strachan, Calder advised him that Strachan was a friend of Norris 'and, as such, would not meet with any sympathetic hearing ...As a last resort it might be a good plan to have Norris himself tackle the problem – if he cared to, which I am inclined to doubt.'[51]

Given McLaughlin's attitude, the proposed move to Chicago was a dead end for Ottawa. Just before the semi-annual meeting in September, Calder notified McLaughlin that Tom Shaughnessy, on behalf of Norris, would be requesting the transfer of the Ottawa club, to be operated as a second club in Chicago. Calder also told McLaughlin that he had advised Shaughnessy that the application could not proceed without first having McLaughlin's consent.[52] On September 26 the League governors voted to suspend both Pittsburgh's and Ottawa's franchises for one year. The League purchased the rights of players on both clubs for the season and redistributed them to the remaining eight clubs in a draft according to the reverse order of their standings the previous season. Pittsburgh was to receive $20,000 for its players. For Ottawa, the League promised to endorse a $28,000 Bank of Montreal note for the club and $25,000 for its players. Interestingly enough, the motion to suspend Ottawa's operation also included provisions in case Ottawa failed to operate for the two seasons after the current one. The League apparently doubted that Ottawa would operate again.[53]

Despite the suspension, Ottawa did hope to operate again. For one thing, its former owner, Ahearn, believed that Ottawa had a good club that would be an asset to another city. In the aftermath of the semi-annual meeting, Ahearn compared the situation in Pittsburgh with the one in Ottawa. He thought the suspension of the franchise and the loaning of players got Ottawa out of 'an impossible situation. But we had a team and they hadn't. That is proved today ... I could make a few trades that would make a reassembled Ottawa squad a useful team. Philadelphia [Pittsburgh] couldn't do that.'[54]

Ahearn did have other options, or at least possibilities, for his investment. Chicago, Boston, Toronto, and Cleveland were four possible locations if he decided against operating in Ottawa. Of the four, Chicago and Toronto represented real opportunities. Chicago Stadium wanted a second tenant. Conn Smythe, the Toronto owner, had begun building a new arena for his Maple Leafs to begin the 1931-2 season and was eager to find a second tenant.[55] Between these two, Ahearn favoured Toronto, because he wanted to retain 'the Canadian end of major league hockey.' Talks with Smythe on the proposal to move Ottawa to Toronto did not go smoothly, however, because 'a $100,000 guarantee on a 40/60 split ... [was] ... too stiff to tackle. It was $85,000 when we first talked.'[56] Ahearn preferred the Auditorium to keep half an interest and to go to Toronto rather than move to an American city. '[I]t would pay Connie, Joe, and Jim Strachan to buy in [*sic*] the other half interest personally in equal shares. It would be a good gamble and would stop the menace of American control.'[57] Nothing came from these initiatives.

After one year's absence from professional hockey, Ottawa was operating again. Relatively healthy League income and measures to control costs probably convinced Ottawa to re-enter the NHL. During the annual meeting in 1932, Charles Adams moved to remit a $1500 dividend from a $16,460.97 surplus to each of the ten teams operating for the 1930–1 season and a $3000 dividend from a $34,348.48 surplus to each of the eight teams operating in 1931-2. But Dwyer of the Americans added an amendment to the motion to leave the surplus for both seasons in the treasury, with the understanding that only teams operating for the season were eligible to be recipients of the surplus for that season. Over Quain's objection, the governors voted for the Dwyer amendment. At the governors' meeting the same day, the governors also took steps to counter the Depression's effects by cutting roster sizes and instituting a team salary cap of $70,000. Moreover, they agreed to limit an individual player's salary to no more than $7500. Offenders faced a penalty of 'five times the difference between the Seventy Thousand Dollars and the amount actually paid in excess of that amount [and] ten times the difference between Seventy-Five Hundred Dollars and the sum actually paid to any individual player.'[58] Ahearn applauded the measures and especially approved the proposal that the League, instead of the rinks, set dates because it would mean saving on travel costs.[59]

Throughout Ottawa's ordeal, Ahearn had injected nationalistic sentiment into his arguments. One of the proceedings at that May meeting seemed to prove Ahearn's concern correct. Adams of Boston submitted a proposal to move the league's headquarters from Montreal to Detroit during the playing season. All the American governors, except Dwyer of the New York Americans, who abstained, voted in favour; the four Canadian governors voted against the motion. Ahearn lamented the fact that the Canadian teams did not try to control the Ottawa and Philadelphia situations and doubted that Dwyer could be a safeguard for the Canadian clubs much longer. He was especially angry with Toronto's Smythe, who declined to include Ottawa in the new Maple Leaf Gardens. Ahearn fumed: 'Damned if I want to see the team go across the border – *whether Norris comes to terms with McLaughlin or not.* [If the Canadian clubs do not help Ottawa and Dwyer], Adams & Co. would be hard masters.'[60]

During the summer of 1932, Ahearn agonized over the decision to operate. For civic and nationalistic reasons, Ahearn wanted Ottawa back in the league. Since the Auditorium was sinking further by virtue of its losses, Ahearn knew that he would have to 'shoulder the white man's burden again.'[61] He managed to get the players to agree to a pay cut if he kept the club in Ottawa. On October 8 Quain notified Calder that Ahearn would once again assume the presidency of the Ottawa hockey club.[62]

Under Ahearn, Ottawa continued for two more seasons, before moving to St Louis for its last season in professional hockey. The same problems persisted, however, with Ahearn back at the helm of the club. In June of 1933, Ahearn informed Calder that he had given Harvey Pulford an option to buy the team and relocate it in Baltimore. Ahearn did not think Pulford would exercise the option, but the club was in default to the Auditorium's bond-holders and therefore 'must show willingness to sell if the price is right.'[63] The club had lost $17,500 for the 1932–3 season, and by late fall it had only enough funds to operate until December 7.[64] When Ottawa hosted Detroit on November 21, advanced ticket sales to that day amounted to $500.[65] With the country deep into the Depression, Ahearn had given up hope of asking the League for any meaningful long-term solution. Besides, other clubs were beginning to suffer. Along with Ottawa, Pittsburgh, and the New York Americans, Detroit had gone into receivership. Even Madison Square Garden Corporation, the parent of the NHL's financial flagship, the New York Rangers, had shown a net loss for the first time in the 1933–4 fiscal year.[66] Near the end of the 1933–4 season Quain asked Calder for 'the address of the man from St. Louis who approached the League in connection with the franchise there, together with any other information you may have either in your files or in your mind regarding the St Louis situation.'[67] Ottawa became the St Louis Eagles in 1934, but the club's long history came to an end after that season.

Ottawa's demise illustrated the changing nature of the NHL organization. Whatever unity had existed among the owners eroded when the League eliminated its top enemy, Livingstone, from professional hockey. Every member looked after its own interest. For weak teams such as Ottawa, this attitude of individual greed excluded any meaningful assistance from the other members. Although other alternatives were available to Ottawa to salvage the franchise, the self-interest of the other members prevented Ottawa from successfully pursuing any of the offers, even when Ahearn invoked nationalistic sentiments. When Ottawa began selling off its top players, its usefulness to the others in the league diminished. In the end, the League cancelled its membership after the team failed in St Louis. Whereas its internal troubles with weak franchises would continue after the dissolution of the Ottawa club, a threat from without appeared early in the 1930s.

Chapter 11

The Rebellion

As the NHL struggled to deal with its franchise problems, a threat, in the form of a rival league, emerged within the professional hockey network. A number of minor leagues were displeased with the NHL affiliation agreement, especially its draft provision. A group of people who had been denied entry into the NHL took advantage of this sentiment and aligned themselves with one of the malcontents, the AHA. This other group represented investors who had built the Chicago Stadium before the Depression and now believed that the economic downturn would endanger their investment unless they could get a second major-league franchise as a tenant. Despite the deepening of the Depression, the AHA bolted from the NHL minor-league system. Its timing was off, however, and the NHL's influence was so entrenched within the professional hockey network that the AHA retreated to its former status within two years. This minor revolt did produce a tangible asset for the NHL. In the process of quelling the revolt, the League managed to lure away the rebel league's wealthiest financial backer, thus further strengthening the NHL's financial position.

On March 29, 1929 the Chicago Stadium opened with great fanfare, and no one in Chicago was more proud of the Stadium than Patrick T. (Paddy) Harmon. A product of the Chicago street culture, Harmon became a sports promoter in boxing, six-day bicycle racing, and roller skating. In 1926, he tried unsuccessfully to bid for a Chicago NHL franchise, which eventually went to the McLaughlin group. Harmon did not give up his dream, however. With McLaughlin adamantly refusing a second Chicago franchise to all comers, Harmon recognized that Chicago needed a first-rate indoor arena to host all its major events. The existing Chicago Coliseum could not fit the bill. Using some of his own money and canvassing Chicago's wealthy elite for financing, Harmon saw his project completed six months before the October crash. To top it all, McLaughlin's Chicago Blackhawks moved into the Stadium that December.[1]

James Norris Sr was one of Harmon's wealthy Chicago backers. He was a transplanted Canadian who had made his millions in the grain business. His father moved the family to the United States in 1898. By the age of thirty-one, Norris had inherited his father's vast grain empire and ventured into grain trading. While this was a risky speculative venture, Norris did not simply rely on his intuition or lady luck. He transformed the Norris empire into a horizontally integrated network of business units. From his business base in grain, he acquired and controlled grain elevators and transportation companies. His distribution network allowed Norris Grain Incorporated the luxury of reacting to market price fluctuations. Norris also fancied himself as a sportsman. He had played hockey in his younger days in Montreal and was a capable squash player. Chicago Stadium was Norris's first serious venture in the sports industry.[2]

Facility problems plagued McLaughlin's Blackhawks from its inception in 1926. McLaughlin balked at Madison Square Garden's proposal of erecting a Madison Square Garden in Chicago. Madison Square Garden Corporation subsequently aborted the project. While the Blackhawks played most of their games there, the Chicago Coliseum was not really a suitable venue. As the Chicago Stadium was being constructed, the Stadium authorities began negotiations with McLaughlin to move the Blackhawks into the new building. Having sustained losses since the club's first year of operation, McLaughlin was fighting hard to get a favourable lease. An exasperated Norris appealed to Calder at the beginning of the 1928–9 season to step in as arbitrator between McLaughlin and the Stadium.[3] The Chicago Stadium was not ready in time for the 1928–9 season, and the difficulties between the two parties continued. Near the end of the 1928–9 season, Bill Tobin, the Blackhawks' business manager, advised Calder that the team planned to play in the Coliseum next season and did not anticipate 'deals of any kind with Harmon and Norris and Stadium.'[4]

McLaughlin's hard-nosed negotiations annoyed the Stadium management. It began exploring other alternatives to fill the hockey calendar. In March of 1929 Harmon and Norris held talks with Frank Patrick about the possibility of Patrick organizing a team in Chicago. One proposal had Patrick purchasing an existing NHL club and, together with a few reinforcements from Patrick's new Pacific Coast minor league, moving the club into the Chicago Stadium. Another proposal from Harmon was for Patrick to bring the entire Pacific Coast minor league to Chicago and form a city league, with Patrick as president of the league. Lloyd Turner of the AHA Minneapolis club was apparently in on the second scheme, but was unable to convince the other AHA clubs to go along. On the other hand, McLaughlin had not forgotten that Patrick and Harmon were two of the people who had threatened to start a rival league with a franchise in Chicago in 1926.[5]

In spite of these new developments, McLaughlin continued negotiations with the Stadium. By early April he informed Calder that the two sides were not too far apart, but complained that the Stadium's terms were exorbitant. He doubted that the Blackhawks could fill the Stadium and worried about the 'depressing' effect of 'a small crowd in a big building ... It would seem silly to order much larger shoes when our present ones aren't even tight, and we probably won't be able to walk at all in the new shoes.'[6] McLaughlin's financial analysis of the situation was sound. But what perhaps galled him most in the negotiations with the Stadium was the use of the threat of a rival league by the Stadium management. McLaughlin had enough trouble in his hockey enterprise as it was without having to worry about such threats.

Chicago faced more problems than attendance. Besides financial losses accumulated by the Blackhawks, Livingstone's lawsuit against McLaughlin and the Coliseum was still ongoing. Moreover, McLaughlin was ever suspicious of a conspiracy by some other league governors against him and his club. Being a novice in hockey at the western outpost of the NHL, he felt isolated and had long complained about Chicago's inability to secure players and the reluctance of other clubs to trade players with Chicago. Partly to hedge his interest and partly as a negotiation tactic, McLaughlin submitted to the Coliseum on 20 April a list of possible dates for the following season. At the end of April McLaughlin informed Calder that negotiations with the Chicago Stadium had fallen through because 'we find dealing with Messrs Norris and Harmon too much of an ordeal to continue.'[7] As for the Patrick-Harmon faction, they immediately asked Calder to consider putting a second franchise in Chicago. Calder rejected their request outright and asked them to seek consent from McLaughlin.[8]

McLaughlin had to be an astute businessman to hold his business empire together, and he would not let a good offer slip away. Between the time when he submitted dates to the Coliseum and the beginning of the 1929–30 season, he secured a one-year lease with the Stadium authorities. (There are no details extant on the lease with the Stadium.) The Blackhawks finally moved into the large arena after playing six games in the Coliseum in the 1929–30 season. The gate receipts for the season justified the move. For the first six games, the average gate was $8296.86; it was $14,033.88 for the remainder. In the first game played at the Stadium, the club netted $20,462, even though it played the lowly Pittsburgh club.[9] Yet the brief duration of the lease necessitated the same kind of antagonistic negotiation at the end of the 1929–30 season. Seeing that the Blackhawks had done well, the Stadium wanted a bigger piece of the pie. Whereas the Stadium had allowed the League the first $7500 for the entire playoffs, it now wanted at least $7500 rent per game.[10]

A second component of the rebel group came from the minor-league American Hockey Association (AHA). Around the same time that McLaughlin and the Chicago Stadium authority started their negotiations for a new lease, grumbling from the minor leagues also began to surface. In early April, the AHA's president, A.G. Warren, approached Calder regarding the renewal of the affiliation agreement. Although the agreement would not expire until September, Warren wanted to discuss 'possible modification of [the] draft.'[11] It appeared that many of the AHA clubs were unhappy with the draft, arguing that the drafting of their star players by the NHL clubs affected their gate receipts. In addition, the clubs found that the NHL clubs often immediately sold the drafted players 'to some other clubs which might not be interested in the particular player.'[12] Calder reassured Warren that the NHL would not 'act in arbitrary manner in its relations with minor leagues if ... it can be clearly shown that minor league clubs are to be sufferers by reason of affiliation.'[13] He further suggested that Warren find another man for the office of commissioner (which Calder now held) because critics doubted if the minor leagues could get a fair deal with Calder at the helm. Both men agreed to meet and renegotiate a new affiliation agreement. Since most of the AHA clubs were located in the Midwest and McLaughlin had had a hand in previous negotiations with the AHA, Calder invited the Chicago owner to the meeting. In reply, McLaughlin asked Calder to ensure the presence of the AHA's Tulsa club owner, Walter Whiteside, who seemed 'to be the dominating figure in that league.'[14]

Since the AHA began expanding southward in the 1927–8 season, it had been undergoing a power shift. Old-timers such as Warren were losing their influence. By the end of the 1929–30 season, only three of the original AHA clubs, St Paul, Minneapolis, and Duluth, remained. Three southern clubs, Kansas City, St Louis, and Tulsa, formed the other half of the AHA. Whiteside was present during the May 2 meeting and was very particular in clarifying the terms of the agreement. He also hinted that the AHA might not renew its affiliation with the NHL and might operate as an independent league. When the meeting was over, however, both sides had come to a tentative understanding that the AHA would renew the agreement for another three years if the NHL agreed to Warren's suggestion that each minor-league club's players could be drafted only every other year.[15]

If the meeting between the NHL and AHA representatives placated the AHA's major concern about the draft, it did not address the desire of the AHA's friends at the Chicago Stadium to place another franchise in Chicago. Within five days after the meeting with the AHA, the NHL received an application for a second franchise in Chicago from the Stadium president.[16] During the governors' meeting on May 10 the League reiterated its position that a second Chicago franchise must have the approval of the current Chicago franchise.[17]

These developments were probably not coincidences and suggested that the relationship between the Chicago Stadium and the AHA, established the previous year by Patrick and Harmon, remained strong. Harmon's desire to own a professional hockey team, the Stadium's desire for a second tenant and a better deal with McLaughlin, the dissatisfaction of the minor leagues with the draft, and Whiteside's ambition to enter major-league hockey surfaced, and all these elements converged in that late spring of 1930. On May 21 Calder advised Warren that the International Hockey League (IHL), formerly the Can-Pro, would not agree to Warren's modification of the draft. Instead, it wanted to either eliminate the draft altogether or raise the price to $7500. At the same time, Whiteside approached the IHL's Toronto club owner, Ted Oke, 'with a proposition to link up some of the American Association clubs with a club in the Chicago Stadium, one in Cleveland ... one in Detroit ... and others to be decided on if and as the thing develops.'[18] McLaughlin, who was absent from the May 10 meeting, also informed Calder that the former Blackhawks coach, Tom Shaughnessy, 'presumably backed by Norris or the Stadium,' had been negotiating to buy the Minneapolis team of the AHA in order to move the team to Chicago 'if the rest of his league will back him in that attempt.'[19] Warren confirmed what Calder and McLaughlin had suspected, telling them that Whiteside was 'reaching in all directions for a hook-up which is more satisfying to his taste than his present association.'[20] An insurrection was imminent.

In the summer of 1930, this insurrection was gaining momentum within the AHA. Warren continued to be in the minority, wanting to sign the agreement as proposed on May 2. Within his own league, however, Whiteside had persuaded the southern end of the AHA to join his fight against the NHL and Warren. In the AHA's northern loop, Shaughnessy had bought the Minneapolis club. In a coup d'état, the conspirators revoked an AHA constitutional bylaw forbidding the transfer of franchises to different cities until there were ten clubs in the league. This paved the way for Shaughnessy to move his club to Chicago.[21] Outside the AHA, the Can-Am and the PCHL also advocated the elimination of the draft. By late June it appeared that Warren had lost power in the AHA. He told Calder that if the AHA did not approve the renewal of the affiliation agreement, he would sell his club.[22] At the beginning of July the AHA announced the addition of the Chicago Shamrocks for the coming season. The rebellion was on.

The economic power of the NHL played an important role in the League's dealings with the rebels. As the AHA marched into Chicago, other minor leagues began to fall in line with the NHL. Despite their dissatisfaction with the draft, the other minor leagues also recognized the potential consequences if they sided with the AHA. As the Depression deepened, many minor-league clubs found it difficult to make ends meet. Many could not even afford to pay the full salaries stipulated in the players' contracts, and a few were teetering on the edge of bankruptcy. They realized that an economic war was certain if they joined the rebels. And without a wealthy financier like Norris in their own leagues they knew they did not have the resources to combat the NHL. The NHL also did its part to isolate the AHA in professional hockey by holding out a carrot to the other minor leagues. It agreed not to draft players from the same club in consecutive years. Subsequent to this announcement, all but the AHA renewed the affiliation agreement. In preparation for a showdown with the AHA, the NHL warned players that 'participation in the games of any club or leagues not affiliated with the National League shall render them ineligible for participation in the games of the National Hockey League or of its affiliated leagues.'[23]

As the other minor leagues had agreed to renew their affiliation with the NHL by late August, an awkward situation existed. The affiliation agreement would not expire until September 24, but the AHA had openly placed a club in Chicago without the consent of the Blackhawks. To counter this scenario, Calder chose a persona-non-grata strategy with the new AHA Chicago club. In early September, Shaughnessy tried unsuccessfully to arrange a meeting regarding the renewal of affiliation. Calder rejected any proposed meeting where a Chicago Shamrocks' representative would be present. Failing in his efforts, Shaughnessy and the AHA's Kansas City club owner, William Grant, surprised Calder by paying him an unannounced visit. What followed became somewhat farcical. Calder remained adamant about not discussing league matters in the presence of a Chicago Shamrocks representative. Grant then launched a monologue complaining about his bad treatment by the Blackhawks. As he went on, a circular announcing the opening game of the Chicago Shamrocks on November 27 arrived in Calder's office. When Calder showed the handbill to Shaughnessy and Grant, the two became embarrassed and Shaughnessy suggested that 'if there could be no agreement at least there would be no semblance of fight from [the] Association.'[24]

If Shaughnessy and the AHA did not want an open fight, the NHL more or less obliged. From the outset, Calder's strategy was to ignore and isolate the AHA, now renamed the American Hockey League (AHL). On October 8 Calder wired the various minor-league affiliates, advising them that the AHL had granted franchises in Chicago and Buffalo, where the IHL had a franchise, without the consent of the existing franchises. He reminded them that the affiliation agreement forbade them having any dealings with the AHL.[25] After the League meeting on October 18 Calder publicly denounced the AHL as an outlaw league and warned players who signed with the AHL clubs that they would be 'barred from organized hockey, [and] can expect no protection ... in the matter of salaries.'[26] Moreover, Calder extended the banishment to any NHL referees working in the AHL games.[27]

To further consolidate the alliance with the affiliated minor leagues, the NHL reversed its previous policy and allowed its members to wholly own minor-league clubs. The NHL constitution forbade such ownership unless the governors assented unanimously. Yet some clubs already had a financial interest in minor-league clubs, and Detroit, for example, actually owned the minor-league club Detroit Olympics. McLaughlin and Adams were vocal opponents because they thought the practice would place those clubs without a minor-league club at a disadvantage.[28] During the December 1 meeting, the two protested.[29] Somehow the governors were able to come to an agreement whereby the League permitted the ownership of a minor-league club if such ownership was not 'detrimental to the interests' of the rest of the NHL clubs. Following the agreement, the League granted the two New York teams, Detroit, and Boston such a privilege regarding clubs in the Can-Am and the IHL.[30] With their ownership came voting rights in the affairs of the minor leagues. This action had the effect of tightening the NHL's influence over the professional hockey network.

Calder's strategy departed from the behaviour of rival leagues in previous hockey wars, where parties went at each other's most important assets, the players. In this latest round, there was hardly any talk of player raids. In large part, the AHL was a minor league and thus had few players whom the NHL coveted. Moreover, with the exception of Chicago, the AHL cities were relatively small when compared to NHL cities. Thus, Calder was gambling that the financial burden placed on small-market teams, especially during an economic depression, would eventually destroy the AHL.

Yet, not everyone in the NHL, especially the Chicago club, agreed with Calder's strategy. McLaughlin was particularly impatient with Calder's sit-and-wait attitude. Since the Chicago Stadium was a major force behind the formation of the AHL, the Blackhawks were on the front line in this hockey war. While Shaughnessy suggested civility between the leagues, the Stadium was not making life easy for McLaughlin. Even before the 1930–1 season began, the Stadium gave preferential treatment to the AHL Shamrocks when it was securing dates for its season.[31] In early January McLaughlin complained to Calder about the NHL's policy toward the AHL and asked that a stronger stance be taken. He noted that the Chicago press did not even consider that a war existed between the leagues and questioned why Calder did not publicize the resolution to blacklist anyone found dealing with the AHL.[32]

The new season saw a continuation of McLaughlin's troubles with the AHL operating in his territory. In submitting a list of possible game dates for the 1931–2 season, the Stadium refused to give the Blackhawks Tuesday and Thursday nights, the usual game nights. Instead, the Blackhawks received Wednesdays. Since the League traditionally had Tuesday and Thursday night games, Wednesdays were usually travel days.[33] This greatly inconvenienced the NHL's scheduling. Just before the season began, the Shamrocks placed McLaughlin in an embarrassing situation by agreeing to play a charity game against the Blackhawks for the relief of the unemployed. Calder had to deny permission for the Blackhawks to play in the match.[34]

While the AHL posed a threat to the Chicago franchise, McLaughlin was most incensed about the lack of support from his fellow governors. He knew that Norris was a friend to several NHL governors and that Ottawa was contemplating selling its franchise to Norris, who proposed moving it to Chicago. McLaughlin told Calder that the other NHL owners were all too 'friendly' with the AHL and that such a relationship would not exist when the AHL saw fit to invade other NHL cities. He questioned the attitude of his fellow owners: 'A little loyalty in the NHL might not be a bad idea. Don't you think that it might be to your interest as well as to ours, for you to work up some such feeling among the Governors?'[35] When a newspaper article announcing the signing of an Ottawa player by the Shamrocks appeared, he mailed Calder the clipping as evidence that Ottawa was too friendly with Norris and Shaughnessy.[36] Dissatisfied with Calder's reply, McLaughlin restated his case for a unified front, because if the Blackhawks fell in the standings and the Shamrocks led in the AHL, the Blackhawks might lose support. '[T]he public here are even yet not too hockey wise and so league standings mean a lot to them, irrespective of the worth of the league.'[37]

McLaughlin's apprehension about the AHL disappeared after the 1931–2 season. Calder's strategy of letting the Depression do the work of destroying the AHL succeeded. On the whole, the AHL had not been a successful venture. Of the seven clubs that began the 1930–1 season, Minneapolis dropped out after the season ended. Shortly after the 1931–2 season began, the Buffalo franchise also folded. Moreover, Calder began receiving complaints from AHL players about non-payment of salaries. Most, if not all, of these complainants wanted to be reinstated into the NHL, which, despite having several troubled franchises, did not lapse in paying its players.[38] Three AHL players actually applied for reinstatement, but were turned down. To add weight to the NHL's resolve against the AHL, the governors passed a motion 'to make ipso facto ineligible for reinstatement ... any players playing in any games that involved non-affiliated clubs.'[39]

As a last-ditch effort to legitimize the AHL's major-league status, league president Grant issued a Stanley Cup challenge. Calder immediately rebuffed the challenge by reason of the AHL being an 'outlaw' league.[40] No one was happier over Calder's blunt response than McLaughlin: 'Just heard from Associated Press your statement relative to American Challenge. Congratulate you heartily it was fine.'[41]

The AHL's dream of major-league hockey glory declined quickly in the late winter of 1932. When Calder officially turned down the challenge presented by the Cup trustees, Grant became desperate. Troubles with players had reached the press, as two St Louis players openly jumped their contracts, claiming that the club had not paid their salaries thus making them free agents. Seizing the moment to embarrass the AHL, McLaughlin immediately started contract nego-tiations with the two players.[42] Grant pleaded with Foran to allow an AHL delegation to meet with the trustees and the NHL in order to settle the matter. Grant rebutted Calder's three charges that the AHL was an outlaw league, that it was financially unsound, and that it played an inferior brand of hockey.[43] Foran suggested to Calder that the NHL should consider the request. In deference to the Cup trustee, Calder agreed to bring the matter up during the governors' meeting in March.[44]

Sensing that the AHL was struggling to stay alive, the NHL tightened the noose. It continued its strategy of not acknowledging the AHL as a major league. At the March NHL governors' meeting, league members voted to 'take no further official action in the Stanley Cup controversy' after Calder reported back from his interview with Foran.[45] Without the legitimation of appearing in a Stanley Cup series, the AHL became less and less of a threat. Moreover, the NHL also considered fragmenting the AHL. In late March, McLaughlin told Calder that he had no objection to Norris coming into the league, as long as Shaughnessy remained out. He suggested that there 'would be a speedy parting between the two' if Norris knew that he could be part of the NHL without Shaughnessy.[46]

By hinting to Norris that he might be welcomed into the NHL, the League was poised to separate the AHL's major financial backer from the rest of the clubs. A majority shareholder of the Stadium, James Norris had tried unsuccessfully to break into the NHL clique on several occasions. With the AHL seemingly falling apart at the seams, it was time for him to abandon ship. Looking at different alternatives in order to align himself with the victors, Norris submitted an application for an NHL franchise in St Louis.[47] During the League annual meeting in May, the governors turned down Norris's application 'because of the additional travelling expense ... entailed by the inclusion of the city of St. Louis in the circuit.'[48] It was the right move, but the wrong city, for Norris. He would, however, get another chance.

Although Norris's latest application did not succeed, the bankrupted Detroit franchise presented Norris with another opportunity. Detroit had become an ailing franchise shortly after its inception. Its revenue steadily declined after the first two seasons.[49] By the summer of 1931 the club and the Detroit Olympia, its home arena, had come under the control of its creditors, who formed a bond-holders' committee to oversee the club's affairs. Since Detroit had not fully paid its franchise fees, Calder sat on the bond-holders' committee as an interested creditor. On July 1, 1931 its default payment was more than $21,000 and the club had accumulated more than $47,000 in unpaid taxes.[50] Despite its indebtedness, the bond-holders saw the continued operation of the club as the way to recoup their investment. But by the summer of 1932 the trust company overseeing the Detroit franchise was having trouble getting financing. Detroit's former owner, Charles Hughes, advised Calder that 'the only prospect the Trust Company has for outside money is Mr. Norris of Chicago.'[51]

In the late summer of 1932 the NHL had more or less quelled the rebellion. On August 18 Grant asked to meet with Calder to re-affiliate his league with the NHL after the Shamrocks withdrew from the AHL.[52] Norris was instrumental in dissolving the Shamrocks club. Near the end of August, Calder had successfully negotiated with AHL representatives the re-affiliation of the AHL, based on three conditions: 1. The AHL must vacate the city of Chicago. 2. The AHL was to affiliate with the NHL as a minor league. 3. The AHL must return all players that previously belonged to NHL clubs.[53] On October 1 the NHL governors ratified the affiliation of the AHL, which had now reverted to its old name, the American Hockey Association.[54]

In return for his help in settling the AHL matters, the NHL later approved James Norris's purchase of the Detroit club from its receiver, the Union Guardian Trust Company, which had won the bid in the foreclosure sale of the club in the fall of 1933.[55] Norris officially became the Detroit club governor in November of that year. So ended the latest challenge to the NHL by a rival professional hockey league – a threat that would not reappear for the next forty-odd years.[56]

The saga of the AHL's rebellion demonstrated the superior economic power of the NHL. Even as the Depression was hurting clubs in both leagues, the deep financial pockets of the NHL allowed it to outlast the AHL. Moreover, the NHL's economic muscle also played a part in preventing the rebellion from becoming more widespread. Alone in the rebellion, the AHL struggled. And when Norris decided to change sides, the AHL's dream of major-league glory vanished.

Chapter 12

In the Best Interests of Hockey

Even with the destruction of the AHL as a major league, the NHL could not claim to be the only powerful organization in the world of commercialized hockey. The Canadian Amateur Hockey Association (CAHA) remained the largest hockey organization in Canada and, in the eyes of the NHL governors, held the largest reserve of players. During the twenties, the CAHA enjoyed the same prosperity that the NHL did. Its membership, as well as its influence, grew. With branches in every province of the Dominion, the CAHA had, in terms of control mechanisms, as elaborate a system as the NHL's. An executive board oversaw the policies of the organization. The powerful office of the national registrar considered and ruled on the eligibility of all hockey players under the CAHA's umbrella. To ensure its sphere of influence, the CAHA affiliated with the Amateur Athletic Union of Canada (AAUC) after the First World War, and accepted the rigid AAUC definition of an amateur. Through its affiliation with the AAUC, the CAHA also participated in organized international competition. With the introduction of the Winter Olympics in 1924, the CAHA sent its senior championship club to represent Canada in the quadrennial event.[1]

By the 1930s, however, the CAHA had come under financial strain because the economic downturn adversely affected the commercialized aspect of amateur hockey. Economic pressure eventually magnified the conflicting demands of amateur ideology and the commercialized hockey-player market. Fearing the loss of control over its player supply, the CAHA made an alliance with the NHL that allowed the NHL access to the vast CAHA player reserve and ensured the NHL a steady supply of players. After 1936, when the first agreement was made between the NHL and the CAHA, the latter was, for all intents and purposes, on its way to becoming a subsidiary of the NHL.

At the beginning of the 1930s, the commercial aspect of amateur hockey suffered with the onset of the Great Depression. The CAHA was running a deficit.

Between 1933 and 1936, the CAHA incurred losses of $13,998.58, $11,112.76, $11,325.49, and $12,499.57 respectively. One reason was the decrease in playoff receipts from the Allan Cup, the senior championship, and the Memorial Cup, the junior championship. With the exception of 1935, at least one of the two Cup series lost money in each of these years. In 1936, the Allan and the Memorial Cup series had a combined loss of $4181.71. The expenditure-to-revenue ratio for these years ranged from two to nearly five times.[2]

Economic difficulties were not the only problem facing the CAHA in the 1930s. They also magnified the split in the ideological underpinning of amateur sports between the purists and the liberals. Even in the twenties, some amateur sport administrators, especially those who resided in small isolated towns in the western provinces, advocated a more liberal interpretation of amateurism. They faced the same problems in amateur sports as in earlier times – the difficulty of finding enough players to fill a team and the once-a-professional-always-a-professional dictum of the AAUC, which disallowed the mixing of amateurs and professionals. In 1928 the Saskatchewan delegates to the AAUC meeting petitioned for an amendment to the AAUC constitution that would permit a professional of one sport to be registered as an amateur in another. This petition, which had come to be known as the Saskatchewan Amendment, was a contentious issue. By 1932, however, it had gained support outside the western provinces as the amendment resurfaced at the annual meeting that year. When the AAUC executives moved to establish a committee to study the amendment, the Ottawa delegate to the meeting objected strenuously. He charged the AAUC with pigeonholing the matter of amateurism and pointed to the commercial aspect of amateur hockey. He further referred to the English practice of allowing the mixing of professional and amateur players and hinted that 'some players with politics' were allowed to bypass scrutiny.[3]

Player problems compounded the CAHA's economic woes and ideological struggles. Like the NHL, the CAHA considered players the most important assets of a club. It is true that amateurism defined membership in the CAHA. To stabilize player movement, the residence rule protected the property rights of the clubs. Discussions on player transfers arose often in CAHA meetings and usually generated heated debate. Despite the growth in membership, top CAHA clubs were losing players to the NHL. With a professional minor-league system in place after 1927, there were even more defections from top amateur clubs. While the minor leagues were unhappy with the NHL drafting of their players, they still received compensation. A strict amateur code afforded the CAHA no such arrangement, even its possibility, with the NHL.

A related issue was the signing of underage players. The CAHA started developing players at younger ages in grass-roots programs across Canada. Between 1928 and 1935, the CAHA gave out grants totalling $36,240.02 to develop players in the bantam, juvenile, and midget categories.[4] These development programs aimed to popularize hockey. For the clubs, they served as feeders to the senior squads. The NHL, however, had no qualms about taking underage players as long as the clubs thought the players could perform at the professional level. Moreover, the NHL had increased its roster size from twelve players and two reserves in 1925 to twenty players in 1931, adding to the demand for skilled players.[5] If a young player tried out with a professional club but could not make the team, he would be banned from amateur competition forever under the strict definition of an amateur. With the onset of the Great Depression, some in the CAHA believed that more players would be willing to take that chance. In May of 1930, a CAHA delegation met with the NHL governors during the NHL annual meeting and requested that NHL clubs refrain from drafting junior players.[6] In June William Hewitt, the CAHA's national registrar, submitted a proposal in this regard. It allowed the NHL to try out players over twenty-one years of age, 'without remuneration, except for actual expenses, and without participation in any games' if the professional hockey circuits agreed not to sign anyone under that age.[7] Hewitt explained that the proposal, if accepted, would help to develop an amateur player 'without cost to the professional clubs.' The amateurs 'would ... have their full junior schooling and one year in senior company before going into the money ranks.'[8] For whatever reasons, the NHL tabled the proposal. Beginning in 1933 however, the CAHA began to allow amateur players to try out with professional clubs, with the proviso that such players could not participate in any amateur competitions during the tryout period. If any player failed to make the grade, the CAHA would consider accepting his re-entry into the amateur rank.[9]

The demand for skilled CAHA players did not come from the NHL alone. Canadian hockey players had been crossing the border to the United States for a long time. By the summer of 1935, however, England had become the latest country to promote hockey in earnest. In his annual report on player movement for the 1935–6 season, registrar Hewitt informed the delegates that English hockey representatives had been recruiting players in different parts of Canada since August of 1935. Alarmed by the potential loss of elite players, CAHA president E.A. Gilroy issued a warning to all CAHA players that they must obtain approval from the CAHA before they could play hockey in England. In late September the CAHA met with representatives of the British Ice Hockey Association (BIHA), who agreed not to use any player without the CAHA's sanction. When the CAHA executives decided not to grant further transfers, however, the BIHA ignored the September agreement. Subsequently, the CAHA suspended twenty-two players for the 1935–6 season because they had played in England without the CAHA's approval.[10]

Various commercialized hockey governing bodies, such as the NHL, the

CAHA, and the BIHA, recognized that, in large part, the quality of the players determined the entertainment value of hockey and, hence, the potential gate receipts. During economic hard times, when jobs were scarce, a possible career in professional hockey was likely just as good a prospect for a man as searching for one of the few jobs available. Thus, many hockey players were willing to listen to the hockey promoters when they came calling. The promise of a paycheque seemed worth the risk of a lifetime ban from amateur hockey.[11]

Facing aggressive recruiting efforts from the NHL, the BIHA, and American hockey promoters, the CAHA's executives realized that the lure of monetary compensation in harsh economic times was too tempting for amateur players, and finally confronted this reality at the 1935 CAHA annual meeting. On the recommendation of a special committee, the executives proposed a four-point change in the definition of an amateur. If passed, the resolution would allow players to receive payment 'for salary or wages deducted while playing hockey,' also known as broken-time payment, and would relax the definition of an amateur by allowing a professional in another sport to play amateur hockey.[12]

Heated debate ensued. While some argued the revisions did not go far enough, others worried about their impact on the prestige of the CAHA as the leading amateur-hockey governing body and how these changes might affect the CAHA's relations with other amateur bodies. The president of the AAUC, William Fry, who was attending the meeting as a CAHA lifetime member, was especially vigorous in trying to tone down the proposal, which, he pointed out, would have far-reaching consequences because of the CAHA's affiliation with the AAUC as well as the Ligue Internationale de Hockey sur Glace (LIHG), the ruling international governing body. Fry further argued that the players would be caught in the middle should the AAUC and the LIHG, among others, decide against making the same changes. Since many hockey players also participated in other sports, the changes would effectively ban them from all sports except hockey. In the end, the reformers won the day and the CAHA approved the four-point proposal. Fry, however, gained a reprieve in one respect by having the CAHA agree to meet and discuss the changes with an AAUC committee before proceeding any further.[13]

The CAHA's move towards liberalizing its definition of an amateur was a bold one because it could very well isolate the CAHA in the amateur sports network. In controlling amateur sports, its different governing bodies allied themselves with one another to consolidate the rule of amateurism. If an athlete violated the amateur code, the force of a suspension on that player became much more restrictive when it was honoured by other allied sport bodies. Certainly, the stark economic reality of the Depression pushed the CAHA to depart from the strict amateur definition still adopted by other major national and international sports governing bodies. But the CAHA also took the gamble in part because of its recent unpleasant experiences with the BIHA and the American AAU over the transfer of players, which left the CAHA wondering about the usefulness of its alliances.

Perhaps most disheartening to the CAHA about these alliances was Canada's first-ever defeat in international competition at the 1936 Olympic ice-hockey tournament at Garmisch-Partenkirchen, Germany. Even before the Olympic team left Canada, controversy over the selection of players was plaguing the CAHA. When the team arrived in Germany, it found that Great Britain was insisting on including two suspended CAHA players on its team. In the name of good sportsmanship, the CAHA allowed the two players to play in the tournament. Subsequently, the British team defeated Canada two to one in the semi-final round, the first time Canada had ever lost in Olympic competitions. Canada finished second behind Britain in their group. According to press reports, one of the suspended players, Jimmy Foster, was spectacular as the goalkeeper for Britain. A bigger shock came when the Canadian team found out that unlike the early rounds, where a round-robin format was used to determine the standings for each group of the participating nations, the results from the semi-final round among the four finalists would carry over to the final standings. Thus, Canada would not play Britain again since it had already lost to the British. When the Canadian delegation protested the change in the format, both the American and British representatives were adamant that rules should not be changed in the middle of the tournament. With a victory over Canada already in hand, Britain won the gold medal by defeating Czechoslovakia and tying the United States. Canada took the silver.[14]

Smarting from its Olympic experience and the pressures on its players from other hockey organizations, the CAHA pushed on in late spring of 1936 with its agenda to redefine what an amateur was. It was as if the Athletic War was being fought over again. Amateur purists fired their replies to the CAHA's four-point proposal in May. After convincing the CAHA delegates in the 1935 meeting that he would arrange a meeting between the AAUC and the CAHA, Fry now announced that there would be no meeting. He pointed out that the AAUC delegates in their previous annual meeting had already rejected the various proposals seeking to alter the definition of an amateur and had dismissed one of the CAHA's proposed changes. Fry suggested that a meeting taking up the same issues would not serve any purpose. 'No clearer ultimatum could have been given the sport world that the union was going to stand by its principles,' said Fry.[15]

Sensing an opportunity in the opening of the CAHA player market, the NHL governors voted to establish a committee to deal with 'conditions that have arisen in the amateur situation.'[16] Calder wrote CAHA registrar Hewitt, whose son was an employee of the NHL's Toronto club, and asked him to set up a meeting between the two bodies.[17] On May 23 the representatives from the NHL and the CAHA met at the Royal York Hotel in Toronto and negotiated an agreement that consisted of four points:

1. The Canadian Amateur Hockey Association shall recognise all suspensions imposed on players by the National Hockey League, and its affiliated minor leagues; and the National Hockey League and its affiliated minor leagues shall recognise all suspensions imposed on players by the Canadian Amateur Hockey Association.

2. No player registered with the Canadian Amateur Hockey Association, eligible to play with a junior club, shall be taken by a professional club unless with the consent of the junior club with which the player is registered.

3. Notice shall be given to the Canadian Amateur Hockey Association by a professional club, not later than August 15th in each year, of its intention to sign to a contract or to 'try out' any player registered with the Association; and if the player is not signed by November 15th he shall not be taken during the season commencing on or about that date, unless with the consent of the club with which he is registered.

4. The Canadian Amateur Hockey Association shall adopt the playing rules of the National Hockey League in their entirety, but shall not be required to make any alterations in the rules during the progress of a season.[18]

Yet not everyone was happy about the negotiated agreement.

Certainly the agreement with the CAHA favoured the NHL. Mutual recognition of suspension tightened further the control of player movement. Most important was the adoption of the NHL's playing rules. This, in effect, gave the NHL the decision-making power to mould the product, and implicitly acknowledged the superiority of the NHL brand as well as its authority in the production of commercialized hockey games. Standardizing the game also helped to prepare aspiring amateurs for the professional game and could potentially decrease the cost of developing a player. For its part, the CAHA needed to have a solution to control, if not stop, the draining of its players. As it was on the brink of breaking with the AAUC, the CAHA needed an agreement with one of the sources of its player troubles. In the presence of CAHA officials, the Oshawa coach summed up the amateur-hockey situation during an OHA award ceremony in 1936. He doubted the effectiveness of changing the definition of an amateur in stopping the migration of players to other countries. Instead, he suggested that the CAHA should cooperate with other hockey federations that needed Canadian hockey players. Starting from a position of strength, however, the NHL was able to get even more than the above negotiated points.[19]

The conflict between self-interest and group goals within the NHL surfaced in the agreement with the CAHA. While Hewitt acknowledged acceptance of the terms, a number of NHL governors were unhappy with the agreement. Lester Patrick of the Rangers objected to the CAHA agreement:'[T]he National League is getting very little and the CAHA is getting everything that they want. And they are an amateur group with no investments and a depleted treasury.'[20] He particularly disliked the first and second provisions of the agreement. The Maroons owner also voiced his displeasure with the first clause.[21]

With dissension at work among the governors, the NHL brought up the CAHA agreement in its July league meeting. The governors added further provisions to the agreement. Above all, they wanted a board of appeal where suspensions could be disputed. One member from each of the two governing bodies, as well as Calder, was to serve on the board.[22] In submitting the revised version of the agreement, Calder added that 'the British Ice Hockey Association should respect the negotiation list of the NHL.'[23] He further assured Hewitt that the NHL would honour any agreement reached between the CAHA, the BIHA, and the AAU.

Realizing the unfavourable position it was in, the CAHA tried to form new alliances in order to protect its control over amateur hockey in Canada. It reached an agreement with the BIHA in late June. As in the previous agreement, the BIHA acknowledged the CAHA's authority over Canadian amateur hockey by promising to take only those players who had the CAHA's sanction. Any suspended player from the previous year would revert to the authority of the CAHA. Moreover, the BIHA agreed to take no more than one player from any CAHA club and the CAHA had the power to determine 'to which British Club a transfer may be allowed in the event that there may be applications for more than one player from any Canadian club to a club in the British IHA.'[24]

With an agreement with the BIHA in hand, the CAHA turned to North America. In mid-September 1936 the CAHA executives met with the NHL committee again in Toronto. During the meeting, the CAHA advised the NHL that it was getting close to reaching an agreement with the American amateur-hockey authorities and that its agreement with the BIHA protected the NHL as well. The CAHA however, objected to the make-up of the appeal board.[25] By late September, the CAHA had also reached an agreement with the Americans.[26]

As the new hockey season approached, the CAHA was eager to have the alliance in place. Two days after the NHL-CAHA meeting, CAHA first vice-president W.G. Hardy (who, significantly, also represented the CAHA's Alberta branch) visited with Conn Smthye at Maple Leaf Gardens. Hardy told a surprised Smythe that the CAHA would withdraw its objection about the appeal board. It was not clear what had led to such a change of heart, but on September 21

Hewitt advised Calder that the CAHA executives had approved the agreement as first set out in May, including the NHL amendments that practically gave the NHL everything it wanted.[27] During the NHL semi-annual meeting in September, the NHL governors approved the agreement with the CAHA for one year.[28]

With the alliance set, the CAHA awaited the AAUC's reaction to the four-point proposal. When the conservatives in the AAUC successfully defeated the CAHA's four-point proposal that November, the CAHA broke with its long-time ally.[29] Addressing the delegates to the 1937 CAHA annual meeting, the president justified the move as 'in the best interests of hockey in Canada.'[30]

During much of the 1930s, the NHL solidified its status as a powerful organization. In large part, the Great Depression was instrumental in drawing the League's attention to its internal weaknesses, exposing its disaffected opponents, and subjugating the CAHA. The NHL's responses to these issues reveal the beliefs and values of the decision-makers who shaped the League's organizational policies. Particularly in its handling of the weak franchises within the league, the NHL chose a strategy of minimal intervention, effectively eliminating the possibility of collective action by these clubs. The weak clubs might have survived had economic conditions been better, but the preference for individual initiative doomed clubs such as Ottawa, Pittsburgh, and the New York Americans given the tight market for capital investments and restricted consumer spending. Detroit would have gone the way of the others had the AHA rebellion not taken place. In eliminating its weak clubs, the NHL decreased the market demand for players. Since general unemployment was high, a shrunken league gave the NHL clubs an advantage when negotiating with players.

Without two other important developments, however, the shifting advantage to the NHL clubs in the player market would have been far less significant. The AHA's rebellion and the alliance with the CAHA further tightened the NHL's hold on the player market as well as the distribution of games. Superior economic power underscored the basis of the NHL's position as the top league. While many businesses had failed during the Depression, the NHL's financial status remained healthy and the elimination of weaker clubs strengthened the league's financial picture.[31] The financial instability of the AHL provided further proof to aspiring hockey players that the NHL was the only alternative in major-league hockey. With the elimination of the AHL challenge and its demotion to the minor-league system, the NHL demonstrated to all in the hockey world that it remained the master in professional hockey.

The NHL's economic viability also contributed to its dominance of the hockey marketplace and brought the amateur and professional governing bodies together after almost thirty years of separation. Ailing financially, the CAHA turned away from dogmatic amateurism and acknowledged the effects of the

Great Depression on commercialized amateur hockey. It broke with the AAUC and, in order to maintain its control of amateur hockey in Canada, made a new alliance with the NHL. While stormy sessions continued between the NHL and the CAHA, the alliance of the two governing bodies nevertheless set a precedent for compromise on the part of the amateurs. For the NHL, the agreement with the CAHA acknowledged the supremacy of the professional game and its authority in hockey matters. Moreover, the pact legitimized the NHL's claim on amateur players under the CAHA's jurisdiction. Since the CAHA's alliance with other governing bodies also allowed the NHL to indirectly control hockey markets far beyond its franchise locations, players had even fewer employment options in hockey.

Hence, by the end of 1936, the NHL's influence in hockey had been fairly well established. As NHL franchises and affiliated minor leagues occupied major urban centres in the industrial northeastern United States and Central Canada, the League held a tight grip in the distribution of professional hockey games. After the New York Americans folded in 1942, no NHL franchise had to share its market with another team. Via its alliance with the CAHA, the League had also gained a large degree of influence in the supply of players. With the minor leagues serving as warehouses of talent, the NHL had a steady labour reserve. Much fine tuning in the control of the player supply was still to come. But the days of players having multiple options had passed.

Chapter 13

Overtime

A web of stakeholders contributed to the construction and popularization of hockey – a sport that was eventually dominated by one governing organization, the National Hockey League. But long before the hegemonic rule of the NHL, fans, media, facility owners, players, and administrators established interlocking interests and helped to commercialize and professionalize elite-level hockey. Throughout the development of this hockey network that created an industry, the ties among the media, the facility owners, and the governing bodies were especially close. Sportsmen were investors in facilities. Some reporters, including the first NHL president, Frank Calder, served in the various associations and leagues in assorted capacities. Even today, the media is undoubtedly the most vocal booster of sports in any town or city. The close relationships among the different groups, however, did not mean there was unanimity in the ways sought to promote and develop the sport and the industry. Yet the common interest of these groups in commercialized hockey ensured the continuous existence of the sport. This book, I hope, has provided a coherent story of how and why the NHL emerged as the dominant force in the elite hockey network.

Throughout this narrative, the dynamic nature of the hockey network is evident in the changing organizational structures of its governing bodies. Before the first decade of the twentieth century, clubs and organizations freely entered into the commercialized hockey market via membership in voluntary associations. Membership in these early governing bodies was unstable. In fact, one can argue that the hockey network, especially the professional subunit, did not become stabilized until after the Second World War. Hence, entrepreneurs sought ways to regularize the delivery of games once they discovered that hockey could be profitable. At this writing, business executives and hockey officials are fretting over the possibility of an NHL lock-out in 2004, but they are not the first to recognize that uncertainty is not good for business. In some ways, then, this book is also about organizations competing to lead, and set order within, the hockey network.

In investigating the history of the hockey network in order to trace the emergence of the NHL as its leading organization, this narrative also reveals that there existed alternatives to the structure of the network in its early years, and that the NHL's dominance was not necessary inevitable. The zealous promotion of a sport brand based on skill level – an exclusionary practice that effectively insulated the elite-level clubs from all others – marked a turning point in the development of the hockey network around the turn of the twentieth century. By contrast, international soccer allows promotion and demotion in a hierarchical league structure based on seasonal results. The choice of a closed corporation by the decision makers of hockey's elite-level clubs had far-reaching consequences.

First and foremost, separating the early commercialized hockey network into senior clubs and others restricted elite-level hockey to only a few teams. Fewer clubs also meant less opportunity to develop a larger pool of highly skilled players. Because their focus was on victories, the senior clubs no longer were involved in the development of talent on junior clubs. Whereas intra-club matches helped improve the play of juniors and others of lesser skills, inter-club competitions left the less talented behind. This change in focus contributed to a limited pool of highly skilled players, a fact then used as a main reason to limit the number of teams in the senior series.

A second consequence of this first major split within the network was the distancing of the senior clubs from their roots. While club formation in the early years had depended on several factors, such as social class, ethnicity, and language, a closed corporation of clubs had the tendency to reduce the diversity of hockey communities at the elite level within a locale. The limited number of elite-level clubs, which eventually was narrowed to one per city, restricted supporters' choice in top-notched hockey entertainment. Conversely, a team now had to appeal to a wider range of people who might have little in common. Whereas the Montreals, Victorias, Crystals, and Shamrocks represented differing communities in one city around the turn of the twentieth century, today's NHL franchises supposedly embody the entire city population's identity. Although, as now, the media usually promoted the local team as representatives of civic pride, the fact remains that social standing, gender, and ethnicity separated a club's supporters. Had the senior clubs decided not to form a closed corporation in the early twentieth century, the hockey network's structure could conceivably have taken a form like soccer's given the close ties that existed between Canada and Great Britain at the time. Locality would not have been the only bond for club supporters. Multiple bonds would have made it that much more difficult for clubs to relocate. But senior hockey's decision doomed the presence of a vibrant organizational structure that could foster strong, locally relevant, community-based clubs, and thus eliminated the possibility of promoting the sport at all skill levels.

The lack of a ruling organization connecting different levels of hockey, hence, precipitated the next split between amateur and professional hockey. This division effectively segregated commercialized hockey into two distinct sections and thus further loosened the ties, or as Robert Stern has called it, the degree of system coupling, that existed previously within the commercialized hockey network. Amateur proponents viewed the split in ideological terms. The professionals ended up with most of the highly skilled players.[1]

In explaining the consequences of the Athletic War, Alan Metcalfe has argued that hockey's failure to settle on a more liberal definition of an amateur led to the development of a professional league largely dependent upon American wealth. Bruce Kidd has also pointed to the increase in capitalization during the 1920s as an important reason for the eventual dominance of the NHL. Yet American involvement in professional hockey was not inevitable because of the split between the amateurs and the professionals in Canada. As this narrative has demonstrated, the initiative to expand southward did not come from the NHL nor was the main reason to grant American franchises primarily the desire to increase capitalization, at least not initially. For many American franchises, the lack of a local hockey culture made their survival questionable, and thus the success of a professional hockey league with American markets and investments was by no means a certainty. Canadian hockey purists can perhaps take solace that this still holds true today, when NHL franchises reside in such sun-belt cities as Tampa Bay, Miami, and Phoenix.[2] Despite the disappearance of the Winnipeg and Quebec City franchises in the late twentieth century, one must not forget that Cleveland, San Francisco, and the original NHL franchises in Denver and Atlanta did not survive either.

An organizational structure without human direction remains inert. Many people contributed to the popularization and commercialization of hockey. In the making of the NHL, however, its first president was the 'visible hand' in guiding the organization, and changing the structure, of the network.[3] Frank Calder was more than a competent administrator. Under his guidance, the NHL emerged from being a small regional organization to become an international cartel. Although he did not hesitate to use the power of his office at times, he preferred diplomacy and alliance making, with great attention to details. He did not reign supreme over hockey as some have claimed. One must remember that he was, after all, an employee of the owners. Yet the length his tenure remained second only to that of Clarence Campbell.[4] He would not have remained in office for twenty-six years without support from the majority of the owners.

Unlike Campbell's regime, Calder's presidency began with turmoil within his organization and the larger hockey network. And unlike Kenesaw Mountain Landis, the first commissioner of Major League Baseball, Calder did not have the credentials of a federal judge to provide a calming effect during the crisis. Despite the Chicago owner McLaughlin's assessment, Calder was rarely an autocrat. But he was able to consolidate power in the president's office during a moment of crisis in 1917, long before new owners from the expansion, such as Adams and McLaughlin, could challenge his authority. When those challenges did appear, he was the one constant in the professional hockey network that connected the past and the present. Hence, the league office, controlled by the president, became the linchpin of the professional hockey network.[5]

One important achievement of Calder's was the reintegration of professional and amateur hockey in the commercial hockey network. With the 1936 NHL-CAHA agreement, the NHL secured its dominant status in the hockey industry. The affiliation agreement opened the door for the NHL to the vast amateur hockey empire under the CAHA's control by allowing amateurs to try out with NHL teams without losing their amateur status. As the affiliation agreement loosened the barrier against the NHL's talent search in the amateur ranks, it also helped to tighten its control on the player market, since the CAHA promised to honour the suspensions and expulsions of the professional organization. In effect, the commercialized hockey network came under the hegemonic rule of the NHL.

By no means did the power of the NHL reach its apex after the establishment of the alliance with the CAHA in 1936. While the NHL wielded tremendous influence in its control of the distribution of hockey games as well as the player market, its power in the world of hockey grew further after 1936. After the Second World War, the NHL had an even more profound influence over Canadian amateur hockey when professional clubs were allowed to sponsor amateur teams. With the aid of the radio, and later television, broadcasting of its games, NHL hockey became a national obsession.[6] While amateur hockey had its followers, the 1936 CAHA alliance effectively promoted the NHL brand of hockey as superior to all others. Until the 1998 Winter Olympic Games, when professional hockey players were first allowed to participate, such an acknowledgment had been the excuse used by hockey fans and the media when the Canadian amateurs started to lose in Olympic competitions – that Canada did not have the best players; they were all professionals.[7]

But the accumulated power of the NHL did not come without a price. Minor-league clubs absorbed the brunt of economic hardship during the Depression, as many tried to survive in small markets with second-rate players. The NHL dropped to seven clubs when the Maroons ceased to operate on the eve of the Second World War. By that time the New York Americans had already been operating under League management, and they followed the fate of Pittsburgh, Ottawa, and the Maroons when they disbanded in 1942. After the dissolution of the Americans, owners zealously guarded their territory, and no city had more than one franchise thereafter. But the fall of these four franchises diminished the League's exposure, especially in the American market, and haunted its various expansion attempts in later years. The perception was that the NHL was a Canadian league with a Northeast–Great Lakes cult following. Thus, NHL's ascent as the dominant organization in the hockey world also exposed the limitations of its power in the sport entertainment industry.

Rules of Hockey, 1877

1. The game shall be commenced and renewed by a Bully in the centre of the ground. Goals shall be changed after each game.
2. When a player hits the ball, any one of the same side who at such a moment of hitting is nearer to the opponents' goal line is out of play, and may not touch the ball himself, or in any way whatever prevent any other player from doing so, until the ball has been played. A player must always be on his own side of the ball.
3. The ball may be stopped, but not carried or knocked on by any part of the body. No player shall raise his stick above his shoulder. Charging from behind, tripping, collaring, kicking or shinning shall not be allowed.
4. When the ball is hit behind the goal line by the attacking side, it shall be brought out straight 15 yards, and started again by a Bully; but, if it is hit behind by any of the side whose goal line it is, a player of the opposite side shall (hit) it out from within one yard of the nearest corner, no player of the attacking side at that time shall be within 20 yards of the goal line, and the defenders, with the exception of the goal-keeper, must be behind their goal line.
5. When the ball goes off at the side, a player of the opposite side to that which hit it out shall roll it out from the point on the boundary line at which it went off at right angles with the boundary line, and it shall not be in play until it has touched the ice, and the player rolling it in shall not play it until it has been played by another player, every player being then behind the ball.
6. On the infringement of any of the above rules, the ball shall be brought back and a Bully shall take place.
7. All disputes shall be settled by the Umpires, or in the event of their disagreement, by the Referee.

Source: Montreal Gazette, 27 February 1877

Stanley Cup Regulations

Deed of Gift

The late Governor-General, the Earl of Derby, before his departure from Canada in 1893 donated a challenge cup to be held from year to year by the championship Hockey Club of the Dominion. He appointed Sheriff J. Sweetland and Mr. P.D. Ross, of Ottawa, to act as trustees of the Cup, and requested them to suggest conditions to govern the competition. Meanwhile, His Excellency directed that in 1893 the Cup should be presented to the M.A.A.A. Hockey team of Montreal, champions of the A.H.A. of Canada, to be held by them until the close of the ensuing year. His Excellency laid down the following preliminary conditions:

His Excellency's Conditions

1. The winners to give bond for the return of the cup in good order when required by the trustees for the purpose of being handed over to any other team who may in turn win.
2. Each winning team to have at their own charge engraved on a silver ring fitted on the cup for the purpose the name of the team and the year won. (In the first instance the M.A.A.A. will find the cup already engraved for them.)
3. The Cup shall remain a challenge cup, and will not become the property of any team, even if won more than once.
4. In case of any doubt as to the name of any club to claim the position of champions, the cup shall be held or awarded by the trustees as they might think right, their decision being absolute.
5. Should either trustee resign or otherwise drop out, the remaining trustee shall nominate a substitute.

Lord Stanley, in view of the fact of several hockey associations existing in Canada, also asked the trustees to arrange means of making the cup open to all, and thus representative of the hockey championship as completely as possible, rather than of any one association.

The Trustees' Regulations

In dealing with challenges and matches since 1893, the trustees have observed the following principles:

1. So far as the Amateur Hockey Association of Canada is concerned, the cup goes with the championship each year, without the necessity of any special or extra contests. Similar in any other association.
2. Challenges from outside the Amateur Hockey Association of Canada are recognized by the trustees only from champion clubs of senior provincial associations, and in the order received.
3. When a challenge is accepted, the trustees desire the two competing clubs to arrange by mutual agreement all terms of the contest themselves, such as a choice of date, of rink, division of the gate money, selection of officials, etc., etc. The trustees do not wish to interfere in any way, shape, or form if it can be avoided.
4. Where competing clubs fail to agree the trustees have observed, and will continue to observe, as far as practicable, the following principles.
   (a) Cup to be awarded by the result of one match, or of best two out of three, as seems fairest as regards other fixtures. The trustees would be willing, however, if desired, to allow the contest to be decided by a majority of the goals scored in two matches only (instead of by the best two matches in three).
   (b) Contest to take place on ice in the home city, the date or dates and choice of rink to be made or approved by the trustees.
   (c) The net gate money given by the rink to be equally divided between the competing teams.
   (d) If the clubs fail to agree on a referee, the trustees to appoint one from outside the competing cities, the two clubs to share the expense equally.
   (e) If the clubs fail to agree on other officials, the trustees to authorize the referee to appoint them, the expense, if any, to be shared equally by the competing clubs.
   (f) No second challenge recognized in one season from the same hockey association.

Source: Montreal Daily Star, 3 January 1903, 18.

National Hockey Association Constitution, 1910

Name

Section 1. The association shall be called the National Association.

Objects

Section 2. The objects of the association are: –
(a) To perpetuate hockey as the national game, and to surround it with such safeguards as to warrant public confidence in its integrity and methods.
(b) To protect and promote the mutual interests of professional hockey clubs of this association and its players.
(c) To establish and regulate the hockey championships of the National Association.

Officers

Section 3. The officers of this association shall be a president, secretary, treasurer and one director from each club enjoying membership in the association.

At its annual meeting, the association shall elect a president, secretary, treasurer and six directors, and such committees as may be necessary, to hold office for the term of one year, or until the election and qualification of their successors.

The offices of president, secretary and treasurer, or any two or all thereof, may be held by one and the same person.

President

Section 4. The president shall preside at all meetings of the association and discharge all duties that are imposed upon him by this constitution or by the association.

He shall interpret the playing rules during the championship season.

He shall have power to suspend for a definite period, or impose a fine not exceeding one hundred dollars, or to inflict both such suspension and fine upon any club member or player who in his opinion shall have been guilty of conduct prejudicial to the National Hockey Association or of the welfare of hockey, regardless of whether the same occurred on or off the playing rink.

He shall report to the board of directors any and all violations of the constitution that may come to his knowledge; also the names of all persons fined or suspended, the amounts of such fines and terms of suspension.

Secretary

Section 5. The secretary shall have the care and custody of the official records and papers of the association; shall keep accurate minutes of all meetings of the association and of the board of directors; shall issue all special notices and attend to necessary correspondence; he shall prepare and furnish such reports as may be called for by the board of directors, and shall be entitled to such books, stationery, blanks and official supplies as he may require.

He shall be the treasurer of the association and as such shall be the custodian of all association funds, receive all dues, fines and assessments, and make such payments as shall be ordered by the board or by the association.

He shall annually render a report of all his receipts and disbursements to the board and shall give such bond with approved sureties as the association may require. At the expiration of his term of office, he shall account for and deliver to the board all monies, books, papers and property received by him by virtue of his office.

Salaries

Section 6. The officers shall receive such salaries as the association shall annually determine, and shall be reimbursed for all proper expenses actually incurred by them in the service of the association; the association may exact from them such guaranties for the faithful performance of their duties as it may deem proper.

Vacancies

Section 7. Should any office, except that of director, become vacant the association shall appoint a successor to act until the next annual meeting, or for such shorter period as it may determine.

In case of a vacancy in the board of directors, it shall be filled as provided in Section 10.

Board of Directors

Section 8. Every director shall be an actual member of the club he represents and no club shall be represented by more than one person on the board.

The board shall elect one of its members [acting?] as its chairman for the term of one year, and until his successor is elected.

The board shall have the general supervision and management of all affairs and business of the association.

It shall promptly consider any complaint preferred by a club against a manager or player of another club, for conduct in violation of any provision of this constitution or prejudicial to the good repute of the game of hockey and shall have power to discipline or expel such player or manager, provided that such complaint be preferred in writing, giving such particulars as may enable the board to ascertain all the facts, and be transmitted to the secretary, by whom it shall at once be referred to the board.

The board shall prepare a detailed report of all its transactions and present the same in writing to the association at its next meeting, which report shall be filed with the secretary, together with all official papers, documents and property, which may come into the possession of said board.

Powers

Section 9. The board of directors shall have power to determine disputes between clubs, and to hear and determine appeals from any decision rendered by the president, the facts to be submitted, and the questions adjudicated under such regulations as the board shall prescribe in each case. The findings of the board shall be final, and under no circumstances be reconsidered, reopened or enquired into by any subsequent board.

The board shall also be the tribunal for the hearing of an appeal made by any player or manager who shall have been expelled, suspended or disciplined by his club or by the president of the association. The appeal shall be heard in the following manner: The person appealing shall within thirty days after the date of the expulsion, suspension or discipline, file with the secretary a written statement of his defence, accompanied by a request that an appeal be allowed him. The secretary shall notify the club, if one is involved, of the request for an appeal, accompanying such notice with a copy of the statement; at the next board meeting of the club, by its duly authorized representative, and the appellant in person, by attorney or by written statement, shall appear before the board, with their evidence. The board shall impartially hear the matter and render a decision which shall be final and forever binding on both club and player.

No director shall sit in the trial of a case in which he or his club is interested as a party.

Any expense of trial or arbitration, as fixed by the board, shall be borne by the parties adjudged to be in fault.

Vacancies

Section 10. In case of a vacancy on the board from whatever cause, the club represented by the director whose office has become vacant, shall designate his successor within ten days and at once notify the secretary. But if such vacancy is caused by the withdrawal, disbanding or disqualification of a club represented on the board, the board shall fill the vacancy by appointment within ten days.

Meetings

Section 11. The board shall meet on the same day of, but prior to the annual meeting of the association, and shall hold special meetings, at the call of the chairman or of any two directors, at such times and places as he or they may deem most convenient for the best interests of the association. Three directors shall constitute a quorum.

Membership

Section 12. This association shall consist of [six?] Clubs, the membership of which shall not be increased or diminished.

Admission to Membership

Section 13. No club shall be admitted to membership unless it shall have first delivered to the secretary of the association a written application for membership, accompanied by proof showing that such a club will be regularly and properly recognized, financed and officered. Such application shall at once be transmitted by the secretary to the board, which shall promptly investigate and report to the association at its next meeting, with its recommendations thereon.

Voting upon applications for membership shall be by ballot and at least four favorable votes shall be required for an election, and the retired or retiring club shall not be entitled to vote thereon.

Withdrawal from Membership

Section 14. Any club member of this association finding itself unable to meet the obligations it has assumed, may apply to the association for permission to dispose of its right and franchise as a member of this association to some other organization. In case this association shall consent to such withdrawal and shall elect such proposed organization to membership, such new member shall assume, together with the rights and franchise of said retiring club, all the liabilities, responsibilities and obligations of the retiring club as a member of the association. Provided, however, that the retiring club shall not be relieved or released from any unexpired contracts, responsibilities or obligations entered into by it as a member of this association.

Termination of Membership

Section 15. The membership of any club may be terminated by:
(a) Its resignation duly accepted and the election of a successor.
(b) Failure to present its team at the time and place appointed to play any championship game unless caused by unavoidable accident.
(c) Playing any game of hockey with any club that is disqualified or ineligible under this constitution.
(d) Offering, agreeing, conspiring or attempting to lose any game of hockey or for failure to immediately expel any player who shall be proven guilty of offering, agreeing, conspiring or attempting to lose any game of hockey or of being interested in any pool or wager thereon.
(e) Disbandment of its organization or team during the championship season.
(f) Failing or refusing to fulfil its contractual obligations.
(g) Failing or refusing to comply with any lawful association requirement or requirement of the board of directors.
(h) Wilfully violating any provision of this constitution or any legislation or playing rules made in pursuance thereof.

Expulsion from Membership

Section 16. Any club member of this association may prefer charges against any other club for a violation of any of the provisions of the preceding section.
    Such charges shall be reduced to writing and set forth in detail the grounds of complaint and the same shall be filed with the secretary, who shall cause a copy thereof to be served by mail upon the club against whom such charges have been made. The accused club shall within five days after the receipt of said complaint file with the secretary its written answer thereto. The secretary shall thereupon transmit said complaint and answer to the board of directors, and said board shall proceed to hear, try and determine said case, under such rules and methods of procedure as it shall prescribe. The findings of said board shall be conclusive and binding upon all parties concerned.

The board shall have the power to impose such fine or penalty upon the offending club as it shall deem just and proper, which may include a penalty payable to any other club or clubs as an equivalent for damages sustained by such club or clubs by reason of such violation of this constitution, or

Said board of directors may recommend the expulsion of the offending club, and thereupon the question of such expulsion shall be submitted to a vote of all the clubs in this association other than the offending club. If four or more clubs vote in favor of expulsion, the president shall declare the offending club expelled, and its membership in this association forfeited and terminated.

Vacancies

Section 17. In case a vacancy occurs in the membership of the association between any January 1st and the close of the ensuing championship season, and a new member shall be selected to fill the vacancy, such new membership shall continue only until the next annual meeting; but such club shall be subject to all the rights and privileges of other members, except the right to vote at the annual meeting.

Assessments

Section 18. The president shall levy an assessment on each club of five hundred dollars each, payable at the annual meeting, and such additional assessments as may be required from time to time to defray the actual and necessary expenses and liabilities incurred by this association in conducting and transacting its affairs and business.

Penalty for Default

Section 19. Any club which refuses or neglects to pay any sum of money or to comply with any lawful demand within fifteen days after the receipt of notice from the president, secretary or board of directors requiring it to do so, shall be liable to have its franchise and rights as a member of this association forfeited and be subject to the imposition of such fine or penalty as the board of directors may see fit to inflict.

Clubs – Their Powers and Responsibilities

Section 20. Subject to the provisions of this constitution and the playing rules of this association, each club member hereof shall have the right to regulate its own affairs, to establish its own rules, and to discipline, punish, suspend or expel its own manager, players or other employees, and those powers shall not be limited to cases of dishonest play or open insubordination, but shall include all questions of intemperance, carelessness, indifference or other conduct on or off the ice, that may be regarded by the club as prejudicial to its interests.

Whenever a club releases, suspends or expels a manager or player said club shall at once notify the secretary of this association, stating in case of release the date which the same takes effect, and in case of suspension or expulsion the cause thereof and the president of the association shall immediately notify all clubs of such release, suspension or expulsion.

No player shall, without the consent of the club with which he is under contract or reservation, enter into negotiations with any other club for his future service.

Contracts

Section 21. An agreement between a club and a player made by telegraph or in writing shall constitute a valid contract, but before such player shall be eligible to play in any championship game he shall sign a contract in the form prescribed and adopted by the association.

Before said player shall be eligible to play in more than three games said formal contract shall be filed with the secretary of the association, who shall make a record of same in a book kept by him for that purpose, and he shall thereafter duly promulgate the same.

If a club allows a player to play who has failed to sign the formal contract hereinbefore required it shall not be permitted to count in its favor in the championship race any game won by said club in which the ineligible player engaged.

Clubs in this association are at liberty to buy, release or exchange players up to the 31st of January of each year, but the release with one club and the signing with the other must be sanctioned by the president.

No club shall be permitted to pay more than $5,000 as salaries for [the] entire club, and any player will not be allowed to receive any bonus, directly or indirectly, from interested or disinterested parties.

The association shall approve and adopt a form of contract which shall be printed and furnished in sufficient number to each club by the secretary.

No other form of contract shall be used by said club.

Waivers

Section 22. – If a club desires to release or otherwise dispose of a player to a club of another minor association, such club shall notify the president, and he shall, upon behalf of said club, immediately request all other clubs in this association to waive claim to said player.

No player shall be released or otherwise disposed of unless all other clubs in this association consent thereto, either in writing or by telegram, or such consent will be assumed and claim to said player deemed to have been waived unless a club after receiving notice of such request expressly, by letter or telegram, refuses to waive its said claim.

Notice of such refusal shall be served upon the president during the playing season within forty-eight hours after receipt of such a request at any time within ten days after receipt of such request.

Reservation of Players

Section 23. – The right of reservation of players secured to this association is hereby granted to each and every member of this association provided that at the close of each season and not later than April 15th a draft of players required for next season (and limited to 10) be furnished the president, and all players not drafted are at liberty to sign up with whatever club they may desire.

Discipline of Clubs

Section 24. – No club a member of this association shall tamper with or enter into any negotiations with a player under contract or reservation to any other club a member of this association for or regarding his future or present services without the written consent of the president of the club of which said player is a member.

Any club officer, manager or player violating the provisions of this section shall pay a fine of one hundred ($100.00) dollars to the club making and sustaining the complaint, payable within ten days from receipt of notice from the president of the imposition of said fine.

Disbandment of Clubs

Section 25. – Whenever a club in this association shall disband or in any manner lose its membership in this association the same shall operate as a release of all its claims to all players then under contract or reservation to said club, and title to said players shall thereby vest in the association to be disposed of in such manner as the Board of Directors may determine.

Non-payment of Salaries

Section 26. – If a club defaults in the payment of salary due any of its players, according to the terms of his contract, the president of this association shall, upon being requested so to do by said player, promptly pay same out of the funds of this association and title to said player shall thereby pass to and vest in this association.

Any club which shall fail to reimburse this association for any monies paid for salaries as above provided within ten days after receiving notice from the president requiring it so to do shall be liable to have its franchise and rights as a member declared forfeited.

Additional Penalties

Section 27. – Any manager or player who, in the judgment of the president, or of the Board of Directors, shall be guilty of offending, agreeing, conspiring or attempting to cause any game of hockey to result otherwise than on its own merits shall be expelled and forever thereafter disqualified from participating in any game.

No owner, manager, player or representative of a club in this association shall pay or offer to pay, present or offer to present, any money, present or emulment of any kind to any player or manager of another club to defeat, or for having defeated, or as an inducement to defeat any other club in this association.

Any person found guilty by the president or Board of Directors of a violation of either of the foregoing provisions of this Constitution shall pay a fine of not less than one hundred ($100.00) dollars for each and every offence.

Source: *Montreal Gazette*, 9 November 1910, 10.

Binding Agreement of 1926

AGREEMENT BETWEEN THE OTTAWA HOCKEY ASSOCIATION LIMITED AND THE LES CANADIENS HOCKEY CLUB INC. AND THE MONTREAL PROFESSIONAL HOCKEY CLUB LTD. AND THE ST PATRICK'S PROFESSIONAL HOCKEY LIMITED AND THE BOSTON PROFESSIONAL HOCKEY ASSOCIATION INC. AND THE NEW YORK RANGERS PROFESSIONAL HOCKEY CLUB INC. AND THE PITTSBURGH PROFESSIONAL HOCKEY CLUB INC. being the members of the National Hockey League, and parties hereto.

WHEREAS the parties hereto are members of an association known as the National Hockey League, hereinafter called 'The League' in which each of the parties hereto has entered a team of hockey players who compete annually in a series of matches; and

WHEREAS the parties hereto are desirous of continuing for a period of 15 years their association with one another and with such other parties as may become members of the League from time to time; and

WHEREAS the parties hereto have, through such association with others, built up valuable goodwill among the spectators at its matches both at home and on the road; and

WHEREAS to retain such goodwill it is essential that the parties hereto remain together on friendly terms as members of the said League and resist any effort to disorganize or disband the said League and its players; and

WHEREAS the parties hereto agree that the foregoing recitals truly represent the situation with reference to them and the said League.

NOW THEREFORE THIS INDENTURE WITNESSETH,
and it is hereby agreed:

(a) The parties hereto covenant and agree mutually with one another that they will remain members of the League as at present, or from time to time, constituted.

(b) No member of the League and no officer, agent or employee of any member, shall, with the knowledge, assistance or acquiescence of such member, without the unanimous written consent of the members of the League, enter into, or be a party to, any negotiation, proposal or agreement or do any act, whereby directly or indirectly such member or any officer, agent or employee thereof becomes or proposes to become, a competitor of the League, or interested in the promotion, ownership or operation of any other existing or proposed hockey league or organization or of any hockey team other than the one representing such member in the National Hockey league.

(c) The remedy for breach of this agreement shall be available to each or all of the non-defaulting members of the League, and shall be available to the League itself for such damages as the League itself may be able to establish from such breach, or jointly to such members and the League, and shall be in addition to any remedy available to any party under the constitution of the League as it may be from time to time, or otherwise available.

(d) The damages deemed to have been suffered by every member of this League by breach of this agreement shall be deemed to be not less than $10,000 for each such member who has not been guilty of such breach, and in addition, such amount in excess thereof as (at their respective options) any member, or the League or both jointly, may be able to establish as damages incurred through such breach. Such $10,000 is hereby agreed to be liquidated damages and the minimum damages incurred through such breach, and not a penalty.

(e) The parties hereto agree that any money held by the League or by any other association, corporation or person, on behalf of any member who is guilty of a breach of this agreement, may be paid in equal shares to the non-offending members of the League as a payment on account of such damages. The Trustee or other person holding such funds on behalf of such member who so commits a breach hereof, is hereby directed, authorized and empowered (a) to pay such funds into the Court in which relief is sought, or to another Trustee within the jurisdiction thereof, as he may deem expedient, to be held pending the outcome of any litigation or dispute in respect of such breach, or (b) if there is no such dispute or litigation within one month after such breach is first made by the member alleged to be in default, to pay such funds forthwith to the members objecting to such breach.

(f) This agreement shall replace any agreement hitherto made among the parties hereto, or any of them, (other than the constitution of the League) on the subject of remaining bound to one another as members of any hockey league, and in particular a certain agreement between the Ottawa, St. Patrick's, Hamilton and Canadien Clubs, starting 'For the mutual benefit' and ending 'a suitable guarantee to that end.'

(g) All such agreements are deemed to be cancelled as of the date hereof and shall no longer affect any person or corporation which was a party thereto.

(h) This agreement shall also be binding upon the successors and assigns of the parties hereto; but shall not be for the benefit of such successors and assigns, unless the transaction or transactions by which such succession or assignment was effected has been duly approved by resolution of the League.

(i) The League, by its President, executes this agreement for the purpose of becoming a party thereto to entitle it to secure such damages as it may suffer through breach of this agreement.

IN WITNESS WHEREOF THE parties hereto have hereunto set their corporate seals attested by their proper officers, respectively, in that behalf.

Source: NHL Meeting Minutes, 15 May, NHLA.

Ottawa Gate Receipts, 1927–35[a]

Season	Net revenue[b]	Visitor's share (3.5% of net)	Club's share	Average revenue per game[c]	Std Dev.
1927–8	$92,104.63	$3,223.66	$88,880.97	$4,232.43	$2,187.22
1928–9	$67,823.00	$2,373.81	$65,449.20	$3,272.46	$1,783.59
1929–30	$97,046.29	$3,396.62	$93,649.67	$4,256.80	$1,916.94
1930–1	$78,891.80	$2,761.21	$76,130.59	$3,460.48	$1,650.91
1932–3	$91,823.91	$3,213.84	$88,610.07	$3,692.09	$1,972.30
1933–4	$58,797.94	$2,057.93	$56,740.01	$2,364.17	$1,164.56
1934–5	$61,285.57	$2,145.00	$59,140.58	$2,464.19	$1,715.15
Average	$78,253.31	$2,738.87	$75,514.44	$3,146.44	$1,770.10

a The table was compiled from gate-receipt reports filed by the Ottawa club to the NHL. Ottawa had suspended operation for the 1931–2 season. No provisions have been made for the differences in exchange rates between Canadian and American currencies in League gate-receipt reports.

b Figures are arrived at after deducting 2% Ontario Athletic Commission from gross receipts. Caution must be exercised when interpreting these numbers. From the 1927–8 season onward, Ottawa began transferring some of its home games to cities with bigger arenas. Thus the gross net revenue for each season does not give a true indication of fan support. In all likelihood the numbers would have been lower if Ottawa had not moved some of its home games.

c From 1927 to 1931 there were 22 home games per club. Beginning with the 1931–2 season, the NHL went to a schedule with 24 home games. Due to incomplete records, gate receipts for only 21 home games were on file for the 1927–8 season, and for only 20 in the 1928–9 season.

Appendix F

Detroit Gate Receipts, 1927–35[a]

Season	Net revenue	Visitor's share (3.5% of net)	Club's share	Average revenue per game[b]	Std Dev.
1927–8	$211,025.70	$7,385.90	$203,639.80	$9,256.35	$3,996.35
1928–9	$249,673.43	$8,738.57	$240,934.86	$10,951.58	$4,415.70
1929–30	$153,331.95	$5,366.62	$147,965.33	$7,045.97	$3,337.81
1930–1	$183,425.55	$6,419.89	$177,005.66	$8,045.71	$3,655.46
1932–3	$147,912.25	$5,176.93	$142,735.32	$5,947.31	$2,441.79
1933–4	$132,224.59	$4,627.86	$127,596.73	$5,316.53	$2,535.47
1934–5	$165,371.61	$5,788.01	$159,583.60	$6,649.32	$2,299.15
Average	$177,566.44	$6,214.83	$171,351.61	$7,139.65	$3,240.25

a The table was compiled from gate-receipt reports filed by the Detroit club to the NHL. No provisions have been given for the differences in exchange rates between the Canadian and American currencies in League gate-receipt reports.

b From 1927 to 1931 the NHL season allowed 22 home games per club. Beginning with the 1931–2 season, the NHL went to a schedule with 24 home games. Due to incomplete records, gate receipts for only 21 home games were on file for the 1929–30 season.

Appendix G

NHL Club Net Average Revenues by Year, 1929–45[a]

Season	No. of teams in league	Net average gate per team
1929–30[b]	10	$11,048.67
1930–1[c]	10	$11,020.20
1931–2	9	$11,055.33
1932–3	8	$8,475.34
1933–4	9	$7,574.41
1934–5	9	$7,885.58
1935–6	8	$9,092.81
1936–7	8	$9,797.99
1937–8	8	$10,322.36
1938–9	7	$11,231.47
1939–40	7	$10,195.08
1940–1	7	$10,961.29
1941–2	7	$10,460.88
1942–3	6	$12,413.42
1943–4	6	$13,713.28
1944–5	6	$15,438.76

a Net average revenue per club for each season is calculated based on gate-receipt reports sent to the NHL office by each team. Rink rental has already been deducted from the total gross gate receipts in arriving at the total net revenues, which are then divided by the number of teams for the season. No provisions have been made for the differences in exchange rates between the Canadian and American currencies in League gate-receipt reports.

b For the 1929–30 season, there are two gate-receipt reports missing from Pittsburgh, and one from each of Ottawa, Detroit, and Chicago.

c For the 1930–1 season, one gate-receipt report is missing from the Ottawa team.

Biographies of Hockey Personalities

Adams, Charles   Boston amateur sportsman and millionaire. A director of the Boston Arena, he purchased one of the NHL options from Tom Duggan and established the Boston (Bruins) Professional Hockey Club in 1924.

Ahearn, Frank   His family owned the local traction company in Ottawa. He was owner of the Ottawa Hockey Club. Ahearn was also an elected member of Parliament.

Calder, Frank   Sports editor of the *Montreal Herald*, he assumed the position of secretary-treasurer of the National Hockey Association. He was elected president when the NHL was formed in 1917 and held that post until he died in 1943.

Clapp, Charles   President of the minor-league Canadian-American Hockey League.

Creighton, James George Alywin   Student from McGill University who is generally acknowledged as the father of modern hockey.

Dandurand, Leo   Owner of the Canadiens Hockey Club. Together with two others, he bought the Canadiens franchise when its previous owner, George Kennedy, passed away. He was also a sports promoter, especially in wrestling, and was heavily involved with horse racing.

Dey, Edwin P.   Owner of the Dey rink in Ottawa and later part-owner of the Ottawa Hockey Club. The Ottawa team played in Dey's rink until Frank Ahearn and a group of investors built the Ottawa Auditorium.

Duggan, Tom   Director of the Mount Royal rink in Montreal as well as of the National Sporting Club. He was instrumental in promoting professional hockey in the

United States in the 1920s by approaching the NHL with the idea of expansion and then acting as a salesman of NHL franchises. He eventually became a director of the New York Americans Hockey Club.

Foran, William Ottawa sportsman who was also the president of the short-lived Federal Amateur Hockey League. Foran succeeded Sheriff John Sweetland as the Stanley Cup trustee, and later was governor of the Ottawa Hockey Club in the NHL for one season.

Gorman, Tom Sports editor of the *Ottawa Citizen* and later owner of the Ottawa Hockey Club. He had been involved with horse racing and was secretary of Ottawa Connaught Race Track. Gorman quit hockey in the mid-1920s in a failed attempt to be a resort developer. He returned to the NHL in the late 1920s and was manager of the New York Americans Hockey Club.

Hammond, John Right-hand man of Tex Rickard of Madison Square Garden, New York. He was credited with convincing Rickard to add professional hockey to the Garden's sports calendar. Hammond was the governor of the New York Rangers Hockey Club in its initial years until a power struggle deposed him.

Harmon, 'Paddy' Sports promoter from Chicago. He was unsuccessful in bidding for an NHL franchise in Chicago. He subsequently amassed enough capital to build the Chicago Stadium, which housed the NHL's Chicago team. In his bid to be a franchise owner, he helped the American Hockey Association in its attempt to enter major-league hockey.

Hewitt, William Sports editor of the *Toronto Star* and long-time registrar of the Canadian Amateur Hockey Association. Hewitt was instrumental in affiliating the CAHA with the NHL in the mid-1930s.

Kendall, George Also known as George Kennedy. He was the owner of the Canadiens Hockey Club.

King, Charles President of the minor-league Canadian Professional Hockey League.

Lichtenhein, Sam Owner of the Wanderers Hockey Club. Using the destruction of the Montreal Arena in a fire as a pretext, Lichtenhein folded his club in 1918 after years of financial losses.

Livingstone, Edward J.   Owner of the Toronto Shamrocks in the NHA. Livingstone's fellow owners abandoned him when they formed the NHL with the expressed purpose of excluding him from professional hockey. In an unsuccessful attempt to re-enter professional hockey, he aligned with Percy Quinn. He later owned the Chicago franchise in the minor-league American Hockey Association, but was banished from the AHA when it affiliated with the NHL.

McLaughlin, Frederick   Chicago amateur sportsman and millionaire. He was the owner of the Chicago (Blackhawks) National Hockey Club when the NHL granted a franchise to the city of Chicago.

Norris, James, Sr   A Canadian who had made his millions in the United States overseeing a vast empire of transportation and grain. Norris was reputed to be the richest man in America in the 1930s. He was part of the financing group that built the Chicago Stadium. Norris also backed the American Hockey Association's attempt to enter major-league hockey. He eventually became the owner of the NHL Detroit Hockey Club.

Northey, William   Avid amateur sportsman and later manager of the Montreal (Westmount) Arena, where most senior hockey matches were played. He was also involved in the building of the Toronto Arena Garden in the early 1910s.

O'Brien, James Ambrose   Principal organizer of the National Hockey Association. His family had vast fortunes in various industries. Together with a number of resource-industry barons, he bankrolled the NHA in its initial years. He was the owner of the Renfrew (Creamery Kings / Millionaires) Hockey Club.

Patrick, Frank   Second son in the Patrick family, which operated the Pacific Coast Hockey Association, Frank assumed the duties of president of the PCHA for most of the league's existence. He was also owner of the PCHA Vancouver (Millionaires) Hockey Club.

Patrick, Lester   Oldest member of the Patrick family. Together with his brother Frank, he created the PCHA and was the owner of the Victoria (Aristocrats / Cougars) Hockey Club. After the demise of major-league hockey in the West, he became the manager of the New York Rangers Hockey Club.

Quain, Redmond   Ottawa lawyer and director of the Ottawa Hockey Club. He assumed the position of NHL governor for the club when Frank Ahearn sold it to the Ottawa Auditorium in the early 1930s.

Quinn, Mike   Director of the Quebec Bulldogs, which folded in 1920.

Quinn, Percy   Owner of the expansion Toronto Hockey Club in 1912. He later purchased the the Quebec hockey club shortly after the NHL was formed, and for a time assumed the managership of the Toronto Arena Garden. His association with Eddie Livingstone led to his ostracization by the NHL's owners.

Quinn, T. Emmett   President of the National Hockey Association from 1910 until 1916, when he was replaced by Major Frank Robinson.

Rickard, George L. 'Tex'   One of the most famous boxing promoters of the 1920s, he was also instrumental in building a new Madison Square Garden in New York when he extended his sporting interests to hockey.

Ross, Arthur   Hockey player and later manager of the Boston (Bruins) Professional Hockey Club when the NHL expanded south into the United States.

Ross, Philip Dansken   One of the two original trustees of the Stanley Cup, he was also publisher of the *Ottawa Citizen*.

Shaughnessy, Tom   Former Chicago Blackhawks coach who bought the St Paul (Minn.) franchise of the AHA in order to organize the league to challenge the NHL.

Stanley, Frederick Arthur, Baron Stanley of Preston, 16th Earl of Derby
Governor General of Canada whose love of hockey led him to donate a trophy in 1893 to determine the hockey championship of Canada.

Strachan, James   Director of the Shamrocks Hockey Club in Montreal's senior circuit, he was later governor of the Montreal Maroons of the NHL.

Sweetland, John   One of the two original trustees of the Stanley Cup.

Taylor, Fred 'Cyclone'   Hockey player from the Ottawa area, arguably one of the most famous and sought-after players in elite-level hockey at the beginning of the twentieth century. His signing by the NHA and, later, the PCHA in part helped to legitimize the latter league's status.

Warren, A.G.   President of the American Hockey League until insurgents within the league seized power to challenge the NHL in 1930.

Notes

Chapter 1: Introduction

1 *Toronto Daily Mail*, 23 March 1894, 8.
2 The America's Cup, for yachting, was first presented in 1857, making it the oldest trophy today. The NHL did not come into existence until 1917, 24 years after Stanley Cup competition had begun.
3 Robert N. Stern, 'The Development of an Interorganizational Control Network: The Case of Intercollegiate Athletics,' *Administrative Science Quarterly* 24 (June 1979), 242–66. See *Networks and Organizations: Structure, Form, and Action*, ed. Nitin Nohria and Robert G. Eccles (Boston: Harvard Business School Press, 1992) for an examination of the various approaches in network theory. For stakeholder theory, see for example R. Edward Freeman, *Strategic Management: A Stakeholder Approach* Marshfield, MA: Pitman Publishing, 1984) and Thomas Donaldson and Lee Preston, 'Redefining the Corporation,' in *The Corporation and Its Stakeholders: Classic and Contemporary Readings*, ed. Max Clarkson (Toronto: University of Toronto Press, 1988). There are many studies that have player–management relationship as their foci. In hockey, see for example J.C.H. Jones, 'The Economics of the National Hockey League,' in *Canadian Sport: Sociological Perspectives*, ed. Richard S. Gruneau and John G. Albinson (Don Mills, ON: Addison-Wesley, 1976), 225–48; David Mills, 'The Blue Line and the Bottom Line: Entrepreneurs and the Business of Hockey in Canada, 1927–90,' in *The Business of Professional Sports*, ed. Paul D. Staudohar and James A. Mangan (Urbana and Chicago: University of Illinois Press, 1991), 175–201; and Rob Beamish, 'The Impact of Corporate Ownership on Labour–Management Relations in Hockey,' in *The Business of Professional Sports*, ed. Staudohar and Mangan, 202–21.
4 The three-part sport commodity consists of the activity or game-form, the service, and the goods. This book deals with the first two. Stephen Hardy, 'Entrepreneurs,

Organizations and the Sport Marketplace: Subjects in Search of Historians,' *Journal of Sport History*, Spring 1986, 14–33. I am influenced by Robert Stern's concept of Degree of System Coupling in network analysis. See Stern, 'The Development of an Interorganizational Control Network,' 244. See also Wayne Baker, *Achieving Success through Social Capital* (San Francisco: Jossey-Bass, 2000) for a discussion of power relationships within a network. Baker uses the concept of social capital. For examples of the multifaceted and interrelated forces in the workings of sport organizations, see Bruce Kidd, *The Struggle for Canadian Sport* (Toronto: University of Toronto Press, 1996); Donald Macintosh and Michael Hawes, *Sport and Canadian Diplomacy* (Montreal: McGill-Queen's University Press, 1994); and Donald Macintosh and David Whitson, *The Game Planners: Transforming Canada's Sport System* (Montreal: McGill-Queen's University Press, 1990). For a discussion of the importance of examining an organization's decision-making process, see Hardy, 'Entrepreneurs,' 14–33.

5 I am especially influenced by Paul DiMaggio's notion of network dynamics in a fluid environment. See Di Maggio, 'Nadel's Paradox Revisited: Relational and Cultural Aspects of Organizational Structure,' in *Networks and Organizations*, ed. Nohria and Eccles, 118–42.

6 Kidd, *The Struggle for Canadian Sport*, 190.

7 As a matter of fact, one historian has traced at least eight categories of modern athletes in the amateur-professional dichotomy. See David C. Young, *Myth of Greek Amateur Athletics* (Chicago: Ares Publishers, 1984), 182–3.

8 For jockeys as independent contractors, see Edward Hotaling, *The Great Black Jockeys: The Lives and Times of the Men Who Dominated America's First National Sport* (Rocklin, CA: Forum, 1999). For prize fighting, see Elliott J. Gorn, *The Manly Art: Bare-Knuckle Prize Fighting in America* (Ithaca, NY: Cornell University Press, 1986). For baseball, see Warren Goldstein, *Playing for Keeps: A History of Early Baseball* (Ithaca and London: Cornell University Press, 1989), 84–100.

9 Thomas J. Peters and Robert H. Waterman, Jr, *In Search of Excellence: Lessons from America's Best-Run Companies* (New York: Warner Books with Harper and Row, Publishers, 1982), 75–9. Peters and Waterman argued that initiatives must come from the employees if a company is to be successful. Far too often, management dictates its will to the employees, which invariably leads to confusion and perhaps non-compliance. For a study of the Japanese corporate culture that employs a group approach, see William G. Ouchi, *Theory Z* (New York: Avon Books, 1981). For a wonderful analysis of the struggles between management and workers to control work, see Lizabeth Cohen, *Making a New Deal: Industrial Workers in Chicago, 1919–1939* (New York: Cambridge University Press, 1990), 160–211.

10 For colonial and early Republic commercialized sports, see Nancy Struna, 'Taverns and Sports' and 'Epilogue: People of Prowess,' in *People of Prowess: Sport, Leisure, and*

Labour in Early Anglo-America (Urbana and Chicago: University of Illinois Press, 1996).

11 For the influence of technology on American sports, see John R. Betts, 'The Technological Revolution and the Rise of Sport, 1850–1900,' *Mississippi Valley Historical Review*, September 1953, 231–56. For an examination of work and leisure in the two different economies, see Keith Thomas, 'Work and Leisure in Pre-Industrial Society,' *Past and Present* 29 (1964), 50–66; and E.P. Thompson, 'Time, Work-Discipline and Industrial Capitalism,' *Past and Present* 38 (1967), 56–97.

12 For urbanization and the park movement, see John R. Betts, 'Public Recreation, Public Parks, and Public Health before the Civil War,' in *Big Ten Symposium on the History of Physical Education and Sport, Ohio State University, 1971*, ed. Bruce L. Bennett (Chicago: Athletic Institute, 1972), 33–52; Stephen Hardy, *How Boston Played: Sport, Recreation, and Community, 1865–1915* (Boston: Northeastern University Press, 1982); and Steven A. Riess, *City Games: The Evolution of American Urban Society and the Rise of Sports* (Urbana: University of Illinois Press, 1989). For a good analysis on one particular tavern sport, prize fighting, see Gorn, *The Manly Art.*

13 There are plenty of works on the history of baseball. Of importance for its general history is Harold Seymour, *Baseball*, 3 vols. (New York: Oxford University Press, 1960). An excellent early history of baseball can also be found in Melvin L. Adelman, 'The Early Years of Baseball, 1845–60' and 'Baseball Matures and Turns Professional, 1860–70,' in *A Sporting Time: New York City and the Rise of Modern Athletics* (Champaign: University of Illinois Press, 1986). For a detailed analysis of the development of baseball from amateur play to commercialization to professionalization, see Goldstein, *Playing for Keeps.*

14 Adelman, *A Sporting Time*, 122, 131–4; Goldstein, *Playing for Keeps*, 70–1, 84–100; Robert F. Burk, *Never Just a Game: Players, Owners, and American Baseball to 1920* (Chapel Hill, NC: University of North Carolina Press, 1994), 12–14, 26–49.

15 For early Canadian commercialized sports, see Alan Metcalfe, *Canada Learns to Play* (Toronto: McClelland & Stewart, 1987), 138, 141. See also Edwin C. Guillet, *Early Life in Upper Canada* (Toronto: University of Toronto Press, 1963), 298–302, 311–14, 340–1, 354; Donald Guay, 'Problèmes de l'intégration du sport dans la société canadienne, 1830–1865: Le cas des courses de chevaux,' *Canadian Journal of the History of Sport and Physical Education* 4, no. 2 (1973), 70–92; and Peter DeLottinville, 'Joe Beef of Montreal: Working Class Culture and the Tavern, 1869–1889,' *Labour / Le Travailleur*, Autumn/Spring 1981–2, 9–40. For the impact of industrialization and urbanization on sports in Canada, see Ian F. Jobling, 'Urbanization and Sport in Canada, 1867–1900,' in *Canadian Sport*, ed. Gruneau and Albinson, 64–77. For a discussion of Canadian immigration policies in the nineteenth century, see Ninette Kelley and Michael Trebilcock, *The Making of the Mosaic: A History of Canadian Immigration Policy* (Toronto: University of Toronto Press, 1998), 3–163. For the

Anglo-American relationship before Canadian Confederation, see Martin Craw-
ford, *The Anglo-American Crisis of the Mid-Nineteenth Century* (Athens: University of
Georgia Press, 1987).

16 See Frank Cosentino, 'A History of the Concept of Professionalism in Canadian
Sport,' PhD diss., University of Alberta, 1973, 24–43; Metcalfe, *Canada Learns to
Play*, 133–59; Kidd, *The Struggle for Canadian Sport*, 30; and Greg Gillespie, 'Roderick
McLennan, Professionalism, and the Emergence of the Athlete in Caledonian
Games,' *Sport History Review* 31, no. 1 (2000), 43–63.

17 Kenneth McNaught, *The Penguin History of Canada* (Toronto: Penguin Books
Canada, 1988), 165, 168. Carl Berger, 'Introduction,' in *Imperialism and Nationalism,
1884–1914: A Conflict in Canadian Thought* (Toronto: Copp Clark, 1969). For early
Canadian sports development from a social-class perspective, see Alan Metcalfe,
'The Roots of Organized Sport: Sport in British North America, 1807–1867,' in
Canada Learns to Play, and, for an analysis of class and ethnicity, Metcalfe, 'Organized
Sport and Social Stratification in Montreal: 1840–1901,' in *Canadian Sport*, ed.
Gruneau and Albinson, 77–101. For the British influence, see Peter Lindsay, 'The
Impact of the Military Garrisons on the Development of Sport in British North
America,' *Canadian Journal of History of Sport and Physical Education* 1, no. 1 (1970),
33–44; Henry Roxborough, 'There Always Was an England' and 'By Way of Scot-
land,' in *One Hundred-Not Out: The Story of Nineteenth-Century Canadian Sport*
(Toronto: Ryerson Press, 1966); and Gerald Redmond, *The Sporting Scots of Nine-
teenth-Century Canada* (London and Toronto: Associated University Press, 1982).

Chapter 2: From Fraternal Hockey Clubs to Closed Corporation

1 Richard Gruneau and David Whitson, *Hockey Night in Canada: Sport, Identities, and
Cultural Politics* (Toronto: Garamond Press, 1993), 44.

2 Gruneau and Whitson, *Hockey Night in Canada*, 41–3.

3 Michel Vigneault, 'Out of the Mists of Memory: Montreal's Hockey History,
1875–1910,' in *Total Hockey*, ed. Dan Diamond (New York: Total Sports, 1998), 10.

4 Vigneault has disputed the claims by three McGill students, Robert F. Smith,
W.L. Murray, and W.R. Robertson, who supposedly wrote the rules in 1879. Ibid.,
11.

5 For example, the *Montreal Gazette* reported three hockey matches in the beginning
months of 1879. Of the three, only the last one appeared in the sports and pastimes
section. See *Montreal Gazette*, 14 January and 1, 7, and 10 March 1879, 2.

6 Vigneault, 'Out of the Mists of Memory,' 10. According to another source, the two
sides represented the Montreal Football Club, a member of the Montreal Amateur
Athletic Association (MAAA), and the Victoria Skating Rink. While the reports
themselves neither confirm nor contradict this fact, the participants were undoubt-

edly members of the Victoria rink and/or guests. See Garth Vaughan, *The Puck Starts Here: The Origin of Canada's Great Winter Game Ice Hockey* (Fredericton, NB: Goose Lane Editions and Four East Publications, 1996), 48.

7 *Montreal Gazette*, 4 March 1875.

8 Ibid., 7 March 1879, 2. See appendix A, on hockey rules.

9 Vigneault, 'Out of the Mists of Memory,' 11.

10 *Montreal Gazette*, 4 December 1899, 2. Henry Roxborough, *One Hundred-Not Out: The Story of Nineteenth-Century Canadian Sport* (Toronto: Ryerson Press, 1966), 142, 144; Neil D. Isaacs, *Checking Back* (New York: W.W. Norton & Co., 1977), 26.

11 Vigneault, 'Out of the Mists of Memory,' 13.

12 *Montreal Gazette*, 27 February 1877.

13 Vigneault, 'Out of the Mists of Memory,' 12.

14 *Montreal Gazette*, 14 December 1893, 8.

15 A copy of the letter from Lord Stanley on the purpose of the Cup can be found in Roxborough, *One Hundred-Not Out*, 143. In keeping with the challenge format used by hockey clubs at the time, the original name of the trophy was the Dominion Hockey Challenge Cup, but it has generally been referred to as the Stanley Cup.

16 Gruneau and Whitson, *Hockey Night in Canada*, 40.

17 For the early rules of Stanley Cup competition, see appendix B.

18 *Montreal Gazette*, 9 November 1878, 2.

19 The annual grand masquerade hosted by the Victoria rink was an important event in the Montreal winter social calendar. See, for example, *Montreal Gazette*, 20 February 1879, 2. The rink also hosted skating championships. See *Montreal Gazette*, 28 February and 1 March 1879, 2.

20 The Montreal Gymnasium was taken over by the MAAA.

21 Alan Metcalfe, *Canada Learns to Play* (Toronto: McClelland & Stewart, 1987), 136–7. See also *Montreal Gazette*, 1 January 1879, 2.

22 Unlike the Victoria rink, the Crystal rink was built as a commercial enterprise from the beginning. *Montreal Gazette*, 20 November 1878, 2, and 6 January 1879, 2. See also Gruneau and Whitson, *Hockey Night in Canada*, 64.

23 *Montreal Gazette*, 4 December 1893, 8. Early clubs usually consisted of a number of teams. In the case of the Wanderers, there were four teams that played a regular schedule as well as taking challenges from outside clubs. This was not the same Wanderers club as the one created in 1903.

24 Ibid., 4 March 1893, 8.

25 Ibid., 17 March 1894, 8.

26 For a discussion of the notion and importance of time in industrial capitalism, see E.P. Thompson, 'Time, Work-Discipline, and Industrial Capitalism,' *Past and Present* 38 (1967), 56–97, and also Nancy L. Struna, *People of Prowess: Sport, Leisure, and*

Labor in Early Anglo-America (Urbana and Chicago: University of Illinois Press, 1996), 166–8.

27 The complaint appeared in the *Montreal Gazette*, 21 March 1894, 8. Reports of late starts were quite regular. See for example *Montreal Gazette*, 11 February 1893, 8; 4 March 1894, 8; 8 March 1894, 8; and Charles L. Coleman, *The Trail of the Stanley Cup*, 3 vols. (Sherbrooke, QC: Sherbrooke Daily Record Co., 1964), 1: 20.

28 *Montreal Gazette*, 1 and 30 December 1898, 2. For a description of the new arena and its services, see *Montreal Gazette*, 22 December 1898, 2 and 2 January 1899, 2. See also Coleman, *The Trail of the Stanley Cup*, 1: 46.

29 National Archives of Canada, Gault W. Lea Papers, MG 30 E, 419, Northey to Gault, 12 March 1959.

30 Metcalfe, *Canada Learns to Play*, 104–19.

31 Don Morrow, *A Sporting Evolution: The Montreal Amateur Athletic Association, 1881–1981* (n.p.: Montreal Amateur Athletic Association and Don Morrow, 1981), 14.

32 Ibid., 182–3.

33 In 1888, the MAAA added a ten-dollar initiation fee, and in 1903 increased its annual membership fees to $15. Ibid., 58–9.

34 Frank Cosentino, 'A History of the Concept of Professionalism in Canadian Sport,' PhD diss., University of Alberta, 1973, 42.

35 Morrow, *A Sporting Evolution*, 58. For a description of the MAAA structure, see ibid., 29–31.

36 Ibid., 228.

37 Metcalfe, *Canada Learns to Play*, 112.

38 For lacrosse and professionalism, see ibid., 211–17.

39 Ibid., 114, and Kevin G. Jones, 'Sports and Games from 1900–20,' in *History of Sport in Canada*, ed. M.L. Howell and R.A. Howell (Champaign, IL: Stipes Publishing Co., 1981), 187–8.

40 Metcalfe, *Canada Learns to Play*, 113–14

41 Coleman, *The Trail of the Stanley Cup*, 1: 20–1.

42 Gruneau and Whitson, *Hockey Night in Canada*, 200–1. The original passage actually includes national conversation about the game as part of hockey's appeal to Canadians. For the period in this chapter, however, it would be too soon to speak of a national conversation.

43 *Winnipeg Free Press*, 1 and 11 February 1896, as quoted in Brian McFarlane, 'Our Electrifying Game: Hockey in the Era of Gaslight,' in Diamond, *Total Hockey*, 24.

44 *Winnipeg Free Press*, 15 February 1896, as quoted ibid., 24–5.

45 This is based on the *Montreal Gazette* and is generally true for the other major English-language newspaper, the *Star*, in Montreal. Hockey coverage in the French press in Montreal, *La Presse* and *La Patrie*, did not begin until around the end of the nineteenth century. By the mid-1890s, media coverage also increased significantly

in Ottawa. See Peter Wilson, 'How Early Hockey Was Reported,' in *Total Hockey*, ed. Diamond, 27. Regarding increased sport coverage and the growth of daily newspapers, see Stacy L. Lorenz, '"A Lively Interest on the Prairies": Western Canada, the Mass Media, and a "World of Sport," 1870–1939,' *Journal of Sport History* 27 (Summer 2000), 195–227 and 'In the Field of Sport at Home and Abroad': Sports Coverage in Canadian Daily Newspapers,' *Sport History Review*, November 2003, 133–67.

46 *Montreal Gazette*, 20 January 1886, p. 8. At the end of that season, the *Gazette* again evaluated the season's games as 'for the most part ... rough.' Ibid., 26 March 1886, 8.
47 Ibid., 26 March 1886, 8. The game report originally appeared on 20 March.
48 The AHAC executives rejected the Crystals' protest. *Montreal Gazette*, 13 March 1893, 2. There were three protests that prompted the AHAC to call a special meeting, two of which involved the senior league clubs. For the rulings on the protests, see ibid., 14 March 1893, 8.
49 Ibid., 14 December 1893, 8.
50 Ibid., 23 March 1894, 8.
51 Ibid., 7 January 1904, 2. Pittsburgh had started a professional league at the Duquesne Garden and had been luring players away from the Canadian leagues. For a social-historical analysis of hockey and violence, see Lyle Allen Hallowell, 'The Political Economy of Violence and Control: A Sociological History of Professional Ice Hockey,' PhD diss., University of Minnesota, 1981.
52 Warren Goldstein, *Playing for Keeps: A History of Early Baseball* (Ithaca, NY: Cornell University Press, 1989), 84–100.
53 *Montreal Gazette*, 2 December 1893, 8.
54 Ibid., 4 December 1899, 2.
55 Coleman, *The Trail of the Stanley Cup*, 1: 47.
56 *Montreal Gazette*, 11 December 1899, 2. For the breakup of the AHAC, see Coleman, *The Trail of the Stanley Cup*, 1: 40, 45.
57 Coleman, *The Trail of the Stanley Cup*, 1: 61.

Chapter 3: The Hockey Front in the Athletic War

1 Alan Metcalfe, *Canada Learns to Play* (Toronto: McClelland & Stewart, 1987), 114–16. See also Don Morrow, 'A Case Study in Amateur Conflict: The Athletic War in Canada, 1906–1909,' in *Sports in Canada: Historical Readings* ed. Morris Mott (Toronto: Copp Clark Pitman Ltd, 1989), 201–19.
2 Charles L. Coleman, *The Trail of the Stanley Cup* (Sherbrooke, QC: Sherbrooke Daily Record Co., 1964), 1: 68.
3 Ibid. See also *Montreal Gazette*, 9 December 1903, 2 regarding the supply of and demand for ice rinks in Montreal.

4 Coleman, *The Trail of the Stanley Cup*, 1: 65.

5 Ibid., 1: 76–7, 83. It must be remembered that the Stanley Cup series remained a challenge series, even though the CAHL and other associations were playing a regular schedule. Thus, a challenge for the Cup could be issued at any time during the season. The challenge for the Stanley Cup as part of post–regular season play would not appear until the next decade. For detailed reports of the quarrels between the Stanley Cup Trustees and the CAHL directors, see *Montreal Star*, 8 January 1903, 18, 5 January 1903, 2, and 8 January 1903, 2.

6 *Montreal Star*, 9 January 1903, 2.

7 *Montreal Gazette*, 5 December 1904, 2.

8 Coleman, *The Trail of the Stanley Cup*, 1: 24, 38, 51, 71–2, 84–5, and 96–7.

9 Donald Swainson, 'Ontario on the Rise,' *Horizon Canada* 66 (1986), 1561–7.

10 In the 1900 Stanley Cup series between the Shamrocks and Winnipeg, for example, the second game drew about 5000. The third game also brought out a large audience, including the governor-general. Coleman, *The Trail of the Stanley Cup*, 1: 57–8. The next year, when the Winnipeg challenger won the cup, the second-game gate receipts totalled $2700, supposedly the largest up to that time. Ibid., 1: 65.

11 *Montreal Gazette*, 3 December 1903, 2. As a further insult, the report lauded the brand of hockey played in Manitoba as superior.

12 Coleman, *The Trail of the Stanley Cup*, 1: 54.

13 *Montreal Gazette*, 9 December 1903, 2. A different article on the same page stated that the Montagnard rink was going to make several changes in order to 'induce the Wanderers to play matches and practice' there. The changes included conforming the size of the ice surface to that of the Montreal Arena and furnishing 3500 seats.

14 *Montreal Gazette*, 5 December 1899, 2. For a brief history of refrigeration technology in ice hockey, see Donald M. Clark, 'Early Artificial Ice,' in *Total Hockey*, ed. Dan Diamond (New York: Total Sports, 1998), 564–5.

15 *Montreal Gazette*, 14 and 15 December 1899, 2. See also Coleman, *The Trail of the Stanley Cup*, 1: 61, 76.

16 *Montreal Gazette*, 3 November 1903, 2. Cornwall is about 100 kilometres to the west of Montreal and was linked with it by railroads. By comparison, Ottawa was 180 kilometres, and Quebec City over 250 kilometres, away.

17 Ibid., 13 November 1903, 2. There were no particulars as to why the players were unhappy. Even at this stage of hierarchical development in senior hockey, players were active members of the clubs and sometimes served on the executive board or the various committees. Thus, they had voting rights in determining the policies of the club. Similarly, club directors consisted of businessmen who were supporters of, and past players on, the clubs. Besides managing the club businesses, they also

contributed by acting as referees and goal judges. The line between club management and players was still not sharp.

18 See for example, three articles, one each from Montreal, Ottawa, and Cornwall, that appeared in the *Montreal Gazette*, 2 December 1903, 2, and 3 December 1903, 2; and a dispatch from Ottawa, ibid., 9 December 1903, 2.

19 Ibid., 2 December 1903, 2.

20 The other French-Canadian club, the Montagnards, threatened to form another league if it failed to gained admission into the FAHL. But the FAHL insisted on one French-Canadian team only in order to draw the French-Canadian spectators. The second new league never materialized. See *Montreal Gazette*, 4 December 1903, 2. William Foran would later become a Stanley Cup trustee.

21 Ibid., 5 December 1903, 2.

22 Ibid., 7 December 1903, 2.

23 Ibid., 7 January 1904, 2.

24 Ibid., 8 February 1904, 2. See also Coleman, *The Trail of the Stanley Cup*, 1: 88.

25 Up until 1904, only two non-AHAC/CAHL clubs had won the Stanley Cup, Winnipeg in February 1896 (the AHAC's Victorias quickly regained the Cup before the start of the following season) and Winnipeg again in 1901. Reportedly, it cost the Winnipeg club over $1000 for their first successful bid in 1896, and the Victorias around $1200 to get the Cup back. The system was decidedly against the challengers economically. See *Montreal Gazette*, 9 February 1899, 2.

26 See the various articles and out-of-town despatches that appeared in the *Montreal Gazette*, 9 February 1904, 2; and also the editorials in the *Gazette*, 10 and 15 February 1904, 2, under the title 'One Man's View.' See also Coleman, *The Trail of the Stanley Cup*, 1: 88–9.

27 *Montreal Gazette*, 10 February 1904, 2.

28 Ibid., 15 February 1904, 2.

29 Actually, the Ottawas played the FAHL champions, the Wanderers, to a draw in the first game of a two-game series. When asked to replay the first match in Montreal, Ottawa refused and the trustees again sided with the Ottawa club. The Wanderers subsequently withdrew from competition, again with much public bickering. Coleman, *The Trail of the Stanley Cup*, 1: 94–100.

30 *Montreal Gazette*, 25 February 1904, 2.

31 To follow the development of the proposed amalgamation, see page 2 in the *Montreal Gazette*, 28, 29, and 30 November 1904. See also Coleman, *The Trail of the Stanley Cup*, 1: 102.

32 Reports on the two games can be found in *Montreal Gazette*, 15 February 1904, 2 and 25 February 1904, 2, respectively.

33 The Michigan franchises were in Calumet, Houghton, and Sault Ste Marie; the Canadian city of the same name, across the border, also had a team. Studies on the IHL have been few. See Daniel Scott Mason, 'The Origins and Development of the International Hockey League and Its Effects on the Sport of Professional Ice Hockey in North America,' MA thesis, University of British Columbia, August, 1994; Daniel S. Mason, 'The International Hockey League and the Professionalization of Ice Hockey, 1904–1907,' *Journal of Sport History* 25 (Spring 1998), 1–17; and Daniel Mason and Barbara Schrodt, 'Hockey's First Professional Team: The Portage Lakes Hockey Club of Houghton, Michigan,' *Sport History Review* 27 (May 1996), 49–71.

34 *Montreal Gazette*, 22 November 1904, 2. A copy of a contract signed by E.J. Schaeffer to play with the professional hockey team of Sault Ste Marie for $22 a week appeared in the press. See *Montreal Gazette*, 16 December 1904, 2.

35 Houghton and Calumet, for example, had populations of 3359 and 4668 respectively around the turn of the twentieth century. Mason, 'The International Hockey League,' 5.

36 Take, for example, the case of Kenneth Mallon, a former Wanderer player who had moved to Brockville by 'October 1st, so as to be eligible' to play for the local FAHL entry. Calumet of the IHL supposedly lured him away at $500 for the season. See *Montreal Gazette*, 26 November 1904, 2, and 12 December 1904, 2. The first-year salary limit, set at $25 a week, was increased to $40 in the second season. But it is doubtful that the salary cap was strictly adhered to given the competitive bidding among the IHL clubs as well as the incentive needed to lure players away from Canada. See *Montreal Gazette*, 30 December 1904, 2, and 4 December 1905, p. 2. See also Eric Whitehead, 'Houghton,' in *Cyclone Taylor: A Hockey Legend* (Toronto: Doubleday Canada, 1977).

37 The OHA suspended Hummel and McDonald of Brockville as well as E.J. Schaeffer of Midland for playing in the professional league that season. See *Montreal Gazette*, 31 December 1904, 2.

38 The seven clubs included the Wanderers and the French-Canadian Montagnards of the FAHL (the latter club joined the FAHL after the Nationals defected to the CAHL) and the CAHL's Montreal-based clubs: the Montreal Hockey Club, the Victorias, the Shamrocks, the Nationals, and the Westmount Hockey Club. The last two were admitted instead of the proposed Ottawa-Wanderers entry.

39 *Montreal Gazette*, 18 and 20 November 1905, 2. See also page 2 of the *Gazette*, 30 November and 1 and 6 December 1905, for the wrangling about admission to the ECAHA.

40 Sheppard noted that the Wanderers had netted approximately 'almost a thousand dollars more than the Montreal, Shamrock and Westmount clubs,' and the estimated

revenue from the Wanderers was '$4,400 and the C.A.H.L. clubs $3,500.' Ibid., 8 December 1905, 2.

41 For problems with ice time, see *Montreal Gazette*, 9 December 1905, 2. For the almost verbatim text of the meeting, see ibid., 11 December 1905, 2. A copy of the signed agreement, sometimes known as the 'offensive and defensive' alliance, can be found ibid., 8 December 1905, 2. It included all the CAHL clubs except the Nationals.

42 Ibid., 12 December 1905, 2.

43 Wilson's last active role was his election in 1905 as the president of the Victoria club, and he had served as secretary-treasurer of the AHAC in 1897. Between 1901 and 1906, he was the honorary patron of the Victoria Hockey Club. Coleman, *The Trail of the Stanley Cup*, 1: 40. See also *Montreal Gazette*, 9 November 1905, 2.

44 *Montreal Gazette*, 12 December 1905, 2. See also Coleman, *The Trail of the Stanley Cup*, 1: 117–18.

45 *Montreal Gazette*, 14 December 1905, 2.

46 Ibid., 18 December 1905, 2.

47 Ibid.

48 Ibid., 2 November 1906, 4. For the Victoria's club reaction to this development, see ibid., 14 November 1906, 2.

49 The statement was made in the context of the lacrosse situation. See ibid., 20 November 1906, 4.

50 Ibid., 12 November 1906, 4. See also Coleman, *The Trail of the Stanley Cup*, 1: 131.

51 *Montreal Gazette*, 14 November 1906, 2.

52 Ibid., 13 November 1906, 2.

53 See Coleman, *The Trail of the Stanley Cup*, 1: 132–3.

54 William Foran was also the president of the FAHL at the time. He eventually succeeded Sheriff John Sweetland, one of the two original appointees by Lord Stanley, as a trustee for the Stanley Cup when Sweetland passed away on 5 May 1907. Coleman, *The Trail of the Stanley Cup*, 1: 144–7.

55 Their geographical locations were so close that the public generally referred to the league as the Trolley League.

56 Coleman, *The Trail of the Stanley Cup*, 1: 158. Actually Manitoba had also formed a professional league consisting of three clubs, Kenora, Portage, and the Winnipeg Strathconas. Morris Mott, 'The Problem of Professionalism: The Manitoba Amateur Athletic Association and the Fight against Pro Hockey, 1904–1911,' in ed. E.A. Corbet and A.W. Rasporich, *Winter Sports in the West* (Calgary: Historical Society of Alberta, 1990).

57 For the Ottawa troubles, see *Montreal Gazette*, 9 November 1907, 2, and 12 and 14 November 1907, 4.

58 For the Wanderers, see ibid., 16 November 1907, 2. For Montreal, see National
    Archives of Canada (hereafter NAC), Montreal Amateur Athletic Association, MG
    28, I 351, vol. 6, file 3, p. 40, in which the treasurer's statement lists salaries for
    players, coach, and trainers totalling $2,004.35; gate receipts for the 1907–8 season
    were $1,741.10. See also Coleman, *The Trail of the Stanley Cup*, 1: 151–2. For the
    Victoria club, see *Montreal Gazette*, 9 November 1907, 2.

Chapter 4: Leagues of Their Own

 1 Paul DiMaggio, 'Nadel's Paradox Revisited: Relational and Cultural Aspects of
    Organizational Structure,' in *Networks and Organizations: Structure, Form, and Action*,
    ed. Nitin Nohria and Robert G. Eccles (Boston: Harvard Business School Press,
    1992), 118–42. Quote is on 124. For the importance of legitimation in generating
    sport policies, see also Laurence L. Chalip, 'Policy Analysis in Sport Management,'
    Journal of Sport Management, January 1995, 1–13.
 2 For the struggles between the CAAU and the AAFC in general, and the Olympic
    incident in particular, see Alan Metcalfe, *Canada Learns to Play* (Toronto: McClel-
    land & Stewart, 1987), 115–17; and Don Morrow, 'A Case Study in Amateur
    Conflict: The Athletic War in Canada, 1906–1909,' in *Sports in Canada: Historical
    Readings*, ed. Morris Mott (Toronto: Copp Clark Pitman, 1989), 211–14.
 3 Charles L. Coleman, *The Trail of the Stanley Cup* (Sherbrooke, QC: Sherbrooke Daily
    Record Co., 1964), 1: 152.
 4 *Montreal Gazette*, 4 and 5 November 1908, 2.
 5 Ibid., 23 November 1907, 16.
 6 Ibid., 16 November 1908, 2. The trustees denounced the 'promiscuous buying and
    selling of players' in a letter sent to the ECAHA and thereby precipitated the de-
    parture of the Montreal and Victoria clubs. For a more detailed account of this
    incident, see John Chi-Kit Wong, 'The Development of Professional Hockey and
    the Making of the National Hockey League,' PhD diss., University of Maryland,
    2001, 117–19.
 7 *Montreal Gazette*, 23 November 1908, 2.
 8 See ibid., 20 and 28 November 1908 and 2 December 1908, 2.
 9 Coleman, *The Trail of the Stanley Cup*, 1: 166.
10 National Archives of Canada (NAC), Montreal Amateur Athletic Association, MG
    28, I 351, vol. 6, file 3, p. 40. There were no itemized details, but the amount
    included payments to players, trainers, and coach. When Montreal was bidding for
    the services of Ross, Hern, and Pitre before it resigned from the ECAHA, the club
    offered $1500, $600, and $900 respectively. Ibid., pp. 45, 47.
11 *Montreal Gazette*, 1 December 1908, 2.
12 Ibid., 3 December 1908, 2.

13 'Series D280–287: Annual Earnings in Manufacturing Industries, Production and Other Workers, by Sex, Canada, 1905, 1910 and 1917 to 1959,' in *Historical Statistics of Canada*, ed. M.C. Urquhart, asst. ed. K.A.H. Buckley (Cambridge: At the University Press, Toronto: MacMillan Co. of Canada, 1965), 99.

14 *Montreal Gazette*, 16 December 1908, 2.

15 Coleman, *The Trail of the Stanley Cup*, 1: 174–6. For Lester Patrick's early hockey travels, see Eric Whitehead, *The Patricks: Hockey's Royal Family* (Toronto: Doubleday Canada, 1980), 23–4, 26–40, 46–8. According to Patrick's account, he only received expenses for the Edmonton challenge and was not paid a salary.

16 *Montreal Gazette*, 13 November 1909, 2.

17 It must be remembered that the origin of the Wanderers was quite different from that of the other clubs. Its birth was owed to the defection of disaffected players and was financed by some backers. For the Wanderers' buyout, see Coleman, *The Trail of the Stanley Cup*, 1: 178. See also *Montreal Gazette*, 15 November 1909, 6.

18 *Montreal Gazette*, 2 November 1909, 2, and 13 December 1909, 2 (quote).

19 Ibid., 16 November 1909, 2.

20 Coleman, *The Trail of the Stanley Cup*, 1: 179. See *Montreal Gazette*, 26 November 1909, 4. See also ibid., 27 November 1909, 2, for an assessment of Ottawa's role in this coup.

21 *Montreal Gazette*, 4 December 1909, 2. See also Frank Cosentino, *The Renfrew Millionaires: The Valley Boys of Winter 1910* (Burnstown, ON: General Store Publishing House, 1990), 35–50.

22 Scott Young and Astrid Young, *O'Brien* (Toronto: Ryerson Press, 1967).

23 *Montreal Gazette*, 4 December 1909, 2.

24 Coleman, *The Trail of the Stanley Cup*, 1: 180. See also Eric Whitehead, *Cyclone Taylor: A Hockey Legend* (Toronto: Doubleday Canada Ltd, 1977), 103–6. For more player dealings, see *Montreal Gazette* for 1, 4, 6, 16, 17, and 20 December 1909, 2.

25 Renfrew is less than 100 kilometres west of Ottawa. *Montreal Gazette*, 16 December 1909, 2.

26 Ibid., 3, 4, and 6 December 1909, 2.

27 Ibid., 18 December 1909, 2.

28 Ibid., 30 December 1909, 2. Coleman, *The Trail of the Stanley Cup*, 1: 183.

29 *Montreal Gazette*, 6 January 1910, 5. Coleman, *The Trail of the Stanley Cup*, 1: 183.

30 *Montreal Gazette*, 10 January 1910, 2. It must be remembered that the Jubilee rink was located in the francophone east end, the poorer side of town; its full capacity was only a little over 3000.

31 *Montreal Gazette*, 10 January 1910, 9. The Arena seated 7000.

32 Ibid., 11 January 1910, 2.

33 Ibid., 12 and 13 January 1910, 2.

34 Ibid., 15 January 1910, 2.

35 Ibid., 6 and 8 January 1910, 2.

36 Neither Barnet nor O'Brien, for example, came from an upper-class background. Barnet, who had only a country school education, began working as a lumberman at age 15. O'Brien was the son of Irish immigrants.

37 A brief biography of Quinn can be found in *Ottawa Citizen*, 11 February 1930, 10.

38 *Montreal Gazette*, 17 January 1910, 5.

Chapter 5: In Search of Hockey Order

1 R. Edward Freeman, *Strategic Management: A Stakeholder Approach* (Marshfield, MA: Pitman Publishing Inc., 1984), vii.

2 *Montreal Gazette*, 10 November 1910, 10.

3 Ibid., 12 October 1911, 11.

4 The Shamrocks wanted to hold on to the franchise for one year, but this was rejected by the league. See *Montreal Gazette*, 15 November, 1910, 10, and 21 November 1910, 12.

5 Ibid., 17 November 1910, 7. See also ibid., 25 November 1910, 10, on the proposed new league organized by the players.

6 With the media taking the side of management in the salary issue, a letter from the star defenceman Art Ross appeared in the *Montreal Herald* on 25 November 1910 presenting the players' case. He pointed out that, unlike professional baseball players, professional hockey players had to have another job due to the short season. Injuries sustained in hockey could seriously hurt the players' other careers. Most importantly, skilled professionals should be compensated 'as revenue producers.' As reprinted in Charles L. Coleman, *The Trail of the Stanley Cup* (Sherbrooke, QC: Sherbrooke Daily Record Co., 1964), 1: 202–3.

7 *Montreal Gazette*, 24 November 1910, 11. For comment by the league president, see ibid., 25 November 1910, 10.

8 Ibid., 28 November 1910, 12.

9 News of the players' revolt filled the pages of the press from the end of November to about mid-December. See, for example, *Montreal Gazette*, 6 December 1910, 13. The Arena's announcement of the rink accommodation situation appeared ibid., 12 December 1910, 12.

10 Ibid., 5 January 1911, 10.

11 Ibid., 23 January 1911, 12.

12 Ibid., 31 January 1911, 10. The players eventually received $300 each, and made the news when they complained that the clubs were carrying 'too many officials to New York and Boston and charged their expenses to the general receipts,' which cut into the $450 promised to them. Ibid., 10 April 1911, 12.

13 See appendix C, NHA Constitution, sect. 4.

14 Montreal Gazette, 20 January 1911, 10. It is worth noting that the English news-paper, the *Gazette*, admonished the Canadiens' complaint as poor sportsmanship and noted the partisanship of all the French newspapers in town supporting the Canadiens' claim. See also Coleman, *The Trail of the Stanley Cup*, 1: 206.

15 *Montreal Gazette*, 2 February 1911, 10.

16 Ibid., 24 January 1911, 10.

17 Ibid., 27 January 1911, 12. See also Quebec Chronicle, 27 December 1911, 6.

18 Coleman, *The Trail of the Stanley Cup*, 1: 206. Two years later, referee Leo Dandurand, also the future owner of the Canadiens, wrote an open letter to Emmett Quinn detailing the verbal and physical abuses he received from George Kennedy during and after a game between the Canadiens and the Wanderers. There was no record of Quinn taking any action. Ibid., 1: 252.

19 Indeed, ex-Victoria (amateur) players officiated in the first four NHA games of the 1910–11 season. See *Montreal Gazette*, 11 January 1911, 10.

20 See *Montreal Gazette*, 19 October, 1911, 11, and 4 December 1911, 13.

21 The rover played both offence and defence. Protecting its own strength, Ottawa tried in vain to mount a campaign to return to seven-men hockey before the season started. See *Montreal Gazette*, 2 November 1911, 10, and 1 January 1912, 12. For comments by Ottawa players criticizing the new rules, see also ibid., 5 January 1912, 10. For an anecdote on the economic justification in converting seven- to six-man hockey, see Morey Holzman and Joseph Nieforth, *Deceptions and Doublecross: How the NHL Conquered Hockey* (Toronto: Dundurn Group, 2002), 25.

22 *Montreal Gazette*, 11 November 1912, 16.

23 Ibid., 15 and 16 November 1912, 13. It might be important to note here that the Torontos' NHA representative was Percy Quinn, who would later be one of the central figures in the establishment of the NHL.

24 Besides the positive report on league finances for the 1911–12 season, the 1910–11 season had also been a good one. Of the five clubs, four made money. Ottawa netted from $6000 to $8000 in profits; the Canadiens, $3000–$4000; the Wanderers, $2000–$3000; and Quebec about $900. See *Montreal Gazette*, 7 March 1911, 10. Renfrew, which subsequently withdrew, lost money, but not for lack of customers. Even when a small population, its rink could not accommodate the local demand for tickets. See ibid., 10 March 1911, 10.

25 Also among these ranks were the Maritime Professional Hockey League, the New Ontario League, and the Saskatchewan Hockey League.

26 Thomas D. Picard, 'The Pacific Coast Hockey Association,' in *Total Hockey*, ed. Dan Diamond (New York: Total Sports, 1998), 35. See also Eric Whitehead, *The Patricks: Hockey's Royal Family*, 1st ed. (Toronto: Doubleday, 1980), 104.

27 Their father, Joe Patrick, had sold the family timber business for $440,000. Rewarding the two sons' work in the business, he had given both of them $50,000 from the sale. When the brothers decided to go into the professional hockey business, Joe went along with them. Despite the tidy sum of profit from the sale of the timber business, the family had to take out a mortgage of $100,000 to finance the arena venture after a public offering of stocks failed to attract much interest. Whitehead, *The Patricks*, 97. The Vancouver Arena's estimated cost of $220,000 would rise to $275,000. Ibid., 109. A contrary account of the building cost and seating capacity of the Vancouver Arena can be found in Picard, 'The Pacific Coast Hockey Association,' 35. For the total capital investment see Whitehead, *The Patricks*, 111.

28 For an account of the development of the Canadian railway system and its contribution to the growth of Canada, see G.P. de T. Glazebrook, *A History of Transportation in Canada* (New York: Greenwood Press, 1938), 191–341; A.W. Currie, *The Grand Trunk Railway of Canada* (Toronto: University of Toronto Press, 1957), 394–415; and G.R. Stevens, *History of the Canadian National Railways* (New York: Macmillan, 1973), 208–37. For an analysis of the British Columbian economy at the turn of the century, see Allen Seager, 'The Resource Economy, 1871–1921,' in *The Pacific Province: A History of British Columbia*, ed. Hugh J.M. Johnston (Vancouver/Toronto: Douglas & McIntyre, 1996), 205–52.

29 For comments on the early-twentieth-century Canadian economy, see Kenneth McNaught, *The Penguin History of Canada* (London: Penguin Books, 1988), 214–15; and John Herd Thompson, with Allen Seager, *Canada, 1922–1939: Decades of Discord* (Toronto: McClelland & Stewart, 1994), 24–5. See also, on Canadian anti-trust policy, Michael Bliss, 'Another Anti-Trust Tradition: Canadian Anti-Combines Policy, 1889–1910,' *Business History Review* 47, no. 2 (Summer 1973), 177–88; and Russell Smandych, 'The Origins of Canadian Anti-Combines Legislation, 1890–1910,' in *The Social Basis Law: Critical Readings in the Sociology of Law*, 2nd ed. Elizabeth Comack and Stephen Brickey, eds., (Halifax: Garamond Press, 1991), 35–47. Capitalization of Canadian industry in 1900 stood just over $12.9 million and reached over $490.5 million in 1912. Paul W. Bennett and Cornelius J. Jaenen, *Emerging Identities: Selected Problems and Interpretations in Canadian History* (Scarborough, ON: Prentice-Hall Canada, 1986), 356–7.

30 Whitehead, *The Patricks*, 106–7. Quote is on page 107.

31 Coleman, *The Trail of the Stanley Cup*, 1: 228.

32 *Montreal Gazette*, 15 December 1911, 12.

33 Ibid., 4 November 1911, 12.

34 Ibid., 13 November 1911, 13.

35 Ibid., 23 November 1911, 11; and 2 December 1910, 12.

36 Ibid., 15 December 1911, 12.

37 Ibid., 18 December 1911, 14.

38 Ibid., 13 December 1911, 10; 14 and 15 December 1911, 12.

39 For reports on problems and squabbles over the PCHA's challenge to the Stanley Cup, see *Montreal Gazette*, 1, 9, and 10 February 1912, 12. At one time during the debate, Boston proposed to have the PCHA and the NHA champions play the Cup series in Boston. Cup trustee Foran rejected the proposal outright, stating that '[t]he cup was donated for the championship of Canada, and we will certainly oppose any move to play for it outside the Dominion.' Ibid., 6 February 1910, 10. See also *Vancouver Province*, 21 February 1912, 10 for a copy of the telegram to Foran from the PCHA challenging for the Stanley Cup.

40 *Montreal Gazette*, 6 November 1912, 10, and 11 November 1912, 16.

41 Ibid., 22 November 1912, 12. Ironically, it was the Wanderers' owner, Sam Lichtenhein, who had the worst feud with the Patricks. Ibid., 8 November 1912, 11.

42 Whitehead, *The Patricks*, 118. A different source suggested it was otherwise: 7068 paid to see the first game and 6620 the second game in the 1912–13 season. Nevertheless, the same source said Vancouver had 'gone hockey crazy and appreciate[d] the class of hockey that is being served up to them.' *Montreal Gazette*, 27 December 1912, 10.

43 The PCHA had retained the seven-man format as the NHA clubs employed the six-man unit. Although the western style featured an extra man, forward-passing allowed an even speedier game than eastern-style six-man hockey. For game innovations by the PCHA, see Whitehead, *The Patricks*, 127–30.

44 The NHA actually had a playoff system before the PCHA did. In the NHA playoff, the leader in the first half of the season played the winner of the second half. Theoretically speaking, there might not be a playoff at all if the same team won both halves of the season. The PCHA system called for the first and second place finishers of the season to play each other, thus guaranteeing a playoff series.

45 Frank Patrick to Frank Calder, 27 January 1918, 1922–3, Vancouver Arena Company file, National Hockey League Archives (hereafter NHLA). Franchise instability plagued the PCHA. The league never had more than four franchises in any one year, and only Vancouver lasted the whole PCHA's existence.

46 Frank Patrick to Frank Calder, 22 July 1919, 1922–3, Vancouver Arena Company file, NHLA.

47 Details of the agreement, which appeared in the *Montreal Gazette* on 5 September 1913 (p. 11), credited the NHA president as the prime mover behind the agreement. A similar agreement was reached between the NHA and the Maritime professional league. But for all intents and purposes, the Maritime league was a minor league compared to the NHA and the PCHA, and would never be involved in Stanley Cup playoffs. *Montreal Gazette*, 10 November 1913, 18.

48 Buoyed by good gate receipts, Emmett Quinn, the NHA president, had explored

the possibility of establishing an American section of the league in 1911. The NHA had played some exhibition games in New York and Boston, and generated some interest among local entrepreneurs in entering professional hockey. See *Montreal Gazette*, 21 and 27 March 1911, 10.

49 Ibid., 6 April 1917, 14. For an enthusiastic report in anticipation of the Stanley Cup series in Seattle, see *Seattle Post-Intelligencer*, 11 March 1917, 1.

Chapter 6: An Inglorious End and an Inauspicious Beginning

1 Livingstone was arguably the most important person in the establishment of the NHL, yet little is known about him. Two authors recently rescued Livingstone from anonymity. See Morey Holzman and Joseph Nieforth, *Deceptions and Doublecross: How the NHL Conquered Hockey* (Toronto: Dundurn Group, 2002). For Living-stone's background in amateur sports in Toronto, see ibid., 52–8.

2 It must be noted that when the TRAA members first heard about the purchase of the professional club by Livingstone, at least two TRAA players wanted to remain as amateurs. Some TRAA members eventually turned professional. Harry Meeking, in particular, joined Livingstone's club the following season. *Toronto Globe*, 9 December 1914, 13. See also Holzman and Nieforth, *Deceptions and Doublecross*, 59, 64, 90.

3 *Montreal Gazette*, 27 September 1915, 12. Paul W. Bennett and Cornelius J. Jaenen, *Emerging Identities: Selected Problems and Interpretations in Canadian History* (Scar-borough, ON: Prentice-Hall Canada, 1986), 439. For a useful analysis of Quebec's relatively low figure of enlistments, see Elizabeth H. Armstrong, *The Crisis of Quebec, 1914–1918*, with an introduction by Joseph Levitt (Toronto: McClelland & Stewart, 1974).

4 One accusation that Frank Patrick made was that the Canadiens failed to pay for the transfer of the star player Newsy Lalonde from the PCHA to the NHA. Patrick held Quinn responsible for not seeing that the Canadiens lived up to the agree-ment. *Montreal Gazette*, 26 October 1915, 13, 27 October 1915, 15, and 29 October 1915, 14. For the situation in Toronto, see Charles L. Coleman, *The Trail of the Stanley Cup* (Sherbrooke, QC: Sherbrooke Daily Record Co., 1964), 1: 286 and *Montreal Gazette*, 5 November 1915, 13. For the dispute between the two leagues, see Holzman and Nieforth, *Deceptions and Doublecross*, 61–7, 71–2, 76, and 84–91. Holzman and Nieforth have suggested there might have been some backroom agreement between Livingstone and the Patricks, although there is no evidence to support this claim.

5 *Montreal Gazette*, 8 November 1915, 15.

6 For Livingstone's trouble with the 228th, see *Montreal Gazette*, 14 November 1916, 14, and Holzman and Nieforth, *Deceptions and Doublecross*, 105–6, 116. For his other quarrels with Ottawa see *Toronto Daily Mail and Empire*, 16 November 1916, 8, and

Montreal Gazette, 18 November 1916, 18, and 20 November 1916, 16; and with the Wanderers, see *Montreal Gazette*, 2 February 1917, 14. See *Montreal Gazette*, 20 November 1915, 16, and 24 November 1915, 12, for his troubles with the Toronto Arena Gardens management. According to Toronto Arena Company president Lawrence Solmon, Livingstone demanded a $14,000 guarantee.

7 *Montreal Gazette*, 12 February 1917, 16. There was no clarification of exactly what rule the Toronto club had violated. See also *Toronto Daily Mail and Empire*, 12 February 1917, 8.

8 In a sworn statement, the 228th representative, Leon Reade, attested that both George Kennedy and Sam Lichtenhein wanted Livingstone out before the season actually started. See Archives of Ontario, RG22-5800, 'The Toronto Hockey Club Limited and Ottawa Hockey Association Limited, The National Hockey Association of Canada Limited, Wanderers' Hockey Club Limited, The Canadian Hockey Club Incorporated, and Quebec Hockey Club Incorporated,' Court File no. 434, 1917. The news first came from Ottawa via the *Ottawa Citizen*, whose sports editor, Tommy Gorman, was involved with the Ottawa club. See *Montreal Gazette*, 14 February 1917, 9. The Toronto suspension was only for the remainder of the season and was lifted by president Robinson in March. *Toronto Globe*, 9 March 1917, 11.

9 *Toronto Globe*, 10 March 1917, 17. Livingstone never released any details except that he had demanded an investigation into the games played by the Wanderers and the Canadiens against the Quebec club. Robinson dismissed Livingstone's demands.

10 *Toronto Globe*, 13 March 1917, 9. For the detailed claims against the NHA and its member clubs, see Ontario Archives, RG22-5800, Court File no. 434 (1917).

11 In fact, Holzman and Nieforth have interpreted the establishment of the NHL as one gigantic conspiracy engineered by its president, Frank Calder. Holzman and Nieforth, *Deceptions and Doublecross*.

12 *Montreal Gazette*, 6 November 1917, 18. For enlistment figures, see Bennett and Jaenen, *Emerging Identities*, 439.

13 *Montreal Gazette*, 2 November 1917, 14.

14 Ibid., 12 November 1917, 18. For the issue of conscription, see Kenneth McNaught, *The Penguin History of Canada* (London: Penguin Books, 1988), 215; and Armstrong, *The Crisis of Quebec*. For contemporary comments, see *Toronto Globe*, 22 November 1915, 11; and *Montreal Gazette*, 14 September 1917, 12, and 29 September 1917, 20. For Livingstone's troubles with Lichtenhein, see Holzman and Nieforth, *Deceptions and Doublecross*, 67, 74–81, 113, and 119.

15 *Montreal Gazette*, 27 November 1917, 16. See also Brain McFarlane, 'The Founding of a New League,' in *Total Hockey*, ed. Dan Diamond (New York: Total Sports, 1998), 52.

16 Brian McFarlane, *One Hundred Years of Hockey* (Toronto: Summerhill Press, 1990), 13.

17 1917 NHL Meeting Minutes, 22 November, Hockey Hall of Fame, Toronto (hereafter HHOF).

18 In a confidential letter to Calder, Quinn had warned him about the possibility of Quebec suspending operations and asked him to consider it (instead of expelling the club). Mike Quinn to Frank Calder, 4 November 1917, 1917–20 Quebec Bulldogs file, National Hockey League Archives (hereafter NHLA).

19 1917 NHL Meeting Minutes, 22 November, HHOF. Quinn did not declare his intention to suspend operations at the meeting until after Northey gave assurances that Toronto Arena would fill out a team and that he would retain the rights to the Quebec club players. See also *Montreal Gazette*, 26 November 1917, 16. It was also clear that Calder had laid down the conditions under which the Toronto club would be admitted before the meeting. The Toronto club should be 'in responsible hands and free from the present objectionable interest.' Frank Calder to William Northey, 7 November 1917, 1918–19 Miscellaneous Correspondence file, NHLA. For quite a different interpretation of the events, see Holzman and Nieforth, *Deceptions and Doublecross*, 152–9.

20 1918 NHL Meeting Minutes, 3 January, HHOF.

21 Lichtenhein cited losses of $30,000. See Bob Duff, 'Setting the Foundation, 1917–18 to 1925–26,' in *Total Hockey*, ed. Diamond, 53. The Wanderers had first declared a loss in 1914 in the amount of $3987. From that point on, the team had never announced a profit in its annual meetings. See *Montreal Gazette*, 29 October 1914, 10. In the examination of Livingstone in his lawsuit against the NHA, the defence lawyer cited Lichtenhein saying that he had incurred losses of $6000 during the 1915–16 season and $7000 in 1916–17. See Archives of Ontario, RG22-5800, Court File no. 434 (1917).

22 See 1918 NHL Meeting Minutes, 2 February, HHOF. There was no evidence that Lichtenhein ever paid the fine. Toronto actually threatened to sue the Wanderers for lost revenues. A.G. Claxton to Calder, 7 January 1918, 1918–19 Toronto Arena Hockey Club file, NHLA.

23 A report of the failed appeal can be found in the *Toronto Globe*, 20 November 1919, 12. For the NHA lawsuit, see Holzman and Nieforth, *Deceptions and Doublecross*, 140–2, and 199. Quinn first notified Calder that he had purchased the Quebec franchise in August (Percy Quinn to Calder, 8 August 1918, 1918–19 Miscellaneous Correspondence file, NHLA). A brief biography of Percy Quinn can be found in Holzman and Nieforth, *Deceptions and Doublecross*, 172–3, and 192.

24 The Arena Gardens, however, had other plans. They set up their auditor, Hubert Vearcombe, to run the club under the name Toronto Arena Hockey Club and refused to return the Torontos' contracts after the 1917–18 season was over. This eventually led to a lawsuit against the Arena Gardens that lasted until 1926, with several appeals. *Toronto Hockey Club v. Arena Gardens of Toronto Ltd.*, vol. 55, Ontario Law Reports (1923–4), 516.

25 Quinn had also applied for ice time at the Toronto Arena Gardens in the hope that he might move the Quebec franchise to Toronto. See Charles Querrie to Calder, 1 October 1918, T-1, 1918–19 Toronto Arena Hockey Club, NHLA.

26 Livingstone filed two suits, one for money owed for the use of the players, on July 20, 1918, and the other, on December 21, 1918, for breach of contract. Writs of summons for these two cases can be found in Ontario Archives, RG22-5800, Court File no. 849 (1918) and Court File no. 2668 respectively. See also *Montreal Gazette*, 5 November 1918, 14, for Livingstone's claim that the Arena Gardens wanted to settle the lawsuit. See also Holzman and Nieforth, *Deceptions and Doublecross*, 201–11, 214, and 221–9.

27 *Montreal Gazette*, 22 October 1918, 12. This announcement was made before Livingstone hinted that the Toronto Arena Gardens may want to settle his lawsuit. Rumours of a new league actually surfaced in early October. George Kennedy of the Canadiens accused Percy Quinn of tampering with his players even before Percy Quinn had bought the Quebec franchise. When questioned by Calder, Quinn refused to deny any involvement, stating that 'if a man makes no statements, he has no reason whatever for giving a denial.' P. Quinn to Calder, 11 October 1918, 1917–20 Quebec Bulldogs file, NHLA.

28 Vearcombe to Calder, 14 November 1918, 1918–19 Toronto Arena Hockey Club, NHLA. In a later letter Vearcombe said that the Toronto Arena Gardens attorney, Claxton, wanted to settle with Livingstone, but the Arena directorate did not. 'They further decided that only N.H.L. teams should be allowed to play here this winter … [which] together with my exclusive privileges for Professional Hockey gives this end to the League entirely.' Vearcombe to Calder, 30 November 1918, 1918–19 Toronto Arena Hockey Club file, NHLA.

29 According to the owner, Ted Dey, Livingstone had an option until 2 November, but let it expired. *Montreal Gazette*, 12 November 1918, 12.

30 As late as the end of November, when the Livingstone faction seemed to be running out of options, Calder was still hoping to have Quinn in the NHL. 'Percy Quinn is a man I would like to see with us because he has a certain following in Toronto for one thing and for another because his coming in would break up a troublesome combination.' Calder to Vearcombe, 28 November 1918, 1918–19 Toronto Arena Hockey Club file, NHLA.

31 The first revelation that the Brunswick-Balke-Collender Company owned 12 shares of the Canadiens club came in a letter to president Robinson from the company's lawyers in 1917. Murphy, Perrault, Raymond & Gouin to Frank Robinson, 28 September 1917, 1918–19 Miscellaneous Correspondence file, NHLA. According to the NHA constitution, member clubs must hold their entire 50 shares of capital stock in order to remain a member of the league.

32 Letters were sent out to five NHA owners to levy an assessment of $200 to cover court costs for the case against Ocean Accident and Guarantee Corporation,

which involved the retrieval of the $3000 bond forfeited by the 228th battalion team for not finishing the season. Calder to Lichtenhein, Kendall, Quinn, Livingstone, and Wall, 23 October 1918, 1918–19 Miscellaneous Correspondence file, NHLA.

33 *Montreal Gazette*, 12 December 1918, 12; Charles Fremont to Calder, 18 November 1918, 1918–19 Miscellaneous Correspondence file, NHLA. Calder had told at least one NHL owner about Quinn not having paid for the franchise in full. Calder to Vearcombe, 28 November 1918, 1918–19 Toronto Arena Hockey Club file, NHLA.

34 Calder to Claxton, 12 January 1918, 1918–19 Miscellaneous Correspondence file, NHLA.

35 Calder to M.J. Quinn, 5 February 1918, 1917–20 Quebec Bulldogs file, NHLA.

36 Calder to M.J. Quinn, 25 March 1919, 1918–19 Miscellaneous Correspondence file, NHLA.

37 M.J. Quinn to Calder, 21 May 1919, ibid. The proposal called for Percy Quinn to pay Mike Quinn $1100, which included part of the arrears in the former's payment for the Quebec club, as well as to return franchise ownership to M.J. Quinn; M.J. Quinn would not ask for the full amount that was due. The original proposal appeared in a handwritten letter, M.J. Quinn to Calder, 20 March 1919, ibid.

38 1919 NHL Meeting Minutes, 2 December, HHOF. The handwritten entries in the meeting minutes book had December 22 as the date. But its content indicated that it was unlikely the meeting was held on December 22. The writing was not clear enough to indicate the last word in the condition attached to the motion. A note in the Quebec club file indicated that agreement to the condition was known to, if not obtained from, Mike Quinn long before the meeting. See 22 November 1919, 1917–20 Quebec Bulldogs file, NHLA.

39 For Quebec's woes on the ice, see the review at season's end that appeared in the *Quebec Chronicle*, 12 March 1920, 6.

40 The first intimation of Hambly's suggestion to include Hamilton came in a letter from Calder, who replied to Hambly's proposal. See Calder to Hambly, 15 July 1920, 1919–20 Miscellaneous Correspondence file, NHLA. Hambly's letter was not in the file. Holzman and Nieforth, *Deceptions and Doublecross*, 216.

41 Calder to Hambly, 5 August 1920, 1919–20 Miscellaneous Correspondence file, NHLA.

42 Gorman to Calder, 16 July 1920, ibid.

43 Calder to Gorman, 5 August 1920, ibid.

44 Querrie to Calder, 18 August 1920, ibid.

45 Contract agreement to Hamilton Professional Hockey Club, 22 September 1920, ibid.

46 1920 NHL Meeting Minutes, 24 November, HHOF. The minutes never suggested

that the Quebec franchise was transferred to Hamilton, as some writers have claimed. See also *Quebec Chronicle*, 28 November 1920, 6.

47 1920 NHL Meeting Minutes, 24 November, HHOF.

48 Calder to Hambly, 5 January 1921, 1919–20 Miscellaneous Correspondence file, NHLA.

49 Hamilton's request to suspend Harry Broadbent, the loaned Ottawa player, came two days after the meeting that sent Broadbent to Hamilton for the season. Thompson to Calder, telegram, 1 January 1921, 1921 Miscellaneous Correspondence file, NHLA.

50 See Hambly to Calder, 9 January 1921, ibid.

51 See Calder to Hambly, 10 January 1921, ibid. For the Cleghorn agreement, see Calder to Thompson, 21 January 1921, ibid. The agreement called for the Canadiens to make up the difference between what Cleghorn demanded and what the St Patricks were willing to pay. Then the Canadiens received Cully Wilson from Toronto.

52 Calder to Leo Dandurand, Calder to Hambly, Calder to Gorman, and Calder to Thompson, 14 March 1922, 1922–3 Miscellaneous Correspondence file, NHLA.

53 Frank Patrick to Calder, 2 April 1923, 1922–3 Vancouver Arena Company file, NHLA. Frank Patrick apologized to Calder in the letter that the six-game playoff receipts were less than those of two years before. Patrick pointed out that the winning-team players, including the subs, received $700 per person. The 1920–1 NHL Stanley Cup share was $1094.35. The drop might say more about the state of affairs of the PCHA than anything else, as the games were played in the West both these years. See Calder to Frank Patrick, 13 April 1921, ibid.

54 Calder to Hambly, 10 November 1921, 1921 Miscellaneous Correspondence file, NHLA.

55 1921 NHL Meeting Minutes, 29 May, HHOF.

56 1921 NHL Meeting Minutes, 26 November, HHOF.

57 1922 NHL Meeting Minutes, 20 August, HHOF.

Chapter 7: Going South, Part 1

1 1923 NHL Meeting Minutes, 27 January, Hockey Hall of Fame, Toronto (hereafter HHOF).

2 Between 1917 and 1925, Canada was the second leading nation in import/export trade with the United States. For each year within this period, the value of imports from the United States far outstripped the value of Canadian exports to the United States. See *Historical Statistics of the United States: Colonial Times to 1970*, part 2 (White Plains, NY: Kraus International Publication, 1989), 903 and 906.

3 See, for example, Calder to R.B. Nickerson, 7 March 1922 and Nickerson to

Calder, 17 March 1922, 1922–3 Miscellaneous Correspondence file, National Hockey League Archives (hereafter NHLA); George Brown to Calder, 4 March 1924, 1924 Miscellaneous Correspondence file, NHLA. Nickerson was a director, and Brown was the manager, of the Boston Arena. See also S.A. Dion to Sam Lichtenhein, telegram, 11 November, and Calder to Dion, 13 November 1920, 1919–20 Miscellaneous Correspondence file, NHLA. Dion represented the Aero Club of New York, which wanted to arrange a series between the Wanderers and either the Ottawa or Montreal team. The Wanderers had disbanded by then. See also Neil D. Issacs, *Checking Back* (New York: W.W. Norton & Co., 1977), 60; and Conn Smythe with Scott Young, *Conn Smythe: If You Can't Beat 'Em in the Alley* (Markham, ON: Paper Jacks Ltd., 1982), 79.

4 For the intimation of an American section of the NHA, see *Montreal Gazette*, 21 and 27 March 1911, 10. For Boston's recruitment of Canadian players, see ibid., 27 October 1911, 10.

5 Frank Calder to Frank Patrick, 14 December 1920, 1922–3 Vancouver Arena Company file, NHLA. Both American economic nationalism and Canadian 'budgetary parsimony' contributed to this recession. Recovery did not begin until 1924. See John Herd Thompson, with Allen Seager, *Canada, 1922–1939: Decades of Discord* (Toronto: McClelland & Stewart Ltd., 1994), 76.

6 Calder to Hambly, 15 July 1920, 1919–20 Miscellaneous Correspondence file, NHLA. Livingstone had taken his NHA team to play exhibition matches in Cleveland. Morey Holzman and Joseph Nieforth, *Deceptions and Doublecross: How the NHL Conquered Hockey* (Toronto: Dundurn Group, 2002), 81–2, 99.

7 *Toronto Hockey Club v. Arena Gardens of Toronto Ltd.*, vol. 55, Ontario Law Reports (1923–4), 513.

8 Duggan to Calder, 22 September 1920, 1919–20 Miscellaneous Correspondence file, NHLA. According to this letter, Calder had written Duggan on 20 August regarding the Quebec franchise. This letter is in the files. For Duggan's refusal of Calder's counter-offer, see Duggan to Calder, 23 September 1920, ibid.

9 Calder to Tom Gorman, 24 October 1921, 1921 Miscellaneous Correspondence file, NHLA. Both Duggan and the other bidder, Alphonse Racine, offered $10,000 for the Canadiens. Calder's assessment was based on the value of the players' contracts, which, according to Calder, were worth around $7500.

10 Susan Strasser, *Satisfaction Guaranteed: The Making of the American Mass Market* (Washington and London: Smithsonian Institution Press, 1989), 15–16.

11 Between 1917 and 1924, when the first American franchise, the Boston Bruins, joined the NHL, the U.S. average annual wage earnings in real dollars increased by almost 20%. See *Historical Statistics of the United States*, part 1, 164. The 1917 and 1924 figures stand at $586 million and $702 million respectively. On advertising and mass consumption, see Roland Marchand, *Advertising the American Dream: Making*

Way for Modernity, 1920–1940 (Berkeley and Los Angeles: University of California Press, 1985). For the print media's role in the consumer culture, see Richard Ohmann, 'Where Did Mass Culture Come From? The Case of the Magazines,' *Bershire Review* 16 (1981), 85–101; Christopher P. Wilson, 'The Rhetoric of Consumption: Mass-Market Magazines and the Demise of the Gentle Reader, 1880–1920,' and T.J. Jackson Lears, 'From Salvation to Self-Realization: Advertising and the Therapeutic Roots of the Consumer Culture, 1880–1930,' in *The Culture of Consumption: Critical Essays in American History, 1880–1980*, ed. Richard Wightman Fox and T.J. Jackson Lears (New York: Pantheon Books, 1983); and Jennifer Scanlon, *Inarticulate Longings: The Ladies' Home Journal, Gender, and the Promises of Consumer Culture* (New York: Routledge, 1995). For radio and advertising, see Susan Smulyan, *Selling Radio: The Commercialization of American Broadcasting, 1920–1934* (Washington and London: Smithsonian Institution Press, 1994), 65–92.

12 Jackson Lears, 'From Salvation to Self-Realization,' 27.

13 *Historical Statistics of the United States*, part 1, 401.

14 William E. Leuchtenburg, *The Perils of Prosperity, 1914–32*, 2nd ed. (Chicago: University of Chicago Press, 1993), 195.

15 See Mark Dyreson, 'The Emergence of Consumer Culture and the Transformation of Physical Culture: American Sport in the 1920s,' *Journal of Sport History*, Winter 1990, 276; and Benjamin G. Rader, *American Sports: From the Age of Folk Games to the Age of Televised Sports*, 4th ed. (Upper Saddle River, NJ: Prentice Hall, 1999), 116–23. For a good discussion on the consumer culture and work, see Lynn Dumenil, *The Modern Temper: American Culture and Society in the 1920s* (New York: Hill and Wang, 1995), 56–97. For histories of commercial lesiure, see David Nasaw, *Going Out: The Rise and Fall of Public Amusements* (New York: Basic Books, 1993); Woody Register, *The Kid of Coney Island: Fred Thompson and the Rise of American Amusements* (New York: Oxford University Press, 2001); and Richard Butsch, ed., *For Fun and Profit: The Transformation of Leisure into Consumption* (Philadelphia: Temple University Press, 1990).

16 1923 NHL Meeting Minutes, 5 March, HHOF. Duggan had put down $2000 bond, which was immediately allocated for league operating expenses. A later report put the sum at $2500. Duggan was to 'secure players, sites, and the necessary American support.' See *Montreal Gazette*, 5 February 1924, 16.

17 1923 NHL Meeting Minutes, 13 May, HHOF.

18 *Montreal Gazette*, 5 February 1924, 16. For a biography of Tex Rickard, see Charles Samuels, *The Magnificent Rube: The Life and Gaudy Times of Tex Rickard* (New York: McGraw-Hill Book Co., 1957) esp. 217–25. See also Eric Whitehead, *The Patricks: Hockey's Royal Family* (Toronto: Doubleday, 1980), 155, for one account of Rickard's consent to add hockey to the Garden's activities.

19 Trent Frayne, *The Mad Men of Hockey* (New York: Dodd, Mead and Company,

1974), 57–9. The transfer of Hamilton's players to New York was officially sanctioned in a September NHL meeting. See 1925 NHL Meeting Minutes, 25 September, HHOF. While there was no record on how much the transfer had cost Dwyer, it was at least $25,000, as Hamilton owners later protested the New York club for arbitrarily deducting the fines on the suspended players from the purchase price. See Charles Cotton to Calder, 3 January 1927, 1926–7 Miscellaneous Correspondence file, NHLA.

20 Calder to Adams, 15 February 1924, 1924–5 Boston Professional Hockey Association Inc. file, NHLA.

21 *Boston Globe*, 27 January 1924, 20 and 28 January 1924, morning edition, 9.

22 Ibid., 29 January 1924, morning edition, 10; emphases mine.

23 Ibid., 28 January 1924, evening edition, 9.

24 Ibid.

25 Adams to Calder, 11 March 1924, 1924–5 Boston Professional Hockey Association Inc. file, NHLA. According to his son, Adams attended the 1924 Stanley Cup series in Montreal and was so enthralled with the play that he made up his mind to pur-sue an NHL franchise. See Stan Fischler, 'Boston Bruins,' in *Total Hockey*, ed. Dan Diamond (New York: Total Sports, 1998), 162. Adams was going to travel with Linde Fowler of the *Boston Transcript* to the playoffs. Adams to Calder, 25 February 1924, 1924–5 Boston Professional Hockey Association Inc. file, NHLA.

26 R.B. Nickerson to Calder, 17 March 1922, 1922–3 Miscellaneous Correspondence file, NHLA.

27 Adams to Calder, 2 April 1924, 1924–5 Boston Professional Hockey Association Inc. file, NHLA. Adams, however, assured Calder that the Arena would accept the professional franchise for the next season. See also Calder to Adams, 5 April 1924, ibid.

28 *Boston Globe*, 26 March 1924, morning edition, 12.

29 *Montreal Gazette*, 22 March 1924, 18.

30 Ibid., 31 March 1924, 16; 5 May 1924, 18.

31 Work on the site began in June. *Montreal Gazette*, 26 June 1924, 16.

32 There was a reaction to the proposed new league that had the Pittsburgh group heading the American franchises. Adams to Calder, 21 April 1924, 1924–5 Boston Professional Hockey Association Inc. file, NHLA. See also *Montreal Gazette*, 5 April 1924, 22.

33 1924 NHL Meeting Minutes, 6 July, HHOF. His application was tabled, but nothing ever came of it.

34 For a complete list of stockholders, see National Archives of Canada, MG 28 III 57, vol. 363, Molson Papers, The Canadian Arena Company Limited, Stock Subscribed up till July 24th, 1924. See also William Brown, *The Montreal Maroons: The Forgotten Stanley Cup Champions* (n.p.: Véchule Press, 1999), 37–9.

35 1924 NHL Meeting Minutes, 10 May, HHOF.

36 Ibid., 1 November. The motion was moved by Toronto and seconded by the Canadiens. Both Hamilton and Ottawa objected, but Calder cast the deciding vote to carry the motion. Interestingly, Gorman of Ottawa had previously written Calder approving of the entry of the Forum group, but he also wanted to see that the Canadiens were compensated. Obviously, Gorman's idea of compensation did not involve giving the lion's share of the Forum's franchise fee to the Canadiens. See Gorman to Calder, 28 October 1924, 1923–4 Ottawa Hockey Association file, NHLA. As a further reward for the Canadiens, the League passed a motion granting the Canadiens the 'first claim on all French Canadian players.' 1925 NHL Meeting Minutes, 11 April, HHOF. Not surprisingly, James Strachan, owner of the Maroons, dissented.

37 *Montreal Gazette*, 7 July 1924, 17.

38 1924 NHL Meeting Minutes, 6 July, HHOF. The fear of members leaving the league and forming a rival league was so strong that the NHL reworked the 1924 binding agreement in 1926 to incorporate the expansion franchises. As a condition to their admittance into the league, Chicago and Detroit had to agree to be part of the agreement. See appendix D.

39 *Boston Globe*, 27 September 1924, morning edition, 8.

40 Ibid., 1 October 1924, evening edition, 16.

41 1926 NHL Meeting Minutes, 10 January, NHLA. NHL meeting minutes after 1925 are archived in the Montreal NHL office and have since been moved to Toronto. NHL meeting minutes hereafter will be considered as part of the NHL archival collection.

42 1926 NHL Meeting Minutes, 17 April, NHLA. The five Detroit applicants were P.R. Bierer, B.C. Whitney, J.J. Miller, Charles S. King, and B. McCreath. C.R. Hall and P.T. Harmon represented one group for the Chicago applications, J. Hardwick the other. See also *Montreal Gazette*, 19 April 1926, 16. The *Gazette* identified the five Detroit applicants as McCreath, Miller, Whitney, P.R. Bierer, and Percy Lesueur and listed three different applications for the Chicago franchise: Hardwick, Harmon, and a Mr Gary, representing Tex Rickard of Madison Square Garden.

43 1926 NHL Meeting Minutes, 1 and 2 May, NHLA. For reports of the meetings, see *Montreal Gazette*, 3 May 1926, 18, and 17 May 1926, 19; and *Toronto Globe*, 3 May 1926, 7.

44 1926 NHL Meeting Minutes, 15 May, NHLA. The votes to change the constitutional amendment were as follows: six clubs – Ottawa, Boston, the Maroons, Toronto, Pittsburgh, and the Rangers – for and two – Americans and the Canadiens – against. The New York Americans' representative protested Calder's ruling that the Rangers could vote on this issue because the Rangers had only been admitted to the NHL recently.

45 Reprinted in the *Toronto Globe*, 14 May 1926, 10.

Chapter 8: Going South, Part 2

1 Bruce Kidd, *The Struggle for Canadian Sport* (Toronto: University of Toronto Press, 1996), 196–209.

2 1925 NHL Meeting Minutes, 11 April, Hockey Hall of Fame, Toronto (hereafter HHOF).

3 Calder to Ahearn, 11 January 1926, 1925–6 Ottawa Hockey Association file, National Hockey League Archives (hereafter NHLA).

4 1927 NHL Meeting Minutes, 14 May, NHLA.

5 Charles Adams praised Schooley for threatening to bar two USAHA players from amateur play if they refused to report to Boston. Interestingly, Schooley was instrumental in pursuing Pittsburgh's application to the NHL the following year. Adams to Calder, 14 November 1924, 1924–5 Boston Professional Hockey Association Inc. file, NHLA. A complaint was filed against Ross for tampering with two players who were supposed to go to the Maroons. See W.L. Gillespie to Calder, telegram, 15 November 1924, 1924 Miscellaneous Correspondence file, NHLA. See also Charles L. Coleman, *The Trail of the Stanley Cup* (Sherbrooke, QC: Sherbrooke Daily Record Co., 1964), 1: 466.

6 The two players in question were Hooley Smith and Ed Gorman (no relation to Ottawa owner). See Gorman to Calder, 21 November 1924, 1923–4 Ottawa Hockey Association file, NHLA.

7 Gorman to Calder, 9 December 1924, 1924–5 T.P. Gorman file, NHLA. Calder noted that 'Clause 7 is pretty tough for an amateur breaking into the game.' Calder to Gorman, 22 November 1924, 1923–4 Ottawa Hockey Association file, NHLA. Clause 7 in the standard NHL contract of 1926 stated: 'The club may, at any time, after the beginning and prior to the completion of the period of this contract, give the player one day's written notice to end and determine all its liabilities and obligations hereunder, in which event the liabilities and obligations undertaken by the club shall cease and [be] determine[d] at the expiration of said one day. The player, at the expiration of said one day, shall be freed and discharged from all obligations to render service to the club. If such notice be given to the player while "abroad" with the club, he shall be entitled to his travelling expenses to the city of _____.'

8 1926 NHL Meeting Minutes, 14 February, NHLA.

9 Dwyer's arrest was front-page news. A total of 18 people, including members of the coast guard, were detained. Dwyer's bail was set at $40,000. *New York Times*, 4 December 1926, 1. See also Trent Frayne, *The Mad Men of Hockey* (New York: Dodd, Mead and Co., 1974), 58.

10 Calder to Strachan, 24 February 1926, 1925–6 Montreal Professional Hockey Club file, NHLA.

11 Adams to Hammond, 24 February 1926, 1925–6 Boston Professional Hockey Association Inc. file, NHLA.

12 1926 NHL Meeting Minutes, 17 April, NHLA. The lone dissenter was the New York Americans.

13 Frank Patrick to Calder, 1 February 1923, 1922–3, Vancouver Arena Company file, NHLA.

14 *Montreal Gazette*, 5 April 1926, 16.

15 Ibid., 28 April 1926, 18.

16 *Vancouver Morning Star*, 3 May 1926, 3. See also 1926 NHL Meeting Minutes, 2 May, NHLA.

17 Although the matter has not been documented fully, Ross was apparently working closely with the Patricks. At the May 2 NHL meeting Ross assured the governors that Frank Patrick had authority to sell the WHL players and that the inter-league agreement was no longer in force. Calder to Adams, 25 August 1926, 1925–6 Boston Professional Hockey Association Inc. file, NHLA. Amid all the chaos that transpired from the sale of the WHL players, Calder later sought to call a meeting to clear the air because 'Ross is abroad with threats of vengeance on my poor devoted head, claiming I have stood in his way of making a great deal of money.' Calder to Ahearn, 31 August 1926, 1925–6 Ottawa Hockey Association file, NHLA. See also Eric Whitehead, *The Patricks: Hockey's Royal Family* (Toronto: Doubleday, 1980), 153 and 157.

18 See memo, 2 May 1926, 1925–6 Western Hockey League file, NHLA. The Hardwick deal called for a payment of $50,000 on May 25 and the rest on September 1. It also included a purchase by Adams of seven players for $50,000.

19 See memo, 3 May 1926, 1925–6 Western Hockey League file, NHLA.

20 *Vancouver Morning Star*, 4 May 1926, 2.

21 Friedberg was with the Bierer application. Calder to Charles Adams, 23 August 1926, 1925–6 Boston Professional Hockey Association file, NHLA.

22 Calder to Charles Adams, 25 August 1926, 1925–6 Boston Professional Hockey Association file, NHLA. Letters concerning the purchasing of the ice plant and the hiring of Lester Patrick to act as the manager of the Detroit hockey team, as well as manager of the auditorium, can be found in two separate pieces of correspondence (same date) from P.R. Bierer to Frank Patrick, 5 May 1926, 1933–4 Detroit Red Wings file, NHLA.

23 Ottawa director Raymond Quain was visiting the West Coast at the time and discovered the Patricks' problem. He informed the Ottawa club owner, Frank Ahearn, who then relayed the information to Calder. Ahearn to Calder, telegram, 30 July 1926, 1925–6 Ottawa Hockey Association file, NHLA. The cost of repairs was reported to be around $50,000. Calder told Adams about the amount when he tried to explain Patrick's tactics in selling the WHL. See Calder to Adams, 1 September 1926, 1925–6 Boston Professional Hockey Association Inc. file, NHLA.

24 *Detroit Free Press*, 15 August 1926. A clipping of the article regarding the new league was filed in the 1925–6 Detroit Red Wings (Olympia Incorporated) file, NHLA.

25 Townsend to Calder, telegram, 20 August 1926, 1925–6 Detroit Red Wings (Olympia Incorporated) file, NHLA. There were two telegrams sent to Calder from Townsend on this day. One, sent at 3:10 pm, advised Calder that Friedberg was to meet with the Townsend group the next day. In the second telegram, sent at 11:31 pm, Townsend stated that Friedberg's demand was excessive. Friedberg apparently wanted an extra $35,000 for his expenses.

26 C. Hughes to Calder, telegram, 4 October 1926, 1925–6 Detroit Red Wings (Olympia Incorporated) file, NHLA.

27 While most of the playing rules were similar, there were some significant departures between the PCHA and the eastern professional hockey development. Until the 1922–3 season, for example, the PCHA retained the rover position and played seven men on the ice. The NHA, the NHL's forerunner, had abandoned seven-man hockey in favour of six men beginning in the 1911–12 season.

28 The amount is taken from the 1918–19 Playoffs file, NHLA, which contains playoff financial statements from 1918 to 1925. 'Playoff' refers to the league playoff series only and not the Stanley Cup series.

29 1926 NHL Meeting Minutes, 14 February, NHLA.

30 1925–6 Playoffs file, NHLA.

31 1925 NHL Meeting Minutes, 7 November, HHOF. At the time, Hammond was acting on behalf of the New York Americans as Madison Square Garden had yet to submit its application for the Rangers franchise.

32 1926 NHL Meeting Minutes, 25 September, NHLA. Ottawa president Frank Ahearn, who could not attend the meeting, sent Calder a telegram asking him to tell the others that 'if clubs ignore contracts the Western clubs will appeal to government authorities and such appeal will be backed by western members of parliament and will result in action that will make it almost impossible to operate our league.' Ahearn to Calder, telegram, 25 September 1926, 1925–6 Ottawa Hockey Association file, NHLA. It is important to note that Ottawa at the time had negotiated a deal with the Saskatoon club, which was not represented by the Patricks. Thus, it would be to Ottawa's interest for the NHL to honour all player sales. Detroit at the time had not completed its deal with the Patricks, which perhaps accounted for its position in the vote.

33 Adams to Calder, 21 January 1925, 1924–5 Boston Professional Hockey Association Inc. file, NHLA.

34 Calder to Adams, 13 January 1926, 1925–6 Boston Professional Hockey Association Inc. file, NHLA. Adams made the suggestion of appointing American referees in Adams to Calder, 18 January 1926, ibid. It should be noted that Boston was in last place by mid-season. Frustration no doubt added to the suspicion.

35 Calder to Adams, 21 January 1926, ibid.

36 Calder to Adams, 29 September 1926, ibid. The letter from Adams was missing from the file.

37 1926 NHL Meeting Minutes, 16 October NHLA. See also *Vancouver Morning Star,* 27 September 1926, 2. Adams's resignation lasted only one year, but his involvement in the hockey club considerably diminished. Ross, for all intents and purposes, ran the Boston club after 1933.

38 1926 NHL Meeting Minutes, 15 May NHLA. See also Hardwick to Calder, 5 August 1926, 1925–6 Chicago National Hockey Team Inc. file, NHLA. This letter informed Calder that McLaughlin had assumed the presidency of the hockey club.

39 Irene Castle was half of the famed Irene and Vernon Castle dance team. For a brief biography of Frederick McLaughlin, see George Vass, *The Chicago Black Hawks Story* (Chicago: Follett Publishing Co., 1970), 11–12, and Morey Holzman and Joseph Nieforth, *Deceptions and Doublecross: How the NHL Conquered Hockey* (Toronto: The Dundurn Group, 2002), 274–5.

40 McLaughlin to Calder, 25 August 1926, 1926–7 Chicago National Hockey Team Inc. file, NHLA. For examples of Chicago's use of sports to booster its reputation, see Douglas Bukowski, *Big Bill Thompson, Chicago, and the Politics of Image* (Urbana and Chicago: University of Illinois Press, 1998), 41, and Gregg Lee Carter, 'Baseball in Saint Louis, 1867–1875: An Historical Case Study in Civic Pride,' *The Bulletin – Missouri Historical Society* 31 (1975), 253–63.

41 McLaughlin to Calder, 26 November 1926, 1926–7 Chicago National Hockey Team Inc. file, NHLA.

42 Holzman and Nieforth, *Deceptions and Doublecross,* 278. For more on the AHA, see the next chapter, on the minor leagues.

43 McLaughlin to Calder, 21 December 1926, 1926–7 Chicago National Hockey Team Inc. file, NHLA.

44 McLaughlin to Calder, 4 January 1927, ibid. McLaughlin had brought up the question of the offside system from the first Chicago home game. He thought Calder had brushed him off by suggesting that his team, the former Portland club, was not adapting well to the NHL rules. Before its demise, the PCHA had abandoned offside in each of the three ice zones.

45 Ibid.

46 McLaughlin to Calder, 10 January 1927, 1926–7 Chicago National Hockey Team Inc. file, NHLA. McLaughlin had sought legal advice from a law firm that had done work for the NHL in drawing up the binding agreement. The barrister had affirmed Chicago's right to refuse a second franchise, as the agreement to such was made between the NHL and Hardwick, not with the Chicago club; and there was no proof that the Chicago club accepted what Hardwick had agreed to. Furthermore, the NHL had amended the bylaws during the September 25, 1926 meeting,

when Chicago was already a full-blown member. In redrafting sections 1 and 9 of the constitution at that meeting, the League reaffirmed an NHL club's territorial rights. See N.K. LaFlame to McLaughlin, 7 January 1927, ibid.

47 McLaughlin to Calder, 10 January 1927, ibid.

48 McLaughlin to Calder, 10 January 1927, ibid.

49 Calder to McLaughlin, 12 January 1927, ibid.

50 Calder to Hardwick, 12 January 1927, ibid.

51 Hardwick to Calder, 31 January 1927, ibid.

52 McLaughlin to Calder, 2 February 1927, ibid.

53 Calder to Hardwick, 11 February 1927, ibid.

54 Harmon to Calder, 14 February 1927, 1926–7 Miscellaneous Correspondence file, NHLA.

55 Calder to McLaughlin, 19 February 1927, 1926–7 Chicago National Hockey Team file, NHLA. McLaughlin's suspicion had gotten so bad that he refused to send in the Chicago club's stock ownership information. According to Calder, the information was needed to ensure that there was no interlocking ownership between clubs. Calder retracted his request for Chicago's list until the subject was discussed at a meeting. The original refusal by McLaughlin, dated 17 February, is missing from the file.

56 McLaughlin to Calder, 23 March 1927, 1926–7 Chicago National Hockey Team Inc. file, NHLA. For Livingstone's suit against McLaughlin, see Holzman and Nieforth, *Deceptions and Doublecross*, 303–5 and 307–9.

57 For the motion rescinding the agreement and appointment of McLaughlin to the negotiating committee, see NHL Meeting Minutes, 14 February 1927, NHLA. See chapter 9 on McLaughlin and Calder's negotiations with the AHA. The second franchise issue finally came to an end when McLaughlin informed Calder that the original agreement, which McLaughlin claimed he had never seen, was found in the files of the club's ex-secretary. Without actually apologizing, McLaughlin wrote, '[H]ad I ever seen it a lot of acrimonious correspondence between you and me last fall would never have materialized.' For Calder's part, he was gracious enough to plead with McLaughlin to forget about the whole thing. See McLaughlin to Calder, 25 May 1927, and Calder to McLaughlin, 27 May 1927, 1926–7 Chicago National Hockey Team Inc. file, NHLA.

58 Adams to Calder, 31 December 1924, 1924–5 Boston Professional Hockey Association Inc. file, NHLA.

59 Calder to McLaughlin, 26 April 1927, 1926–7 Chicago National Hockey Team Inc. file, NHLA. Billy Couture sometimes appeared as Billy Coutu. For a list of players fined and the amounts, see Coleman, *The Trail of the Stanley Cup*, 2: 27.

60 McLaughlin to Calder, 29 April 1927, 1926–7 Chicago National Hockey Team Inc. file, NHLA.

61 McLaughlin to Calder, 22 April 1927, ibid. Using a rough estimate, the team that incurred the most penalty minutes was not Boston. Boston came in third (495 minutes) in this category after the Maroons (686 minutes) and Ottawa (605 minutes). The minutes are compiled through player statistics in Coleman, *The Trail of the Stanley Cup*, 2: 18–21. One must be cautious in using these numbers, as they do not differentiate between a major and a minor foul nor do they indicate if any injuries were incurred from the infractions. This compilation also does not take into consideration players changing teams during the season.

62 McLaughlin to Calder, 29 June 1927, 1926–7 Chicago National Hockey Team Inc. file, NHLA. The Couture in question was not the Billy Couture who was suspended for life. Ross apparently had signed away Couture, even though he had a contract with the Winnipeg club of the AHA.

63 Calder to McLaughlin, 2 July 1927, ibid.

64 McLaughlin to Calder, 5 July 1927, ibid.

65 For Conn Smythe's battles with Ross, see Conn Smythe with Scott Young, *Conn Smythe* (Markham, ON: Paper Jacks Ltd., 1982), 79, 94, 128–9. For conflicts among other owners as well as those between McLaughlin and Norris, see David Cruise and Alison Griffiths, *Net Worth: Exploding the Myths of Pro Hockey* (Toronto: Penguin Books, 1992), 28–41.

Chapter 9: Birth of the Minor League System

1 1926 NHL Meeting Minutes, 14 February, National Hockey League Archives (hereafter NHLA). The motion also demanded that a certified cheque of $12,500 must accompany any application. Charles Adams was the first one to suggest that the previous franchise fee of $15,000 was too low. Calder to Adams, 18 January 1926, 1925–6 Boston Professional Hockey Association Inc. file, NHLA.

2 The other two leagues were the Prairie League, which folded within a year, and the California Hockey League, which lasted until 1933.

3 Leo Dandurand was the NHL's point man for investigating the Central Association. He found that more than $350,000 had been invested in the Minneapolis club; both Winnipeg and Duluth had about $250,000. Beyond these three, Dandurand did not think the other clubs' investments amounted much. Under the inter-league agreement between the NHL and the WHL, this part of the United States belonged to the WHL. This, perhaps, was one reason why they appointed Frank Patrick to be their representative. More likely, a director of the Minneapolis club, Lloyd Turner, who was also the owner of the Calgary club in the WHL, had convinced the others that Patrick carried some weight in his dealings with the NHL. Interestingly, Patrick had also promised to supply players to the Central Association to replace those who had signed with the NHL clubs. All this happened about a week before

the May 2 NHL meeting when Patrick sold most of the WHL players. See Dandurand to Calder, 26 April 1926, 1925–6 Club de Hockey Canadien Inc. file, NHLA.

4 A.G. Warren to Calder, 28 September 1926, 1926–7 Central Hockey Association file, NHLA.

5 McLaughlin to Calder, 6 December 1926, 1926–7 Chicago National Hockey Team Inc. file, NHLA.

6 Geiger to Calder, 2 June 1926, 1925–6 Miscellaneous Correspondence file, NHLA.

7 Geiger to Calder, 9 June 1926, ibid.

8 The clubs listed by Calder were in Hamilton, Niagara Falls, Windsor, London, and Stratford. Calder to Geiger, 8 June 1926, ibid.

9 Clapp to Calder, 17 August 1926, 1926–7 Canadian American Hockey League file, NHLA. Calder was influential in the Can-Am's organizational structure. He met with Geiger on August 10 regarding such matters as the binding agreement among member clubs, incorporation, and the adoption of NHL playing rules. See Calder to Geiger, 11 August 1926, 1925–6 Miscellaneous Correspondence file, NHLA.

10 London, for example, had only one local player and all players on the Owen Sound roster came from other parts of the province. See *Toronto Globe*, 4 March 1926, 8.

11 The quote, from the *Peterboro Examiner*, appeared in the *Toronto Globe*, 6 March 1926, 12.

12 J.A. Anderson to Calder, 22 February 1926, 1925–6 Miscellaneous Correspondence file, NHLA.

13 *Toronto Globe*, 2 March 1926, 6. The six clubs rumoured to be forming the circuit were Windsor, Niagara Falls, Stratford, London, and Hamilton, and possibly Peterborough, Toronto, or Grimsby. For criticism of the pro-league proposal, see *Toronto Globe*, 5 March 1926, 8.

14 For a discussion of the state of amateurism in Canada in the 1920s, see Bruce Kidd, *The Struggle for Canadian Sport* (Toronto: University of Toronto Press, 1996), 55–63.

15 *Toronto Globe*, 29 March 1926, 6.

16 Ibid., 15 May 1926, 14.

17 The Windsor dispatch appeared in the *Toronto Globe*, 19 May 1926, 8. The 'OBAA' that the dispatch refers to was the Ontario Baseball Amateur Association, which had its own showdown with the Intercounty Baseball League on the question of residence earlier.

18 Calder to J. Anderson, 10 June 1926, 1925–6 Miscellaneous Correspondence file, NHLA.

19 For the result of the certification, see *Toronto Globe*, 16 June 1926, 9.

20 Ibid., 17 June 1926, 9.

21 Anderson to Calder, 28 June 1926, 1925–6 Miscellaneous Correspondence file,

NHLA. See also *Toronto Globe*, 28 June 1926, 9. Besides the original five clubs, Brantford and Toronto also sent representatives. Brantford had five players refused OHA certificates and Toronto two. Also of interest, Hamilton owner Percy Thompson owned the NHL Hamilton franchise until it became inactive due to the players' strike, while Toronto owner Charlie Querrie was then part-owner of the NHL's Toronto St Patricks.

22 *Toronto Globe*, 29 June 1926, 9, and 30 June 1926, 8.

23 Charles King to Calder, telegram, 5 August 1926, 1926–7 Canadian Professional Hockey League file, NHLA. See also *Toronto Globe*, 5 August 1926, 6. Toronto was at the meeting, but dropped out of the league before the season began.

24 Calder to Adams, 26 October 1926, 1925–6 Boston Professional Hockey Association Inc. file, NHLA. The agreement referred to here was for the Can-Am, Can-Pro, and Prairie leagues. The NHL had a separate agreement with the AHA.

25 Dandurand to Calder, telegram, 9 August 1926, 1925–6 Club de Hockey Canadien Inc. file, NHLA.

26 Clapp to Calder, 26 February 1927, 1926–7 Canadian-American Hockey League file, NHLA.

27 Calder to Clapp, 4 March 1927, ibid. Clapp had told Calder there was already a group in Brooklyn ready to build a rink, provided it was assured of a Can-Am franchise.

28 Calder to Hammond, 28 February 1927, 1926–7 New York Rangers file, NHLA. Springfield was the Rangers' minor-league affiliate in the Can-Am.

29 Hammond to Calder, 2 March 1927, ibid. It was unclear why Clapp would think that his application could bypass the New York Rangers' notice, as the Rangers sponsored the Springfield club.

30 Howard Crane to J.L. Woods, 16 April 1926, 1925–6 Detroit Red Wings, Plans for Arena file, NHLA. Woods was with the Townsend-Hughes group.

31 Livingstone to Calder, telegram, 7 August 1926, 1925–6 Miscellaneous Correspondence file, NHLA. Livingstone made the denial to Calder in person, but wrote again to confirm their conversation.

32 At least according to A.G. Warren, president of the AHA, the Chicago situation was still unclear as to who the owner(s) would be as late as August 16. Warren to Calder, telegram, 16 August 1926, 1926–7 Central Hockey Association file, NHLA.

33 The first warning about Livingstone came at the end of August. McLaughlin was unfamiliar with the past relationship between Livingstone and the NHL. Calder to McLaughlin, 31 August 1926, 1926–7 Chicago National Hockey Team Inc. file, NHLA. There was at least one more letter, which is missing from the file, between Calder and McLaughlin on this matter. By about mid-September Livingstone had already secured ice in the Stadium. McLaughlin to Calder, 13 September 1926, ibid.

See also Morey Holzman and Joseph Nieforth, *Deceptions and Doublecross: How the NHL Conquered Hockey* (Toronto: Dundurn Group, 2002), 278, 280–2. Holzman and Nieforth argue that McLaughlin willingly rented the Coliseum to Livingstone. Letters in the above NHL files suggest that McLaughlin was not aware of Livingstone's lease until it was too late.

34 Warren to Calder, 9 and 12 May 1927, 1926–7 American Hockey Association file, NHLA.

35 McLaughlin to Calder, telegram, 23 May 1927, 1926–7 Chicago National Hockey Team Inc. file, NHLA.

36 McLaughlin to Calder, 25 May 1927, ibid.

37 McLaughlin to Calder, 6 June 1927, ibid.

38 McLaughlin to Calder, telegram, 17 June 1927, ibid.

39 Warren to Calder, 11 August 1927, 1926–7 American Hockey Association file, NHLA. The list was submitted on July 19. Warren to Calder, 19 July 1927, ibid.

40 Calder to McLaughlin, 7 July 1927, 1926–7 Chicago National Hockey Team Inc. file, NHLA

41 Warren to Calder, 24 August 1927, 1926–7 American Hockey Association file, NHLA. In ousting Livingstone, the AHA accused him of failing to abide by the contract made between his Chicago franchise and the AHA: specifically, in the non-payment of $750 before the January 1, 1927 deadline and in the failure to have 'the right to use the Coliseum in Chicago, Illinois, for the full agreed number of nights, to-wit, twenty-four nights, in the winter hockey season of 1926–1927.' Calder to Warren, 30 August 1927, ibid.

42 Calder to Clapp, 4 March 1927, 1926–7 Canadian-American Hockey League file, NHLA.

43 Within this system of control, there was room for negotiation. Highly skilled players could command a higher price than those who were not as skilled. Nevertheless, these star players certainly would have received a much higher salary if open bidding were allowed for their services.

44 1926 NHL Meeting Minutes, 16 October, NHLA. The original draft price was $3500. Then Strachan of the Maroons and Hammond of the Rangers moved to amend the price to $5000.

45 Clapp to Calder, 27 April 1927, 1926–7 Canadian-American Hockey League file, NHLA.

46 King to Calder, 20 December 1926, 1926–7 Canadian Professional Hockey League file, NHLA.

47 Calder to McLaughlin, 19 May 1927, 1926–7 Chicago National Hockey Team Inc. file, NHLA.

48 A series of correspondence exists on this incident between Calder and the Pro-Can

president, Charles King. For London's and the Pro-Can's side of the story, see King to Calder, 30 May 1927 and Anderson to King, 23 June 1927, 1926–7 Canadian Professional Hockey League file, NHLA. For the Detroit side of things, see Calder to King, 10 June 1927, ibid. It is not clear whether or not Calder knew that Detroit had made a counter offer of $7500. In the end, Calder ruled that there was no concrete evidence a deal had been consummated before the agreement was reached. See also *Toronto Globe*, 18 May 1927, 11, and *Montreal Gazette*, 18 May 1927, 16.

49 Clapp had suggested two changes: he wanted to clarify that the NHL president only had power to settle inter-league rather than intra-league disputes, and he wanted a clause binding the parties to recognize the territorial rights of each franchise. See Clapp to Calder, 7 June 1927, 1926–7 Canadian-American Hockey League file, NHLA.

50 Calder to Clapp, 17 June 1927, ibid.

51 Clapp to Calder, 20 June 1927, ibid.

52 W.M. Van Valkenburg to Calder, 6 March 1926, 1925–6 Miscellaneous Correspondence file, NHLA.

53 This secondary market extended from important hockey markets in the Northeast and the Great Lakes to the Far West. The Prairie League was organized on 4 February 1926 and sought affiliation with the NHL. It was originally named the Western Canada Hockey League, which name, of course, belonged to the WCL. It was officially named the Prairie League in its first meeting on February 24 with the franchise fee set at $100. See 4 and 24 February 1926, 1926–7 Prairie Hockey League – Constitution and Meetings file, NHLA. The Pacific League of Professional Hockey Clubs, with proposed franchises in Oakland, Sacramento, San Francisco, Los Angeles, and San Diego, was formed on February 7 in San Francisco. See H.H. Dempsey to Calder, telegram, 12 February 1926, 1925–6 Miscellaneous Correspondence file, NHLA.

54 For studies on the NHL that have focused on its internal relationships and structure, see J.C.H. Jones, 'The Economics of the National Hockey League,' in *Canadian Sport: Sociological Perspectives*, ed. Richard S. Gruneau and John G. Albinson (Don Mills, ON: Addison-Wesley, 1976), 225–48; Rob Beamish, 'The Impact of Corporate Ownership on Labour–Management Relations in Hockey,' in *The Business of Professional Sports*, ed. Paul D. Staudohar and James A. Mangan (Urbana and Chicago: University of Illinois Press, 1991), 202–21; and David Mills, 'The Blue Line and the Bottom Line,' in *The Business of Professional Sports*, ed. Staudohar and Mangan, 175–201. In addition, in a study of the OHA Alan Metcalfe has contended that its organizational structure favoured the retention of power by the ruling executives. Alan Metcalfe, 'Power: A Case Study of the Ontario Hockey Association, 1890–1936,' *Journal of Sport History* 19, no. 1 (1992), 5–25.

Chapter 10: Decline of the Ottawa Empire

1 Revenue figures are from the 1928 NHL Meeting Minutes, 13 February, National Hockey League Archives (hereafter NHLA). Only 45,949 customers paid to attend Pittsburgh's 22 home games, the lowest paid attendance in the league; Detroit drew slightly more at 48,097. By contrast, the Canadiens topped the league in attendance with 182,741. The highest paid attendance of an American team was the Rangers', with 156,661, third in the league. Admission figures for the 1926–7 season can be found in Calder to B. Taggert, 30 April 1927, 1926–7 Miscellaneous Correspondence file, NHLA. Taggert was a reporter from the *Pittsburgh Sun*. In responding to Taggert's inquiry about league attendance, Calder noted that the figures excluded complimentary tickets which the American clubs apparently were giving away freely.

2 This belief was grounded in the Elizabethan poor law of 1601 and was based on the concept of local rather than central relief for the economically destitute. See Paul A. Kurzman, *Harry Hopkins and the New Deal* (Fair Lawn, NJ: R.E. Burdick, Inc., Publishers, 1974), 45–52.

3 John Herd Thompson, with Allen Seager, *Canada, 1922–1939: Decades of Discord* (Toronto: McClelland & Stewart, 1994), 197–8.

4 See Appendix E. Toronto's figure was arrived at from gate receipts in the 1929–30 Box Office Statements – Toronto file, NHLA. The 1929–30 season was the first season for which there was a complete set of gate-receipt records from Ottawa on file. Toronto is a more appropriate comparison than Montreal as Toronto was still playing in the small Arena Gardens, which had fewer than 10,000 seats. Also, Toronto had the second smallest market within the NHL at the time.

5 1927 NHL Meeting Minutes, 24 September, NHLA. The previous salary limit was set at $35,000 in 1925 with the exception of the two new entries, the New York Americans and Pittsburgh, which had a limit of $45,000 for two seasons. It should also be remembered that the Chicago and Detroit teams paid $100,000 to the Patricks for a complete roster in 1926. The roster limit had increased to 15 active and 3 inactive players since 1926.

6 Calder to Taggert, 30 April 1927, 1926–7 Miscellaneous Correspondence file, NHLA. The attendance for Ottawa was 80,834, Chicago 73,948, and Detroit 48,097. See also note 1.

7 *Seventh Census of Canada*, 1931, vol. 2 (Ottawa: J.O. Paternaude, 1931), 9. Toronto's population was listed as 631,207.

8 Calder to Hughes, 23 September 1930, 1929–30 Detroit Red Wings file, NHLA. As Detroit was also in financial trouble at the time, Hughes had asked for the price scale for each club. Calder sent him a list based on the previous season's prices and advised that none of the clubs had indicated that they would change the price scale.

According to the list, Toronto had 384 seats that sold at $2.75. This list must be used judiciously, however, as clubs changed the prices for some games, as indicated in a review of the gate-receipt reports. Also the seating capacity relating to the prices fluctuated, although the high-price seats generally held true for most of the season. Ottawa's scale was as follows: 293 at $2, 150 at $1.35, 2044 at $1.25, 76 at $1.05, 900 at $1, 180 at $0.80, 340 at $0.70, 74 at $0.60, 750 at $0.50, and 750 at $0.25. This yields a seating capacity of 6804 excluding standing-room patrons. Official gate receipts indicated, however, a capacity of 5304 excluding standees.

9 1927 NHL Meeting Minutes, 24 September, NHLA.

10 Ibid. The 3.5% was originally instituted to cover additional travelling expenses when the league expanded in the mid-twenties.

11 1927 NHL Meeting Minutes, 12 December, NHLA. The committee consisted of Calder, Charles Adams of the Bruins, Leo Dandurand of the Canadiens, and Colonel John Hammond of the New York Rangers. None of the three governors in the committee had clubs in financial trouble.

12 Ahearn to Calder, 23 January 1928, 1927–8 Ottawa Hockey Association file, NHLA.

13 Ahearn to Calder, telegram, 11 March 1928, ibid.

14 1928 NHL Meeting Minutes, 12 March, NHLA. Only 8 governors attended the meeting, and hence only 8 votes were recorded. Of the majority that voted against the transfer were the Bruins, Maroons, Detroit Cougars, Canadiens, and Rangers. Toronto, the New York Americans, and Pittsburgh voted for the motion. The meeting minutes at the NHLA are not verbatim minutes but a summarized version of the meeting proceedings. Conceivably, there might have been a discussion on Ahearn's proposal.

15 Ahearn to Calder, 22 March 1928, 1927–8 Ottawa Hockey Association file, NHLA. Calder had written to Ahearn earlier indicating preference of a check over a deduction from the franchise account. See Calder to Ahearn, 20 March 1928, ibid.

16 Calder to McLaughlin, 17 January 1929, 1928–9 Chicago Blackhawks file, NHLA. This analysis of the Ottawa and Pittsburgh situations was unsolicited. It would seem that Calder was preparing the governors before Ahearn brought up the subject of revenue sharing again.

17 Average home gate receipts for Chicago have been calculated on the gate-receipt reports for those seasons. For the 1929–30 season, Chicago's total net revenue (after taxes and the 3.5% paid to the visitors, but before deducting rink rental) was at least $260,289.45 (one gate-receipt report is missing in the file). Its average net gate receipt was $12,394.74. See 1927–8, 1928–9, and 1929–30 Box Office Statements – Chicago file, NHLA.

18 McLaughlin to Calder, 21 January 1929, 1928–9 Chicago Blackhawks file, NHLA.

19 McLaughlin's disdain for, and perhaps frustration with, some of the owners was

obvious. 'I consider it important that the N. H. L. should decide once and for all whether it is composed of enemies or allies. Is it composed of ten teams each of which is constantly trying to do the other in the eye, or of ten teams trying to promote each others sporting and financial welfare? My own impression is that the former is the case, and that the latter would elicit cries of raucous laughter at any league meeting.' Ibid.

20 Jay Scherer and Steven J. Jackson, 'From Corporate Welfare to National Interest: Newspaper Analysis of the Public Subsidization of NHL Hockey Debate in Canada,' *Sociology of Sport Journal* 21, no. 1 (2004), 36–60.

21 Ahearn to Calder, 10 January 1929, 1928–9 Ottawa Hockey Association file, NHLA.

22 Calder to Ahearn, 11 January 1929, ibid.

23 Ahearn to Calder, 13 January 1929, ibid.

24 Cohen to Calder, telegraph, 21 January 1929, 1928–9 Miscellaneous Correspondence file, NHLA.

25 Ahearn to Calder, 13 January 1929, 1928–9 Ottawa Hockey Association file, NHLA. Harmon was the same person who had a failed bid for the Chicago franchise in 1926 and had linked up with Frank Patrick, threatening to start a rival league. He had since raised enough money to build the new Chicago Stadium, which would open in December 1929. For Philadelphia's interest in Ottawa, see I. Wener to Calder, 26 January 1929, 1928–9 Miscellaneous Correspondence file, NHLA.

26 Ahearn to Calder, 15 February 1929, 1928–9, Ottawa Hockey Association file, NHLA. See also *Ottawa Citizen*, 28 september 1929, 18.

27 Burpee to Calder, 23 April 1929, 1928–9 Ottawa Hockey Association file, NHLA.

28 Ahearn to Calder, 20 August 1929, ibid.

29 Calder to McLaughlin, 12 September 1929, 1928–9 Chicago Blackhawks file, NHLA.

30 Foran to President and Members, 26 September 1929, 1929–30 Ottawa Hockey Association file, NHLA. Foran cited the following figures for Ottawa's away and home games: the receipts for two games at Boston were $45,038, plus $6180 when Boston visited Ottawa; one game with the Rangers netted $20,911, plus $6033 for the return game at Ottawa; receipts from three away games with the Canadiens amounted to $30,891, plus $16,493 when the Canadiens visited Ottawa; three away games with the Maroons netted $30,775, plus $10,887 for the return game; Ottawa at Chicago grossed $7731, compared with $3484 when Chicago visited Ottawa.

31 1929 NHL Meeting Minutes, 28 September, NHLA. Only six governors attended the subsequent meeting, and the matter was further tabled.
14 October, ibid.

32 16 December, ibid.

33 Quain to Calder, 12 November 1929, 1929–30 Ottawa Hockey Association file, NHLA. Quain's letter was supplemented by Foran's request, 13 November 1929, ibid.

34 Calder to Foran, 15 November 1929, ibid.

35 Calder to Quain, 15 November 1929, ibid. Calder's reason was that the resolution to disperse the equity account was made in 1926, the majority of that party 'have ceased to have any connection with the league.' No record on this subject is found in the minutes of the next governors' meeting.

36 Calder to McLaughlin, 15 October 1929, 1929–30 Chicago Blackhawks file, NHLA.

37 1930 NHL Meeting Minutes, 10 February, NHLA.

38 Ahearn to Calder, 19 April 1930, 1929–30 Ottawa Hockey Association file, NHLA.

39 Burpee to Calder, 27 December 1930, 1930–1 Ottawa Hockey Association file, NHLA. The Auditorium would receive $1200 for whatever number of home games above the 25% that were played in other rinks.

40 Ahearn to Calder, 29 December 1930, ibid. The dire situation prompted Ahearn to waive his veto power on the sale of the club to expedite its sale. Ahearn to Calder, 31 December 1930, ibid.

41 'Series Y215-216: Commercial Failures in Canada, Number and Liabilities,' in *Historical Statistics of Canada*, ed. M.C. Urquhart and K.A.H. Buckley (Toronto: Macmillan, 1965), 659.

42 Calder to Ahearn, 2 January 1931, 1930–1 Ottawa Hockey Association file, NHLA.

43 Charles L. Coleman, *The Trail of the Stanley Cup* (Sherbrooke, QC: Sherbrooke Daily Record Co., 1964), 2: 110. See also Conn Smythe, with Scott Young, *If You Can't Beat 'Em in the Alley* (Toronto: McClelland & Stewart, 1981), 99–102, and Brian McFarlane, *The King Clancy Story* (Toronto: ECW Press, 1997), 63–7.

44 Quain to Calder, 11 February 1931, 1930–1 Ottawa Hockey Association file, NHLA.

45 The discussion of the compact that Quain spoke about took place during the 10 February meeting in New York. The deliberations, however, were purposely struck off the verbatim minutes, of which Quain had requested a copy. Ahearn to Calder, 28 February 1931, ibid.

46 In a letter to McLaughlin, Calder suggested that Ottawa would need to sell some of its best players, as the club had accrued a $70,000 loss for the 1930–1 season. If that happened, however, Calder wondered, would the replacements have the same drawing power on the road? Calder to McLaughlin, 28 August 1931, 1930–1 Chicago Blackhawks file, NHLA. In the same letter, Calder also revealed that Philadelphia had lost $90,000 the previous season.

47 Ahearn was elected member of Parliament in 1930, which perhaps accounts for his concern regarding American control of the NHL. Shortly after rejecting a bid by

Charles Adams to finance the Ottawa club, he wrote Calder: 'If the Auditorium stock were to get into American control, it would, I think, be just too bad for the three Canadian clubs in the NHL. That would make a 7 to 3 vote, no matter if Ottawa played here or in Timbuctoo. It doesn't very much appeal to me, because I feel that it would not be long before Canadians would be at a disadvantage in hockey compared to the present position.' Ahearn to Calder, 17 March 1931, 1930–1 Ottawa Hockey Association file, NHLA.

48 Actually, the Chicago Stadium had applied for a second franchise the year before. Its president, Sydney N. Strotz, argued that a second franchise would eliminate 'the long intervals (between home games) necessitated with one team' and vowed it would not desert the Blackhawks if granted the second franchise. Strotz to Calder, 7 May 1930, 1929–30 Miscellaneous Correspondence file, NHLA.

49 Quain to Calder, 12 May 1931, 1930–1 Ottawa Hockey Association file, NHLA.

50 For the 1930–1 season, Chicago's net gate was $292,980.59, its average gate $13,317.30. Chicago actually posted a profit for the season.

51 Calder to Quain, 13 May 1931, 1930–1 Ottawa Hockey Association file, NHLA. See also David Cruise and Alison Griffiths, *Net Worth: Exploding the Myths of Pro Hockey* (Toronto: Penguin Books, 1992), 30–5. There is no proper citation in Cruise and Griffiths's book to check the validity of their assertion that 'a vicious feud' between McLaughlin and Norris spurred the latter's interest in hockey. They do, however, cite family members' recollections. In both the NHL meeting minutes and correspondence, no evidence exists to support their claim that Norris had applied for a second franchise in Chicago in 1928 – the beginning of the feud.

52 Calder to McLaughlin, telegraph, 15 September [no year], 1930–1 Chicago Blackhawks file, NHLA. While the telegram did not have a year on it, it mentioned the transfer would be done on the same conditions as the transfer of the Pittsburgh club 'discussed last fall.' Pittsburgh was transferred to Philadelphia in the fall of 1930.

53 1931 NHL Meeting Minutes, 26 September, NHLA. See also Coleman, *The Trail of the Stanley Cup*, 2: 135, and *Detroit Free Press*, 10 October 1931, 13.

54 Ahearn to Calder, 26 December 1931, 1931–2 Ottawa Hockey Association file, NHLA.

55 For the story of the construction of Maple Leaf Gardens, see Coleman, *The Trail of the Stanley Cup*, 2: 139; Young, *If You Can't Beat 'Em*, 102–9; and Frank J. Selke, with Gordon Green, *Behind the Cheering* (Toronto: McClelland & Stewart, 1962), 84–91. A copy of the Maple Leaf Gardens prospectus and promotional material can be found in the Archives of Ontario, F 233, Conn Smythe Papers, MU 5968, box 33, file: Maple Leaf Gardens Prospectus – 1931.

56 Ahearn to Calder, 2 February 1932, 1931–2 Ottawa Hockey Association file, NHLA.

57 Ibid.

58 1932 NHL Meeting Minutes, 10 May, NHLA.

59 Ahearn to Calder, 29 May 1932, 1931–2 Ottawa Hockey Association file, NHLA.

60 Ibid. There was probably no love lost between Dwyer and Madison Square Garden, which operated the New York Rangers. The Americans were beginning to suffer at the box office, in part due to a severe rental agreement imposed on the team by the Madison Square Garden Corporation. The Americans had to pay 56% rental, highest in the league, to the Garden Corp. Calder to Ahearn, 22 March 1932, 1931–2 Ottawa Hockey Association file, NHLA. The information provided was in response to Ahearn's proposal that the visitors' share be fixed at 15% as a precondition for Ottawa's return. Calder used the 56% rental paid by the Americans to the Garden Corp. to illustrate the difficulty in getting the other clubs to lessen their own share.

61 Ahearn to Calder, 3 August 1932, ibid.

62 Quain to Calder, 8 October 1932, ibid.

63 Ahearn to Calder, 20 June 1933, 1932–3 Ottawa Hockey Association file, NHLA.

64 Ahearn to Calder, 20 November 1933, 1933–4 Ottawa Hockey Association file, NHLA.

65 W. McIntyre to Calder, 21 November 1933, ibid.

66 *New York Times*, 19 August 1935, 18. The loss amounted to $59,000. Its subsidiary, the Boston Madison Square Garden, had a loss of $78,550. This precipitated a power struggle within the Madison Square Garden management that lasted for almost two years.

67 Quain to Calder, 13 March 1934, 1933–4 Ottawa Hockey Association file, NHLA.

Chapter 11: The Rebellion

1 George Vass, *The Chicago Black Hawks Story* (Chicago: Follett Publishing Co., 1970), 18–19. As in other popular hockey histories, Vass does not provide a citation. He indicates that the cost of the stadium was $6,000,000, whereas the *Chicago Tribune* puts it at $7,000,000; 29 March 1929, 1.

2 David Cruise and Alison Griffiths, *Net Worth: Exploding the Myths of Pro Hockey* (Toronto: Penguin Books, 1992), 26–30. His son Jimmy Norris eventually entered the world of boxing and was implicated monopolizing the sport of boxing in the 1950s. See Barney Nagler, *James Norris and the Decline of Boxing* (Indianapolis and New York: Bobbs-Merrill Co., a subsidiary of Howard W. Sams & Co., 1964). James Norris Sr had tried to purchase the Pittsburgh club in 1929 and move it to Chicago.

3 Norris to Calder, telegram, 5 November 1928, 1928–9 Miscellaneous Correspondence file, National Hockey League Archives (hereafter NHLA).

4 Tobin to Calder, telegram, 22 February 1929, 1928–9 Chicago Blackhawks file, NHLA.

5 A series of correspondence between Calder and McLaughlin discussed the Harmon-Patrick alliance. Although Norris's name was mentioned, the two generally associated Patrick and Harmon with the scheme. See McLaughlin to Calder, 16 March 1929; Calder to McLaughlin, 18 March 1929; and McLaughlin to Calder, 20 March 1929, 1928–9 Chicago Blackhawks file, NHLA. Turner knew Patrick from Western Hockey League days when Turner was running the Calgary franchise.

6 McLaughlin to Calder, 9 April 1929, ibid.

7 McLaughlin to Calder, 29 April 1929, ibid.

8 Calder to Patrick, 4 May 1929, 1928–9 Miscellaneous Correspondence file, NHLA. Patrick had sent two telegrams, one on May 3 and the other May 4, soliciting Calder's opinion on the second Chicago franchise.

9 Data taken from 1929–30 Box Office Statements – Chicago file, NHLA. For this one season, the gate-receipts report for the March 18 game against Toronto is missing. Thus, the use of the averages is a more accurate assessment than the total net amounts.

10 McLaughlin to Calder, telegram, 22 February 1930, 1929–30 Chicago Blackhawks file, NHLA. See also McLaughlin to Calder, 13 March 1930, ibid. While this request was for the playoffs, which were technically the League's rather than the club's responsibility, there was no doubt that the Stadium had toughened up in its demands.

11 Warren to Calder, telegram, 1 April 1930, 1929–30 American Hockey Association file, NHLA.

12 Warren to Calder, 3 April 1930, ibid.

13 Calder to Warren, 9 April 1930, ibid.

14 McLaughlin to Calder, 28 April 1930, 1929–30 Chicago Blackhawks file, NHLA. The meeting was held on May 2.

15 Warren to Calder, 3 May 1930, and Calder to Warren, 21 May 1930, 1929–30 American Hockey Association file, NHLA. Calder gave the official approval from the League for Warren's proposal on 21 May.

16 S.N. Strotz to Calder, 7 May 1930, 1929–30 Miscellaneous Correspondence file, NHLA.

17 NHL Meeting Minutes, 10 May, NHLA. See also Calder to Strotz, 13 May 1930, 1929–30 Miscellaneous Correspondence file, NHLA.

18 Calder to Warren, 21 May 1930, 1929–30 American Hockey Association file, NHLA.

19 McLaughlin to Calder, 23 May 1930, 1929–30 Chicago Blackhawks file, NHLA.

20 Warren to Calder, 23 May 1930, 1929–30 American Hockey Association file, NHLA.

21 Calder to McLaughlin, 26 May 1930, 1929–30 Chicago Blackhawks file, NHLA.

22 Warren to Calder, 21 June 1930, 1929–30 American Hockey Association file, NHLA.

23 1930 NHL Meeting Minutes, 27 September, NHLA. As early as June, Calder had suggested to McLaughlin that several AHA players had complained about their back wages and that the NHL should take the initiative in the pending war by suspending the affiliation with the AHA until it had fulfilled its contracts with its players. Calder to McLaughlin, 3 June 1930, 1929–30 Chicago Blackhawks file, NHLA. The IHL was the first to fall in line. See Calder to McLaughlin, 27 June 1930, ibid. Then the PCHL and the California League signed in August. See Calder to McLaughlin, 18 August 1930, ibid.

24 Calder to Warren, 18 September 1930, 1929–30 American Hockey Association file, NHLA. James Strachan of the Maroons and Art Ross of the Bruins happened to be with Calder at the time Grant and Shaughnessy dropped in. The handbill, sent in by Tobin earlier, had just been received in the NHL office. Supposedly the bill had been handed out in the Stadium during a boxing match. It advertised the Shamrocks as a major-league club, but did not mention which league the team belonged to. Tobin to Calder, 13 September 1930, 1929–30 Chicago Blackhawks file, NHLA.

25 Calder to J.J. Allen Jr, 8 October 1930, 1929–30 American Hockey Association file, NHLA. Similar telegrams were sent to Judge Dooley of the Can-Am league and King of the IHL.

26 *Chicago Herald Examiner*, 19 October 1930, 5. See also *Chicago Tribune*, 19 October 1930, 4.

27 McLaughlin alerted Calder that referees Rodden, Laflamme, and O'Hara had worked in a few AHL games. Calder quickly warned them to stop. McLaughlin to Calder, 22 December 1930, 1930–1 Chicago Blackhawks file, NHLA.

28 Calder to C. Hughes, 6 December 1930, 1930–1 Detroit Red Wings file, NHLA.

29 1930 NHL Meeting Minutes, 1 December, NHLA.

30 1931 NHL Meeting Minutes, 31 January, NHLA. See also McLaughlin to Calder, 8 January 1931, 1930–1 Chicago Blackhawks file, NHLA.

31 McLaughlin to Calder, 7 November 1930, 1930–1 Chicago Blackhawks file, NHLA. The Blackhawks had submitted and received confirmation of the dates to be used for their games. Yet the Stadium wanted to move the Blackhawks' 1 February game so that the Shamrocks could play there that night.

32 McLaughlin to Calder, 12 January 1931, ibid.

33 Besides Tuesdays and Thursdays, the League also scheduled games on Saturdays, and on Sundays where local laws permitted.

34 Forgan to Calder, 15 October 1931, 1931–2 Miscellaneous Correspondence file, NHLA. J. Russell Forgan was the chairman of the Benefits Division of the Joint

Emergency Relief Fund of Cook County. Calder had denied permission in his 21 October reply to this letter. McLaughlin, however, asked Calder to deny permission publicly after news of the benefit game appeared in the press. McLaughlin to Calder, 2 December 1931, 1931–2 Chicago National Hockey Team file, NHLA.

35 McLaughlin to Calder, 2 December 1931, 1931–2 Chicago National Hockey Team file, NHLA.

36 McLaughlin to Calder, 9 December 1931, ibid.

37 McLaughlin to Calder, 28 December 1931, ibid.

38 Correspondence of this kind seemed to stem from the AHL's St Louis and Tulsa clubs.

39 1931 NHL Meeting Minutes, 19 October, NHLA.

40 *Chicago Tribune*, 4 February 1932, 21.

41 McLaughlin to Calder, telegram, 4 February 1932, 1931–2 Chicago National Hockey Team file, NHLA.

42 *Chicago Tribune*, 5 February 1932, 23.

43 Grant to Foran, 4 March 1932, 1931–2 Ottawa Hockey Association file, NHLA.

44 Calder to Grant, 10 March 1932, ibid.

45 1932 NHL Meeting Minutes, 12 March, NHLA. Foran did suggest a way out for Calder and the NHL: by agreeing to a series played at the beginning of the following season. He reaffirmed the trustees' friendship to the NHL but warned that they were duty-bound to take back the Cup if the NHL did not come up with a counter-proposal. Foran to Calder, 19 March 1932, 1931–2 Ottawa Hockey Association file, NHLA.

46 McLaughlin to Calder, 22 March 1932, 1931–2 Chicago National Hockey Team file, NHLA.

47 Norris to Calder, 9 May 1932, 1931–2 Miscellaneous Correspondence file, NHLA. A $10,000 cheque accompanied the letter of application.

48 1932 NHL Meeting Minutes, 10 May, NHLA. James Strachan of the Maroons was the lone supporter of the application. It is interesting to note the reason for rejecting Norris's application, because two years later the NHL approved the Ottawa franchise's move to St Louis.

49 See Appendix F.

50 Lewis K. Walker to Calder, 18 August 1931, 1930–1 Detroit Red Wings file, NHLA. The actual amounts were $21,450 in defaulted payments and $47,069.13 in back taxes. There was also $100,000 in default in the sinking fund and $429 in the 2% tax rebate account. $800,000 in bonds were issued on 1 July 1927 to finance the building and the two Detroit hockey clubs. $140,000 had been retired since then.

51 Hughes to Calder, 16 July 1932, 1931–2 Detroit Red Wings file, NHLA.

52 Grant to Calder, 18 August 1932, 1931–2 Miscellaneous Correspondence file, NHLA.

53 Calder to Grant, 30 August 1932, 1932–3 American Hockey Association file, NHLA. An interesting note was the presence of the Detroit receiver, Pfleiderer, at the negotiation session. Grant, Norris, and Shaughnessy represented the AHL.

54 1932 NHL Meeting Minutes, 1 October, NHLA. The governors stipulated that the affiliation 'be granted ... on conditions similar to those required from other minor leagues affiliated with this League.'

55 E.C. Lewis to Calder, 26 October 1933, 1933–4 Detroit Red Wings file, NHLA.

56 For a different interpretation of the consequence of the demise of the AHL, see Morey Holzman and Joseph Nieforth, *Deceptions and Doublecross: How the NHL Conquered Hockey* (Toronto: Dundurn Group, 2002), 325–6.

Chapter 12: In the Best Interests of Hockey

1 Although ice hockey was on the 1920 Olympic program in Antwerp, the first Winter Olympics did not occur until 1924.

2 National Archives of Canada, CAHA Minutes of 21st Annual Meeting, 1938, MG 28, I 151, file 21, p. 20 (hereafter NAC, CAHA 21st Annual Meeting Minutes). Its assets decreased from a high of $51,147.97 in the 1931–2 season to $17,547.83 for the 1935–6 season. See also *Toronto Globe*, 13 April 1936, 6.

3 NAC, AAUC Minutes of 45th Annual Meeting, 1932, MG 28, I 151, file 7, p. 95 (hereafter NAC, AAUC 45th Annual Meeting Minutes). See Bruce Kidd, *The Struggle for Canadian Sport* (Toronto: University of Toronto Press, 1996), 80–8, for a discussion of the struggles among factions within the AAUC over the issue of amateurism during the first half of the 1930s.

4 *Toronto Globe*, 13 April 1936, 6.

5 1925 NHL Meeting Minutes, 7 November, NHLA. The 1931 figure excludes goalkeepers, whereas the 1925 figures include a goalkeeper. See 1931 NHL Meeting Minutes, 9 May, NHLA. The NHL began to enact countermeasures against the Depression in 1932 by limiting the roster size to 14 players, excluding goalkeepers. See 1932 NHL Meeting Minutes, 10 May, NHLA.

6 1930 NHL Meeting Minutes, 10 May, NHLA. At the time, junior players were those under 20 years of age.

7 Hewitt to Calder, 30 June 1930, 1929–30 Miscellaneous Correspondence file, NHLA.

8 Ibid.

9 NAC, CAHA 18th Annual Meeting Minutes (1935), 15. It is also interesting to note that in debating the question of setting a deadline for allowing amateur hockey players to try out for a professional club, the delegates gave careful attention to the dates of the NHL training camps. This suggests that the CAHA was at the NHL's mercy in this regard. Ibid., 33–5.

10 NAC, CAHA 19th Annual Meeting Minutes (1936), 8–10. A similar situation regarding non-sanctioned players occurred with the United States. The CAHA suspended 27 players. Repeated efforts to have the American Amateur Athletic Union ban the players were unsuccessful. English clubs had been recruiting Canadian players before 1935, but the clubs placed limits on the number of imported players. See *London Times*, 25 September 1935, 5.

11 Kidd, *The Struggle for Canadian Sport*, 80.

12 NAC, CAHA 19th Annual Meeting Minutes, 20.

13 Ibid, 19–32. For comments on this change of direction, see for example *Toronto Globe*, 11 April 1936, 7, which suggested that the amateur clubs had been paying players for a long time.

14 For accounts of the Canada's 1936 hockey fiasco, see *Toronto Globe*, 6 February 1936, 6; 10 February 1936, 7; 12 February 1936, 1; 13 and 14 February 1936, 6; and 17 February 1936, 1. See also Mark Savoie, 'Broken Time and Broken Hearts: The Maritimes and the Selection of Canada's 1936 Olympic Hockey Team,' *Sport History Review*, November 2000, 120–38, and John Wong, 'Sport Networks on Ice: The Canadian Experience at the 1936 Olympic Hockey Tournament,' *Sport History Review*, November 2003, 190–212. See also NAC, CAHA 19th Annual Meeting Minutes, 12–18, for an explanation of Canada's performance, both on and off the ice, by CAHA president E.A. Gilroy, who accompanied the team to Germany. It must be remembered that, previous to this defeat, Canada had never been beaten, and had only been tied once, in 1932 at Lake Placid by the Americans. Usually Canada won these games by a lopsided score. Even as they finished second in the semi-final round in 1936, the Canadians had scored a total of 22 goals and conceded only 4, compared to England's 8 and 3. Gilroy attributed the problem to the Canadian delegation's deficiency in understanding French, which was used for official business. The LIHG minutes indicate that the Canadian delegation had, however, missed the February 3 meeting where the playoff formats were explained to all participants. For a somewhat different version of the events, see 1936 Meeting Minutes, 3, 4, 5, 10, and 13 February, Ligue Internationale de Hockey sur Glace, copies of which are under the possession of the author. I am indebted to Birger Nordmark for these copies. According to the minutes, the president of the organizing committee explained the format to the Canadian delegation the following day and the Canadians did not raise any objection.

15 *Toronto Globe*, 6 May 1936, 7.

16 Ibid., 8 May 1936, 7.

17 Calder to Hewitt, 12 May 1936, 1935–6 Canadian Amateur Hockey Association file, NHLA. Representing the NHL were Calder, Toronto owner Conn Smythe, and

Boston manager Art Ross. The new CAHA president, Cecil Duncan, 2nd vice-president George Dudley, and registrar Hewitt represented the CAHA. The 1st vice-president, Dr George Hardy, a proponent of the changes, could not make the Toronto meeting due to his duties at the University of Alberta.

18 Calder to Smythe, 26 May 1936, ibid.
19 *Toronto Globe*, 11 May 1936, 8. George Dudley and William Hewitt were the CAHA officials present at the ceremony.
20 L. Patrick to Calder, 16 June 1936, 1935–6 Canadian Amateur Hockey Association file, NHLA. Patrick did a clause-by-clause analysis. Except for the fourth clause, for which he commended the NHL committee, he disputed the other three points as damaging to the NHL. From the letter, it also seems that Art Ross and Conn Smythe were in favour of the agreement.
21 Arnold to Calder, 29 June 1936, ibid.
22 1936 NHL Meeting Minutes, 16 July, NHLA. The second point (forbidding an NHL club to take junior players) was passed by majority vote, with New York Rangers and Detroit dissenting. The governors also wanted to set September 1 instead of August 15 as the transfer date, not only between the CAHA and the NHL but also within the CAHA. The fourth point (on the CAHA adopting NHL rules) was passed unanimously.
23 Calder to Hewitt, 20 July 1936, 1935–6 Canadian Amateur Hockey Association file, NHLA.
24 Hewitt to Calder, 31 July 1936, ibid. See also *Toronto Globe*, 29 June 1936, 6.
25 The meeting was held on September 15. Calder to Hewitt, 16 September 1936, 1935–6 Canadian Amateur Hockey Association file, NHLA.
26 Hewitt to Calder, telegram, 28 September 1936, ibid.
27 Hewitt to Calder, 21 September 1936, ibid.
28 1936 NHL Meeting Minutes, 26 September, NHLA.
29 *Toronto Globe*, 20 November 1936, 9, and 21 November 1936, 8. The CAHA's four-point proposal was the centre of debate during the AAUC annual meeting. Besides the CAHA, the Canadian Amateur Basketball Association, the Canadian Amateur Lacrosse Association, the western and the Maritime branches of the AAUC supported it in one way or another. It became a battle between Central Canada and the rest.
30 NAC, CAHA 20th Annual Meeting Minutes, 5.
31 When the Pittsburgh club became inactive for the 1931–2 season, the net average gate receipt per team actually increased slightly. This figure rose significantly when Ottawa left the league after the 1934–5 season, and by close to $1000 when the New York Americans folded. See Appendix G.

Chapter 13: Overtime

1 Robert N. Stern, 'The Development of an Interorganizational Control Network: The Case of Intercollegiate Athletics,' *Administrative Science Quarterly* 24 (June 1979), 245.
2 Alan Metcalfe, *Canada Learns to Play* (Toronto: McClelland & Stewart, 1987), 223. Bruce Kidd, *The Struggle for Canadian Sport* (Toronto: University of Toronto Press, 1996), 196–209.
3 Alfred Chandler, *The Visible Hand: The Managerial Revolution in American Business* (Cambridge, MA: Belknap Press, 1977).
4 Calder most likely would have been the longest-serving president in the NHL had he not died in 1943. Campbell was president of the NHL for 31 seasons.
5 Stern, 'The Development of an Interorganizational Control Network,' 244. For a portrayal of Calder as a conspiratorial and all-powerful president, see Morey Holzman and Joseph Nieforth, *Deceptions and Doublecross: How the NHL Conquered Hockey* (Toronto: Dundurn Group, 2002). For an unflattering look at a sport league's Chief Executive Officer as an owners' employee, see Marvin Miller, *A Whole Different Ball Game: The Sport and Business of Baseball* (New York: Carol Publishing Group, 1991). Miller is especially critical of baseball commissioner Bowie Kuhn.
6 Kidd, *The Struggle for Canadian Sport*, 254–61.
7 Dan MacKinnon, 'Myth, Memory, and the Kitchener-Waterloo Dutchmen in Canadian International Hockey,' *Sport History Review* 31 (2000), 1–27.

Index